Nobel Lectures

Nobel Lectures

20 YEARS OF THE NOBEL PRIZE FOR LITERATURE LECTURES

ICON BOOKS

This expanded edition published in the UK
in 2007 by Icon Books Ltd, The Old Dairy,
Brook Road, Thriplow,
Cambridge SG8 7RG
email: info@iconbooks.co.uk
www.iconbooks.co.uk

Originally published in Australia in 2006
by Melbourne University Press, Victoria

Sold in the UK, Europe, South Africa and Asia
by Faber & Faber Ltd, 3 Queen Square,
London WC1N 3AU
or their agents

Distributed in the UK, Europe, South Africa and Asia
by TBS Ltd, TBS Distribution Centre, Colchester Road,
Frating Green, Colchester CO7 7DW

ISBN: 978-1840468-34-2

Text copyright © 2006, 2007 The Nobel Foundation

The author has asserted his moral rights.

No part of this book may be reproduced in any form, or by any
means, without prior permission in writing from the publisher

Text designed by Lauren Statham

Printed in the UK by J. H. Haynes & Co. Ltd

Contents

Nobel Literature Laureates: An Index	vii
Introduction by John Sutherland	ix
My Father's Suitcase *Orhan Pamuk*	1
Art, Truth and Politics *Harold Pinter*	18
Sidelined *Elfriede Jelinek*	35
He and His Man *J.M. Coetzee*	51
Heureka! *Imre Kertész*	63
Two Worlds *V.S. Naipaul*	74
The Case for Literature *Gao Xingjian*	90
To Be Continued … *Günter Grass*	107
How Characters Became the Masters and the Author Their Apprentice *José Saramago*	125

Contra Jogulatores Obloquentes
(Against Jesters Who Defame and Insult) 141
Dario Fo

The Poet and the World 158
Wislawa Szymborska

Crediting Poetry 165
Seamus Heaney

Japan, the Ambiguous, and Myself 186
Kenzaburo Oe

The Bird Is In Your Hands 200
Toni Morrison

The Antilles: Fragments of Epic Memory 210
Derek Walcott

Writing and Being 230
Nadine Gordimer

In Search of the Present 243
Octavio Paz

Eulogy to the Fable 259
Camilo José Cela

Mankind's Coming of Age 276
Naguib Mahfouz

Aesthetics and Language 283
Joseph Brodsky

This Past Must Address Its Present 298
Wole Soyinka

Laureates, 1901 to 2005 323

Nobel Literature Laureates: An Index

As at September 2007

Number of literature prizes awarded since 1901: 103
Percentage of laureates from Europe: 73
Percentage of laureates from Oceania: 0.92
Number of laureates from France: 13
Number of laureates from China: 1
Number won by women: 10
Percentage of prizes won by women: 0.09
Percentage of prizes won by Scandinavian countries: 0.13
Number who declined the prize: 1
Number forced by authorities to decline the prize: 1
Number won by Australians: 1
Age of Aleksandr Isayevich Solzhenitsyn, the oldest living laureate: 88
Age of Theodor Mommsen, the oldest laureate when he received the prize in 1902: 85
Age of Rudyard Kipling, the youngest laureate when he received the prize in 1907: 42
Number of living laureates: 19
Number of laureates who wrote in English, the most awarded language: 26
Number who wrote in French, the next most awarded language: 13
Number of nominations for the prize in 1901: 25
Number of nominations today: over 200
Prize amount in 1901: 150,792 kronor (SEK)
Prize amount in 2005: 10,000,000 kronor (SEK)

Introduction

In the Berkeley campus of the University of California there are, cruising visitors are perplexed to find, parking spots marked 'NL Only': Nobel Laureates, any brash interloper will discover. The spaces are reserved for vehicles as honorific as London's Lord Mayor's Coach. The American university at which I teach, Caltech, boasts (the word is wholly appropriate) five Nobellists on its current (2007) teaching strength. It equates to five David Beckhams on the neighbouring LA Galaxy team. Boastworthy indeed.

The innocent pride accompanying these academic possessions witnesses to the supreme status which the Nobel accolade bestows on individuals, on their employing institutions, and on the disciplines they serve. And sometimes (but not always) their countries. The Nobel is the prize of prizes. Or, as Camilo José Cela observes, it is the highest dais human creativity can aspire to.

At Berkeley and Caltech the living laureates are, all of them, scientists or social scientists (historically, Caltech can lay claim to the only double Nobellist, Linus Pauling). The literature prize is typically awarded to writers with no, or no anchored, academic affiliation (although possibly Toni Morrison has Nobellian parking privileges at Princeton, where she has been a professor for many years).

There are other elements in the pedigree of the literature award, and the system by which it is awarded, which invest it with a unique character, along with its pre-eminence. One such element is the fact that the literature prize is given for a lifetime's achievement, but is in no sense a funereal, or end-of-life, monument. ('It's not going to be my tombstone', Saul Bellow once declared. Nor was it.) Nonetheless, most winners go, within a decade or so, to their final reward. 'I am near the end of my work now', says V.S. Naipaul. The statement hovers, unstated, over many of the speeches. The youngest laureate (over a century when in almost every other area of competition, victors have become ever more youthful) remains Rudyard Kipling – a mere 42 years old in 1907. He would survive, laurel-browed, for another 30 years.

As a general rule, no writer wins the Nobel without a more-than-lifetime's achievement behind them. Those lives have, in many cases, been difficult. The Swedish committee has a generous sympathy towards authors who have suffered for their art and who come to the dais more than usually worn out by honourable struggle. 'Perhaps I have lived too long under dictatorships', muses the 73-year-old Imre Kertész. The 2002 laureate had elected to stay in his native Hungary, after the failure of the 1956 uprising, to watch 'how an entire nation could be made to deny its ideals'.

Linger awhile on that last word. Another uniqueness in the Nobel literature award hinges on the sole criterion imposed by the academy. Namely that their prize go to 'the most outstanding work of an *idealistic* tendency' (my stress). The original Swedish is: 'den som inom litteraturen har producerat det utmärktaste i idealisk riktning'. Translation throws up two areas of ambiguity. Does 'work' mean something equivalent to the German *gesamtwerk*, or the French *oeuvre* – 'life's work', that is? Or the Latin *magnum opus* – 'masterwork'? And need the 'work' in question be unequivocally literary? It manifestly was not in the case of Winston Churchill in 1953 (author of one potboiling Ruritanian romance), or Bertrand Russell in

1950 (author of one inferior volume of detective stories). It was their respective work in the war against fascism, and in the post-war peace movement, which earned them the world's premier literary award.

There has been keen debate in the English-speaking world as to how the key adjective should be glossed. More so as one is informed that in the original Swedish, the word 'idealisk' translates as either 'idealistic' or 'ideal'.

The notion of great literature embodying the 'ideal' – or transcendent spiritual values – was very much a 19th-century aesthetic concern; and was still a live issue when the prize was set up in 1901. Conventionally, 'idealistic' was opposed to 'realistic'. Henrik Ibsen, the greatest dramatist of the 19th century, may have been excluded (as common belief has it) on the grounds of his uncompromising 'realism'. But as the 20th century progressed, the category loosened. There was no objectionable subversion of the 'idealisk' criterion observed when, for example, Ibsen's leading British (or is he Irish?) disciple, and avowed 'realist', George Bernard Shaw, won in 1925. Nor when Shaw's dramatic heir, Harold Pinter, won in 2005. The last century has seen the triumph of literary realism. The Nobel Prize has adapted accordingly, shaping its shoe to fit the changing literary foot.

If there is one motto which unites the laureates it is the Faustian 'non serviam' or, to paraphrase, 'I will not create in a condition of servitude'. Hence the paradox that often the laureate bites not the Swedish hand that bestows the accolade (although, famously, Jean-Paul Sartre did, in 1964) but the culture from which the writer sprang. It is, as the USSR famously found (with Boris Pasternak and Alexandr Solzhenitsyn) sometimes uncomfortable to have nurtured a prize-winner. Nobel Prizes do not always sit easily on the national mantelpiece.

Even a country like Britain, vastly and properly proud of its centuries-long liberal heritage, may squirm when 'its' 2005 prize-winner uses the dais to describe the country that gave him birth and fostered his career as 'a bleating little lamb', tagging 'pathetically' behind the US into the Iraq quagmire, to plant not liberalism, but 'a malignant growth'. (The image was the more hard-hitting since, at the time, Pinter himself was recovering from cancer of the throat. Not even carcinoma, however, could silence him, or his raging Anglophobia.) The hand bleeds.

Even the famously neutral and supra-national Swedish Academy can receive – if not quite a bite – a teasing nip from the lectern. See, for example, the hilarious speech by Dario Fo, in 1997, when he turns on his august donors to ask: 'Dear members of the Academy, let's admit it, this time you've overdone it. I mean, come on, first you give the prize to a black man, then to a Jewish writer. Now you give it to a clown. What gives?' No answer was forthcoming. Perhaps a subdued splutter.

Slyer, but equally subversive, is Günter Grass's choosing to offer a fantasia on the subject of his novel, *The Rat*, in which an animal, representing all the rodent kind who have laid down their little lives in laboratories, is awarded a Nobel Prize for 'services to science'. The wit with which the 1999 laureate does it counteracts the insolence. But the underlying 'non serviam' is unmistakably there. 'I mix ink with spit', as Grass (inimitably) puts it. And, continuing the theme: 'It is a fact of life that writers have always and with due consideration and great pleasure spat in the soup of the high and mighty.' One trusts he restrained himself at the banquet that evening.

Literature is the most individualistic and (at its best) unservile of activities. But, at the same time, great authors are characteristically self-effacing. It is their work which matters, not them, they insist time and again. Many of the laureates represented here blink in the Stockholm spotlight. Naipaul, for example, protests: 'I have no lecture to give ... everything of value about me is in my books.' What, as Wislawa Szymborska asks, could be of less of interest to the observer than poets creating?

Their work is hopelessly unphotogenic. Someone sits at a table or lies on a sofa while staring motionless at a wall or ceiling. Once in a while this person writes down seven lines only to cross out one of them fifteen minutes later, and then another hour passes, during which nothing happens ... who could stand to watch this kind of thing?

Literature is one of the greatest productions of the human species. The making of literature is a boring spectacle. And the rewarding of it is often an uneasy thing for the winner. Trophy-winning sports people have it easier.

The performances offered by the speech-givers – unaccustomed to such ceremonial events as they protest themselves to be – are as fascinatingly diverse as their works. Pinter offers fist-flailing political diatribe. J.M. Coetzee – the most mystical of laureates – spins a fable on the Crusoe-like loneliness of the creative mind (complete with Robinson's parrot which, like Grass's 'rat', is an ironic image of the writer). Crusoe's ambiguous partner/chattel, Man Friday, alludes to the South African laureate's investigation of racial themes.

Toni Morrison, also a connoisseur of racial difference, discrimination and oppression, offers a beautifully composed allegory crystallising the wisdom of the slave, and the freedoms which can be aspired to even in that most degraded and disgusting of human conditions. Hers, of all the pieces anthologised here, approaches most closely to pure literary creation.

Kertész used the occasion at Stockholm for a profoundly moving description of the 'nauseous' condition of the free-spirited writer under the totalitarian heel, concluding with the black comedy of reading the record of his own death in the Buchenwald concentration camp register (the most hideous and unliterary kind of book imaginable). 'I died once, so I could live', he concludes, with grim relish. 'Live or half live', that is, under communist tyranny for 40 years. Like Byron's 'Prisoner of Chillon', he recovered his freedom with a sigh – habituated for so long as he was to its opposite.

A number of writers use the high dais to recall their childhoods – with a candour rarely to be found elsewhere in their work. In a keenly evoked memory of his border Ulster/Eire childhood, Seamus Heaney recalls his search for 'his' voice, listening simultaneously to the domestic idiom of his Irish home, and the 'official idioms' of the British broadcaster, on the family radio. What combinations, what resistances, are required so that, in later life, his poetry can be honestly expressed?

Naipaul confides to his Stockholm listeners an exquisitely precise reminiscence of growing up, a migrant Indian in Trinidad, over the bones of the island's exterminated 'aborigines'. What could someone like himself, topped off with a British Oxbridge education, become other than a 'mimic man'? And nonetheless, in his authorial prime, transcend mimicry to become a free voice?

José Saramago offers another autobiographical vignette, recalling his barefoot childhood self, gleaning in the harvest-stripped cornfields of rural Portugal. It evokes nothing so much as a Portuguese Jude Fawley (Hardy, of course, is one of the greatest also-rans in the Nobel race: he may, like Zola, have been too 'realistic' for the turn-of-the-century committee). He is, Saramago says, 'the echo of the conjoined voices of his life'.

Lost integrity of self, and the painful recovery of something to compensate for the loss, is a recurrent theme among the laureates. Derek Walcott describes the condition with a poet's sureness of touch and metaphor:

> Break a vase, and the love that reassembles the
> fragments is stronger than that love which took
> its symmetry for granted when it was whole. The
> glue that fits the pieces is the sealing of its original

> shape. It is such a love that reassembles our African
> and Asiatic fragments, the cracked heirlooms
> whose restoration shows its white scars.

Is the bestowal of the prize, from the Nordic outpost of world culture, another white scar on the African body? Is it what Wole Soyinka opprobriates in the fieriest of the speeches gathered here, 'racist condescension'? Or is it soothing balm for history's injuries? Reparation even?

The vase is forever broken. Life is a 'continuing fracturing', as Octavio Paz puts it, a 'continuous expulsion from the present'. It is the writer's task, and literature's highest achievement, to recover a saving wholeness. This may suggest a certain heroism in the writer's mission and accomplishment. Gao Xingjian (like Kertész a veteran survivor of state oppression) modifies the image in a manifesto speech, anatomising what it is to be an author. Literature may be strong, Xingjian concedes; but authors personally are, typically, feeble; judged, that is, by conventional measures of heroism or athleticism: 'a writer is an ordinary person; perhaps he is more sensitive but people who are highly sensitive are often more frail.'

And often, in their frailty, more victimised than the run of ordinary persons. A majority of writers who have won the literature prize since 1980 have had their careers broken by exile and imprisonment, or have been sanctioned into silence in their native countries to be left, as Xingjian puts it, with only 'themselves' to write for. Internal readerships, like internal exile, are a fact of 20th-century tyranny. Even the limited circulation of the samizdat is often denied. But not to write, even in this extremity of creative loneliness, is – as Xingjian says – 'suicide'. He experienced it, survived it, and rose, finally, above the oppressor to win his prize.

Clearly the writers who win the prize do so by virtue of their individual genius and courage. Nonetheless, they acknowledge themselves members of a larger community. They represent, one apprehends, other great writers. Greater, perhaps. Prizeworthiness is not gladiatorial combat with the victor ludorum standing over the slain bodies of bested opponents. Kenzaburo Oe makes the point allusively, citing in his address, *inter alia*, his compatriot (and predecessor on the platform) Kawabata Yasunari, W.B. Yeats (another winner), W.H. Auden (a runner up, alas), Flannery O'Connor, George Orwell, Mikhail Bakhtin, Kim Ji-ha of Korea, Chon I and Mu Jen of China. The point, delicately insisted on, is that the prize is – however strenuous the cogitations and consultations of the committee – something of a lottery. Others might as well have stood where he stands. Would posterity, for example, have been affronted had Orwell, rather than Bertrand Russell, have won in 1950? I think not.

Disputes over who should have won are, of course, inevitable and whip up headline-making publicity every October, when the actual winner is announced. Accompanying the disputes is a miasma of mythology, suspicion and (probably apocryphal) Nobel-lore. Did Joseph Conrad not get it because of the 'dynamitard' villains in *The Secret Agent*? Did Graham Greene not get it because of the offensive depiction of the Swedish 'safety-match king', Ivar Kreuger, in *England Made Me*? Would the British-born W.H. Auden (widely reported to be a front-runner in 1971) have won had he not been American at the wrong time of his life – namely while the Vietnam War was coming to its bloody conclusion? Was Salman Rushdie out of contention in the early 1990s because it would have been too difficult publicly to reward a writer whom 2 billion Muslims had been commanded to assassinate? Such gossipy imaginings add spice to every year's announcement. And they are, backhandedly, a tribute to the importance attached to the prize.

If there is one literary topic on which the literary prize-winners agree, it is the paramount importance of their medium.

'Language', says Naguib Mahfouz (in 1988 the first Islamic laureate), is 'the real winner'. And language, whatever its national origin, is what the writer is dedicated to purify, preserve, and refine. And, above all, to protect from those who, as Morrison says, would 'molest' and 'loot' it. Pinter savagely assaults those linguistic pimps and prostitutes, politicians, who misuse language 'to keep thought at bay'. The writer, as T.S. Eliot put it, is engaged in an 'intolerable wrestle with words and meaning' – intolerable, but nonetheless necessary. There is no other way. After a long rhapsodic meditation on her relationship with her medium, Elfriede Jelinek concludes: 'I am the prisoner of my language' – and yet, at the same time, its custodian.

The custodian's task has become more pressing in the century that the Nobel Awards have been running. As Kertész instructs:

> Consider what happened to language in the twentieth century, what became of words. I daresay that the first and most shocking discovery made by writers in our time was that language, in the form it came down to us, a legacy of some primordial culture, had simply become unsuitable to convey concepts and processes that had once been unambiguous and real. Think of Kafka, think of Orwell, in whose hands the old language simply disintegrated. It was as if they were turning it round and round in an open fire, only to display its ashes afterward, in which new and previously unknown patterns emerged.

One of the notable features of the period during which the Swedish Academy has (with the interruption of world war) awarded its literary prize is the growing force of literature to alter, or accelerate, world-historical events. The literary voice has never been more potent. Its language never more listened to. Seamus Heaney makes the point astutely, and accurately, with a comparison of what brought down the Third Reich in 1945, and what brought down the USSR in 1989:

> This century has witnessed the defeat of Nazism by force of arms; but the erosion of the Soviet regimes was caused, among other things, by the sheer persistence, beneath the imposed ideological conformity, of cultural values and psychic resistances of a kind that these stories and images enshrine.

By literature, that is. And yet (there is always a 'yet') as Joseph Brodsky, in the wittiest of these lectures, reminds us: 'Lenin was literate, Stalin was literate, so was Hitler; as for Mao Zedong, he even wrote verse. What all these men had in common, though, was that their hit list was longer than their reading list.' Literature's power, like dynamite, depends on those who use it. On 'idealism', or the lack of it. One returns to Stockholm's original formulation.

The question of 'for whom do we write?' is raised by a number of the laureates, directly and indirectly. It is, as Nadine Gordimer puts it, the 'tin can attached to the tail of every work published'. Few writers, it is safe to say, write for the Swedish Literature Academy. Gordimer answers her own question about the irritating tin can with the assertion that 'the writer is of service to mankind'. It's an embarrassingly lofty declaration. But then, as has been said, there is no platform loftier than that erected every October in Stockholm. If writers cannot express their highest ideals there, they can express them nowhere.

John Sutherland
June 2007

Orhan Pamuk

My Father's Suitcase
2006

Orhan Pamuk was born in Istanbul in 1952 into a family of engineers. He was educated in Istanbul at an American school. He dropped out of his architecture course to become a full-time writer and obtained a degree in journalism from Istanbul University. Since 1982, when his first novel was published to great acclaim, Pamuk has been one of Turkey's most successful authors. After three years in the USA, including a stint as visiting fellow at the University of Iowa, he returned to Istanbul, where he lives with his wife and daughter. In 1995 Pamuk was among a group of authors tried for criticising the Turkish regime's treatment of the Kurds in a book of essays exercising the freedom of speech.

He is the author of seven novels. The White Castle *won the 1990 Independent Award for Foreign Fiction, and the publication of* The New Life *caused a sensation in his native land, becoming the fastest-selling book in Turkish history. In 2003 Pamuk was awarded the International IMPAC Award for* My Name is Red.

Two years before his death, my father gave me a small suitcase filled with his writings, manuscripts and notebooks. Assuming his usual joking, mocking air, he told me he wanted me to read them after he was gone, by which he meant after he died.

'Just take a look,' he said, looking slightly embarrassed. 'See if there's anything inside that you can use. Maybe after I'm gone you can make a selection and publish it.'

We were in my study, surrounded by books. My father was searching for a place to set down the suitcase, wandering back and forth like a man who wished to rid himself of a painful burden. In the end, he deposited it quietly in an unobtrusive corner. It was a shaming moment that neither of us ever forgot, but once it had passed and we had gone back into our usual roles, taking life lightly, our joking, mocking personas took over and we relaxed. We talked as we always did, about the trivial things of everyday life, and Turkey's never-ending political troubles, and my father's mostly failed business ventures, without feeling too much sorrow.

I remember that after my father left, I spent several days walking back and forth past the suitcase without once touching it. I was already familiar with this small, black, leather suitcase, and its lock, and its rounded corners. My father would take it with him on short trips and sometimes use it to carry documents to work. I remembered that when I was a child, and my father came home from a trip, I would open this little suitcase and rummage through his things, savouring the scent of cologne and foreign countries. This suitcase was a familiar friend, a powerful reminder of my childhood, my past, but now I couldn't even touch it. Why? No doubt it was because of the mysterious weight of its contents.

I am now going to speak of this weight's meaning. It is what a person creates when he shuts himself up in a room, sits down at a table, and retires to a corner to express his thoughts – that is, the meaning of literature.

When I did touch my father's suitcase, I still could not bring myself to open it, but I did know what was inside some of those notebooks. I had seen my father writing things in a few of them. This was not the first time I had heard of the heavy load inside the suitcase. My father had a large library; in his youth, in the late 1940s, he had wanted to be an Istanbul poet, and had translated Valéry into Turkish, but he had not wanted to live the sort of life that came with writing poetry in a poor country with few readers. My father's father – my grandfather – had been a wealthy businessman; my father had led a comfortable life as a child and a young man, and he had no wish to endure hardship for the sake of literature, for writing. He loved life with all its beauties – this I understood.

The first thing that kept me distant from the contents of my father's suitcase was, of course, the fear that I might not like what I read. Because my father knew this, he had taken the precaution of acting as if he did not take its contents seriously. After working as a writer for 25 years, it pained me to see this. But I did not even want to be angry at my father for failing to take literature seriously enough ... My real fear, the crucial thing that I did not wish to know or discover, was the possibility that my father might be a good writer. I couldn't open my father's suitcase because I feared this. Even worse, I couldn't even admit this myself openly. If true and great literature emerged from my father's suitcase, I would have to acknowledge that inside my father there existed an entirely different man. This was a frightening possibility. Because even at my advanced age I wanted my father to be only my father – not a writer.

A writer is someone who spends years patiently trying to discover the second being inside him, and the world that makes him who he is: when I speak of writing, what comes first to my mind is not a novel, a poem, or literary tradition, it is a person who shuts himself up in a room, sits down at a table, and alone, turns inward; amid its shadows, he builds a new world with words. This man – or this woman – may use a typewriter, profit from the ease of a computer, or write with a pen on paper, as I have done for 30 years. As he writes, he can drink tea or coffee, or smoke cigarettes. From time to time he may rise from his table to look out through the window at the children playing in the street, and, if he is lucky, at trees and a view, or he can gaze out at a black wall. He can write poems, plays, or novels, as I do. All these differences come after the crucial task of sitting down at the table and patiently turning inwards. To write is to turn this inward gaze into words, to study the world into which that person passes when he retires into himself, and to do so with patience, obstinacy, and joy. As I sit at my table, for days, months, years, slowly adding new words to the empty page, I feel as if I am creating a new world, as if I am bringing into being that other person inside me, in the same way someone might build a bridge or a dome, stone by stone. The stones we writers use are words. As we hold them in our hands, sensing the ways in which each of them is connected to the others, looking at them sometimes from afar, sometimes almost caressing them with our fingers and the tips of our pens, weighing them, moving them around, year in and year out, patiently and hopefully, we create new worlds.

The writer's secret is not inspiration – for it is never clear where it comes from – it is his stubbornness, his patience. That lovely Turkish saying – to dig a well with a needle – seems to me to have been said with writers in mind. In the old stories, I love the patience of Ferhat, who digs through mountains for his love – and I understand it, too. In my novel, *My Name is Red*, when I wrote about the old Persian miniaturists who had drawn the same horse with the same passion for so many years, memorising each stroke, that they could recreate that beautiful horse even with their eyes closed, I knew I was talking about the writing profession, and my own life. If a writer is to tell his own story – tell it slowly, and as if it were a story about other people – if he is to feel the power of the story rise up inside him, if he is to sit down at a table and patiently give himself over to this art – this craft – he must first have been given some hope. The angel of inspiration (who pays regular visits to some and rarely calls on others) favours the hopeful and the confident, and it is when a writer feels most lonely, when he feels most doubtful about his efforts, his dreams, and the value of his writing – when he thinks his story is only his story – it is at such moments that the angel chooses to reveal to him stories, images and dreams that will draw out the world he wishes to build. If I think back on the books to which I have devoted my entire life, I am most surprised by those moments when I have felt as if the sentences, dreams, and pages that have made me so ecstatically happy have not come from my own imagination – that another power has found them and generously presented them to me.

I was afraid of opening my father's suitcase and reading his notebooks because I knew that he would not tolerate the difficulties I had endured, that it was not solitude he loved but mixing with friends, crowds, salons, jokes, company. But later my thoughts took a different turn. These thoughts, these dreams of renunciation and patience, were prejudices I had derived from my own life and my own experience as a writer. There were plenty of brilliant writers who wrote surrounded by crowds and family life, in the glow of company and happy chatter. In addition, my father had, when we were young, tired of the monotony of family life, and left us to go to Paris, where – like so many writers – he'd sat in his hotel room filling notebooks. I knew, too, that some of those very notebooks were in this suitcase, because during the years before he brought it to me, my father had finally begun to talk to me about that period in his life. He spoke about those years even when I was a child, but he would not mention his vulnerabilities, his dreams of becoming a writer, or the questions of identity that had plagued him in his hotel room. He would tell me instead about all the times he'd seen Sartre on the pavements of Paris, about the books he'd read and the films he'd seen, all with the elated sincerity of someone imparting very important news. When I became a writer, I never forgot that it was partly thanks to the fact that I had a father who would talk of world writers so much more than he spoke of pashas or great religious leaders. So perhaps I had to read my father's notebooks with this in mind, and remembering how indebted I was to his large library. I had to bear in mind that when he was living with us, my father, like me, enjoyed being alone with his books and his thoughts – and not pay too much attention to the literary quality of his writing.

But as I gazed so anxiously at the suitcase my father had bequeathed me, I also felt that this was the very thing I would not be able to do. My father would sometimes stretch out on the divan in front of his books, abandon the book in his hand, or the magazine, and drift off into a dream, lose himself for the longest time in his thoughts. When I saw on his face an expression so very different from the one he wore amid the joking, teasing, and bickering of family life – when I saw the first signs of an inward gaze – I would, especially during my childhood and my early youth, understand, with trepidation, that he was discontent. Now, so many years later, I know that this discontent is the basic trait that turns a person into a writer. To become a writer, patience and toil are not enough: we must first feel compelled to escape crowds, company, the stuff of ordinary, everyday life, and shut ourselves up in a room. We wish for patience and hope so that we can create a deep world in our writing. But the desire to shut oneself up in a room is what pushes us into action. The precursor of this sort of independent writer – who reads his books to his heart's content, and who, by listening only to the voice of his own conscience, disputes with others' words, who, by entering into conversation with his books, develops his own thoughts, and his own world – was most certainly Montaigne, in the earliest days of modern literature. Montaigne was a writer to whom my father returned often, a writer he recommended to me. I would like to see myself as belonging to the tradition of writers who – wherever they are in the world, in the East or in the West – cut themselves off from society, and shut themselves up with their books in their room. The starting point of true literature is the man who shuts himself up in his room with his books.

But once we shut ourselves away, we soon discover that we are not as alone as we thought. We are in the company of the words of those who came before us, of other people's stories, other people's books, other people's words, the thing we call tradition. I believe literature to be the most valuable hoard that humanity has gathered in its quest to understand itself. Societies, tribes, and peoples grow more intelligent, richer, and more advanced as they pay attention to the troubled words of their authors, and, as we all know, the burning of books and the denigration of writers are both signals that dark and improvident times are upon us. But literature is never just a national concern. The writer who shuts himself up in a room and first goes on a journey inside himself will, over the years, discover literature's eternal rule: he must have the artistry to tell his own stories as if they were other people's stories, and to tell other people's stories as if they were his own, for this is what literature is. But we must first travel through other people's stories and books.

My father had a good library – 1,500 volumes in all – more than enough for a writer. By the age of 22, I had perhaps not read them all, but I was familiar with each book – I knew which were important, which were light but easy to read, which were classics, which an essential part of any education, which were forgettable but amusing accounts of local history, and which French authors my father rated very highly. Sometimes I would look at this library from a distance and imagine that one day, in a different house, I would build my own library, an even better library – build myself a world. When I looked at my father's library from afar, it seemed to me to be a small picture of the real world. But this was a world seen from our own corner, from Istanbul. The library was evidence of this. My father had built his library from his trips abroad, mostly with books from Paris and America, but also with books bought from the shops that sold books in foreign languages in the 40s and 50s and Istanbul's old and new booksellers, whom I also knew. My world is a mixture of the local – the national – and the West. In the 70s, I, too, began, somewhat ambitiously, to build my own library. I had not quite decided to become a writer – as I related in *Istanbul*, I had come to feel that I would not, after all, become a painter, but I was not sure what path my life would take. There was inside me a relentless curiosity, a hope-driven desire to read and learn, but at the same time I felt that my life was in some way lacking, that I would not be able to live like others. Part of this feeling was connected to what I felt when I gazed at my father's library – to be living far from the centre of things, as all of us who lived in Istanbul in those days were made to feel, that feeling of living in the provinces. There was another reason for feeling anxious and somehow lacking, for I knew only too well that I lived in a country that showed little interest in its artists – be they painters or writers – and that gave them no hope. In the 70s, when I would take the money my father gave me and greedily buy faded, dusty, dog-eared books from Istanbul's old booksellers, I would be as affected by the pitiable state of these second-hand bookstores – and by the despairing dishevelment of the poor, bedraggled booksellers who laid out their wares on roadsides, in mosque courtyards, and in the niches of crumbling walls – as I was by their books.

As for my place in the world – in life, as in literature, my basic feeling was that I was 'not in the centre'. In the centre of the world, there was a life richer and more exciting than our own, and with all of Istanbul, all of Turkey, I was outside it. Today I think that I share this feeling with most people in the world. In the same way, there was a world literature, and its centre, too, was very far away from me. Actually what I had in mind was Western, not world, literature, and we Turks were outside it. My father's library was evidence of this. At one end, there were Istanbul's books – our literature, our local world, in all its beloved detail – and at the other end were the books from this other, Western, world, to which our own bore no resemblance, to which our lack of resemblance gave us both pain and hope. To write, to read, was like leaving one world to find consolation in the other world's otherness, the strange and the wondrous. I felt that my father had read novels to escape his life and flee to the West – just as I would do later. Or it seemed to me that books in those days were things we picked up to escape our own culture, which we found so lacking. It wasn't just by reading that we left our Istanbul lives to travel West – it was by writing, too. To fill those notebooks of his, my father had gone to Paris, shut himself up in his room, and then brought his writings back to Turkey. As I gazed at my father's suitcase, it seemed to me that this was what was causing me disquiet. After working in a room for 25 years to survive as a writer in Turkey, it galled me to see my father hide his deep thoughts inside this suitcase, to act as if writing was work that had to be done in secret, far from the eyes of society, the state, the people. Perhaps this was the main reason why I felt angry at my father for not taking literature as seriously as I did.

Actually I was angry at my father because he had not led a life like mine, because he had never quarrelled with his life, and had spent his life happily laughing with his friends and his loved ones. But part of me knew that I could also say that I was not so much 'angry' as 'jealous', that the second word was more accurate, and this, too, made me uneasy. That would be when I would ask myself in my usual scornful, angry voice: 'What is happiness?' Was happiness thinking that I lived a deep life in that lonely room? Or was happiness leading a comfortable life in society, believing in the same things as everyone else, or acting as if you did? Was it happiness, or unhappiness, to go through life writing in secret, while seeming to be in harmony with all around one? But these were overly ill-tempered questions. Wherever had I got this idea that the measure of a good life was happiness? People, papers, everyone acted as if the most important measure of a life was happiness. Did this alone not suggest that it might be worth trying to find out if the exact opposite was true? After all, my father had run away from his family so many times – how well did I know him, and how well could I say I understood his disquiet?

So this was what was driving me when I first opened my father's suitcase. Did my father have a secret, an unhappiness in his life about which I knew nothing, something he could endure only by pouring it into his writing? As soon as I opened the suitcase, I recalled its scent of travel, recognised several notebooks, and noted that my father had shown them to me years earlier, but without dwelling on them very long. Most of the notebooks I now took into my hands he had filled when he had left us and gone to Paris as a young man. Whereas I, like so many writers I admired – writers whose biographies I had read – wished to know what my father had written, and what he had thought, when he was the age I was now. It did not take me long to realise that I would find nothing like that here. What caused me most disquiet was when, here and there in my father's notebooks, I came upon a writerly voice. This was not my father's voice, I told myself; it wasn't authentic, or at least it did not belong to the man I'd known as my father. Underneath my fear that my father might not have been my father when he wrote, was a deeper fear: the fear that deep inside I was not authentic, that I would find nothing good in my father's writing; this increased my fear of finding my father to have been overly influenced by other writers and plunged me into a despair that had afflicted me so badly when I was young, casting my life, my very being, my desire to write, and my work into question. During my first ten years as a writer, I felt these anxieties more deeply, and even as I fought them off, I would sometimes fear that one day, I would have to admit to defeat – just as I had done with painting – and succumbing to disquiet, give up novel-writing, too.

I have already mentioned the two essential feelings that rose up in me as I closed my father's suitcase and put it away: the sense of being marooned in the provinces, and the fear that I lacked authenticity. This was certainly not the first time they had made themselves felt. For years I had, in my reading and my writing, been studying, discovering, deepening these emotions, in all their variety and unintended consequences, their nerve endings, their triggers, and their many colours. Certainly my spirits had been jarred by the confusions, the sensitivities and the fleeting pains that life and books had sprung on me, most often as a young man. But it was only by writing books that I came to a fuller understanding of the problems of authenticity (as in *My Name is Red* and *The Black Book*) and the problems of life on the periphery (as in *Snow* and *Istanbul*). For me, to be a writer is to acknowledge the secret wounds that we carry inside us, the wounds so secret that we ourselves are barely aware of them, and to patiently explore them, know them, illuminate them, to own these pains and wounds, and to make them a conscious part of our spirits and our writing.

A writer talks of things that everyone knows but does not know they know. To explore this knowledge, and to watch it grow, is a pleasurable thing; the reader is visiting a world at once familiar and miraculous. When a writer shuts himself up in a room for years on end to hone his craft – to create a world – if he uses his secret wounds as his starting point, he is, whether he knows it or not, putting a great faith in humanity. My confidence comes from the belief that all human beings resemble each other, that others carry wounds like mine – that they will therefore understand. All true literature rises from this childish, hopeful certainty that all people resemble each other. When a writer shuts himself up in a room for years on end, with this gesture he suggests a single humanity, a world without a centre.

But as can be seen from my father's suitcase and the pale colours of our lives in Istanbul, the world did have a centre, and it was far away from us. In my books I have described in some detail how this basic fact evoked a Chekhovian sense of provinciality, and how, by another route, it led to my questioning my authenticity. I know from experience that the great majority of people on this earth live with these same feelings, and that many suffer from an even deeper sense of insufficiency, lack of security and sense of degradation, than I do. Yes, the greatest dilemmas facing humanity are still landlessness, homelessness, and hunger ... But today our televisions and newspapers tell us about these fundamental problems more quickly and more simply than literature can ever do. What literature needs most to tell and investigate today are humanity's basic fears: the fear of being left outside, and the fear of counting for nothing, and the feelings of worthlessness that come with such fears; the collective humiliations, vulnerabilities, slights, grievances, sensitivities, and imagined insults, and the nationalist boasts and inflations that are their next of kin ... Whenever I am confronted by such sentiments, and by the irrational, overstated language in which they are usually expressed, I know they touch on a darkness inside me. We have often witnessed peoples, societies and nations outside the Western world – and I can identify with them easily – succumbing to fears that sometimes lead them to commit stupidities, all because of their fears of humiliation and their sensitivities. I also know that in the West – a world with which I can identify with the same ease – nations and peoples taking an excessive pride in their wealth, and in their having brought us the Renaissance, the Enlightenment, and Modernism, have, from time to time, succumbed to a self-satisfaction that is almost as stupid.

This means that my father was not the only one, that we all give too much importance to the idea of a world with a centre. Whereas the thing that compels us to shut ourselves up to write in our rooms for years on end is a faith in the opposite; the belief that one day our writings will be read and understood, because people all the world over resemble each other. But this, as I know from my own and my father's writing, is a troubled optimism, scarred by the anger of being consigned to the margins, of being left outside. The love and hate that Dostoyevsky felt towards the West all his life – I have felt this too, on many occasions. But if I have grasped an essential truth, if I have cause for optimism, it is because I have travelled with this great writer through his love-hate relationship with the West, to behold the other world he has built on the other side.

All writers who have devoted their lives to this task know this reality: whatever our original purpose, the world that we create after years and years of hopeful writing will, in the end, move to other very different places. It will take us far away from the table at which we have worked with sadness or anger, take us to the other side of that sadness and anger, into another world. Could my father have not reached such a world himself? Like the land that slowly begins to take shape, slowly rising from the mist in all its colours like an island after a long sea journey, this other world enchants us. We are as beguiled as the western travellers who voyaged from the south to behold Istanbul rising from the mist. At the end of a journey begun in hope and curiosity, there lies before them a city of mosques and minarets, a medley of houses, streets, hills, bridges, and slopes, an entire world. Seeing it, we wish to enter into this world and lose ourselves inside it, just as we might a book. After sitting down at a table because we felt provincial, excluded, on the margins, angry, or deeply melancholic, we have found an entire world beyond these sentiments.

What I feel now is the opposite of what I felt as a child and a young man: for me the centre of the world is Istanbul. This is not just because I have lived there all my life, but because, for the last 33 years, I have been narrating its streets, its bridges, its people, its dogs, its houses, its mosques, its fountains, its strange heroes, its shops, its famous characters, its dark spots, its days and its nights, making them part of me, embracing them all. A point arrived when this world I had made with my own hands, this world that existed only in my head, was more real to me than the city in which I actually lived. That was when all these people and streets, objects and buildings would seem to begin to talk amongst themselves, and begin to interact in ways I had not anticipated, as if they lived not just in my imagination or my books, but for themselves. This world that I had created like a man digging a well with a needle would then seem truer than all else.

My father might also have discovered this kind of happiness during the years he spent writing, I thought as I gazed at my father's suitcase: I should not prejudge him. I was so grateful to him, after all: he'd never been a commanding, forbidding, overpowering, punishing, ordinary father, but a father who always left me free, always showed me the utmost respect. I had often thought that if I had, from time to time, been able to draw from my imagination, be it in freedom or childishness, it was because, unlike so many of my friends from childhood and youth, I had no fear of my father, and I had sometimes believed very deeply that I had been able to become a writer because my father had, in his youth, wished to be one, too. I had to read him with tolerance – seek to understand what he had written in those hotel rooms.

It was with these hopeful thoughts that I walked over to the suitcase, which was still sitting where my father had left it; using all my willpower, I read through a few manuscripts and notebooks. What had my father written about? I recall a few views from the windows of Parisian hotels, a few poems, paradoxes, analyses ... As I write I feel like someone who has just been in a traffic accident and is struggling to remember how it happened, while at the same time dreading the prospect of remembering too much. When I was a child, and my father and mother were on the brink of a quarrel – when they fell into one of those deadly silences – my father would at once turn on the radio, to change the mood, and the music would help us forget it all faster.

Let me change the mood with a few sweet words that will, I hope, serve as well as that music. As you know, the question we writers are asked most often, the favourite question, is; why do you write? I write because I have an innate need to write! I write because I can't do normal work like other people. I write because I want to read books like the ones I write. I write because I am angry at all of you, angry at everyone. I write because I love sitting in a room all day writing. I write because I can partake in real life only by changing it. I write because I want others, all of us, the whole world, to know what sort of life we lived, and continue to live, in Istanbul, in Turkey. I write because I love the smell of paper, pen, and ink. I write because I believe in literature, in the art of the novel, more than I believe in anything else. I write because it is a habit, a passion. I write because I am afraid of being forgotten. I write because I like the glory and interest that writing brings. I write to be alone. Perhaps I write because I hope to understand why I am so very, very angry at all of you, so very, very angry at everyone. I write because I like to be read. I write because once I have begun a novel, an essay, a page, I want to finish it. I write because everyone expects me to write. I write because I have a childish belief in the immortality of libraries, and in the way my books sit on the shelf. I write because it is exciting to turn all of life's beauties and riches into words. I write not to tell a story, but to compose a story. I write because I wish to escape from the foreboding that there is a place I must go but – just as in a dream – I can't quite get there. I write because I have never managed to be happy. I write to be happy.

A week after he came to my office and left me his suitcase, my father came to pay me another visit; as always, he brought me a bar of chocolate (he had forgotten I was 48 years old). As always, we chatted and laughed about life, politics and family gossip. A moment arrived when my father's eyes went to the corner where he had left his suitcase and saw that I had moved it. We looked each other in the eye. There followed a pressing silence. I did not tell him that I had opened the suitcase and tried to read its contents; instead I looked away. But he understood. Just as I understood that he had understood. Just as he understood that I had understood that he had understood. But all this understanding went only so far as it can go in a few seconds. Because my father was a happy, easy-going man who had faith in himself: he smiled at me the way he always did. And as he left the house, he repeated all the lovely and encouraging things that he always said to me, like a father.

As always, I watched him leave, envying his happiness, his carefree and unflappable temperament. But I remember that on that day there was also a flash of joy inside me that made me ashamed. It was prompted by the thought that maybe I wasn't as comfortable in life as he was, maybe I had not led as happy or footloose a life as he had, but that I had devoted it to writing – you've understood ... I was ashamed to be thinking such things at my father's expense. Of all people, my father, who had never been the source of my pain – who had left me free. All this should remind us that writing and literature are intimately linked to a lack at the centre of our lives, and to our feelings of happiness and guilt.

But my story has a symmetry that immediately reminded me of something else that day, and that brought me an even deeper sense of guilt. Twenty-three years before my father left me his suitcase, and four years after I had decided, aged 22, to become a novelist, and, abandoning all else, shut myself up in a room, I finished my first novel, *Cevdet Bey and Sons*; with trembling hands I had given my father a typescript of the still unpublished novel, so that he could read it and tell me what he thought. This was not simply because I had confidence in his taste and his intellect: his opinion was very important to me because he, unlike my mother, had not opposed my wish to become a writer. At that point, my father was not with us, but far away. I waited impatiently for his return. When he arrived two weeks later, I ran to open the door. My father said nothing, but he at once threw his arms around me in a way that told me he had liked it very much. For a while, we were plunged into the sort of awkward silence that so often accompanies moments of great emotion. Then, when we had calmed down and begun to talk, my father resorted to highly charged and exaggerated language to express his confidence in me or my first novel: he told me that one day I would win the prize that I am here to receive with such great happiness.

He said this not because he was trying to convince me of his good opinion, or to set this prize as a goal; he said it like a Turkish father, giving support to his son, encouraging him by saying, 'One day you'll become a pasha!' For years, whenever he saw me, he would encourage me with the same words.

My father died in December 2002.

Today, as I stand before the Swedish Academy and the distinguished members who have awarded me this great prize – this great honour – and their distinguished guests, I dearly wish he could be amongst us.

Translated from Turkish by Maureen Freely

Harold Pinter

Art, Truth and Politics
2005

Harold Pinter is recognized as one of the most important British playwrights of the second half of the 20th century. Originally training as an actor, he made his playwriting debut in 1957 with The Room. *Pinter, whose mother was a Jewish dressmaker, was deeply affected by anti-Semitism in his childhood, and he has credited this as a defining experience for his ambition to become a playwright. Among his 29 plays are* The Birthday Party, The Caretaker, One for the Road, The Homecoming *and* Betrayal.

Since the early 1970s Pinter has become as well known for his political activism as for his writing. His often controversial statements are wide-ranging, but address issues such as the abuse of state power, including NATO's bombing of Serbia. He has been a vocal critic of the conflict in Iraq and has campaigned for an end to torture in all its forms. He has also published poetry, written screenplays—including The Go-Between *and* The French Lieutenant's Woman *—and directed theatre, television and film.*

According to the Academy, Pinter 'uncovers the precipice under everyday prattle and forces entry into oppression's closed rooms'.

In 1958 I wrote the following: 'There are no hard distinctions between what is real and what is unreal, nor between what is true and what is false. A thing is not necessarily either true or false; it can be both true and false.'

I believe that these assertions still make sense and do still apply to the exploration of reality through art. So as a writer I stand by them but as a citizen I cannot. As a citizen I must ask: What is true? What is false?

Truth in drama is forever elusive. You never quite find it but the search for it is compulsive. The search is clearly what drives the endeavor. The search is your task. More often than not you stumble upon the truth in the dark, colliding with it or just glimpsing an image or a shape which seems to correspond to the truth, often without realizing that you have done so. But the real truth is that there never is any such thing as one truth to be found in dramatic art. There are many. These truths challenge each other, recoil from each other, reflect each other, ignore each other, tease each other, are blind to each other. Sometimes you feel you have the truth of a moment in your hand, then it slips through your fingers and is lost.

I have often been asked how my plays come about. I cannot say. Nor can I ever sum up my plays, except to say that this is what happened. That is what they said. That is what they did.

Most of the plays are engendered by a line, a word or an image. The given word is often shortly followed by the image. I shall give two examples of two lines which came right out of the blue into my head, followed by an image, followed by me.

The plays are *The Homecoming* and *Old Times*. The first line of *The Homecoming* is 'What have you done with the scissors?' The first line of *Old Times* is 'Dark.'

In each case I had no further information.

In the first case someone was obviously looking for a pair of scissors and was demanding their whereabouts of someone else he suspected had probably stolen them. But I somehow knew that the person addressed didn't give a damn about the scissors or about the questioner either, for that matter.

'Dark' I took to be a description of someone's hair, the hair of a woman, and was the answer to a question. In each case I found myself compelled to pursue the matter. This happened visually, a very slow fade, through shadow into light.

I always start a play by calling the characters A, B and C.

In the play that became *The Homecoming* I saw a man enter a stark room and ask his question of a younger man sitting on an ugly sofa reading a racing paper. I somehow suspected that A was a father and that B was his son, but I had no proof. This was however confirmed a short time later when B (later to become Lenny) says to A (later to become Max), 'Dad, do you mind if I change the subject? I want to ask you something. The dinner we had before, what was the name of it? What do you call it? Why don't you buy a dog? You're a dog cook. Honest. You think you're cooking for a lot of dogs.' So since B calls A 'Dad' it seemed to me reasonable to assume that they were father and son. A was also clearly the cook and his cooking did not seem to be held in high regard. Did this mean that there was no mother? I didn't know. But, as I told myself at the time, our beginnings never know our ends.

'Dark.' A large window. Evening sky. A man, A (later to become Deeley), and a woman, B (later to become Kate), sitting with drinks. 'Fat or thin?' the man asks. Who are they talking about? But I then see, standing at the window, a woman, C (later to become Anna), in another condition of light, her back to them, her hair dark.

It's a strange moment, the moment of creating characters who up to that moment have had no existence. What follows is fitful, uncertain, even hallucinatory, although sometimes it can be an unstoppable avalanche. The author's position is an odd one. In a sense he is not welcomed by the characters. The characters resist him, they are not easy to live with, they are impossible to define. You certainly can't dictate to them. To a certain extent you play a never-ending game with them, cat and mouse, blind man's buff, hide and seek. But finally you find that you have people of flesh and blood on your hands, people with will and an individual sensibility of their own, made out of component parts you are unable to change, manipulate or distort.

So language in art remains a highly ambiguous transaction, a quicksand, a trampoline, a frozen pool which might give way under you, the author, at any time.

But as I have said, the search for the truth can never stop. It cannot be adjourned, it cannot be postponed. It has to be faced, right there, on the spot.

Political theater presents an entirely different set of problems. Sermonizing has to be avoided at all cost. Objectivity is essential. The characters must be allowed to breathe their own air. The author cannot confine and constrict them to satisfy his own taste or disposition or prejudice. He must be prepared to approach them from a variety of angles, from a full and uninhibited range of perspectives, take them by surprise, perhaps, occasionally, but nevertheless give them the freedom to go which way they will. This does not always work. And political satire, of course, adheres to none of these precepts, in fact does precisely the opposite, which is its proper function.

In my play *The Birthday Party* I think I allow a whole range of options to operate in a dense forest of possibility before finally focusing on an act of subjugation.

Mountain Language pretends to no such range of operation. It remains brutal, short and ugly. But the soldiers in the play do get some fun out of it. One sometimes forgets that torturers become easily bored. They need a bit of a laugh to keep their spirits up. This has been confirmed of course by the events at Abu Ghraib in Baghdad. *Mountain Language* lasts only twenty minutes, but it could go on for hour after hour, on and on and on, the same pattern repeated over and over again, on and on, hour after hour.

Ashes to Ashes, on the other hand, seems to me to be taking place under water. A drowning woman, her hand reaching up through the waves, dropping down out of sight, reaching for others, but finding nobody there, either above or under the water, finding only shadows, reflections, floating; the woman a lost figure in a drowning landscape, a woman unable to escape the doom that seemed to belong only to others.

But as they died, she must die too.

Political language, as used by politicians, does not venture into any of this territory since the majority of politicians, on the evidence available to us, are interested not in truth but in power and in the maintenance of that power. To maintain that power it is essential that people remain in ignorance, that they live in ignorance of the truth, even the truth of their own lives. What surrounds us therefore is a vast tapestry of lies, upon which we feed.

As every single person here knows, the justification for the invasion of Iraq was that Saddam Hussein possessed a highly dangerous body of weapons of mass destruction, some of which could be fired in forty-five minutes, bringing about appalling devastation. We were assured that was true. It was not true. We were told that Iraq had a relationship with Al Qaeda and shared responsibility for the atrocity in New York of 11 September 2001. We were assured that this was true. It was not true. We were told that Iraq threatened the security of the world. We were assured it was true. It was not true.

The truth is something entirely different. The truth is to do with how the United States understands its role in the world and how it chooses to embody it.

But before I come back to the present I would like to look at the recent past, by which I mean United States foreign policy since the end of the Second World War. I believe it is obligatory upon us to subject this period to at least some kind of even limited scrutiny, which is all that time will allow here.

Everyone knows what happened in the Soviet Union and throughout Eastern Europe during the post-war period: the systematic brutality, the widespread atrocities, the ruthless suppression of independent thought. All this has been fully documented and verified.

But my contention here is that the US crimes in the same period have only been superficially recorded, let alone documented, let alone acknowledged, let alone recognized as crimes at all. I believe this must be addressed and that the truth has considerable bearing on where the world stands now. Although constrained, to a certain extent, by the existence of the Soviet Union, the United States' actions throughout the world made it clear that it had concluded it had carte blanche to do what it liked.

Direct invasion of a sovereign state has never in fact been America's favoured method. In the main, it has preferred what it has described as 'low intensity conflict'. Low intensity conflict means that thousands of people die but slower than if you dropped a bomb on them in one fell swoop. It means that you infect the heart of the country, that you establish a malignant growth and watch the gangrene bloom. When the populace has been subdued—or beaten to death—the same thing—and your own friends, the military and the great corporations, sit comfortably in power, you go before the camera and say that democracy has prevailed. This was a commonplace in US foreign policy in the years to which I refer.

The tragedy of Nicaragua was a highly significant case. I choose to offer it here as a potent example of America's view of its role in the world, both then and now.

I was present at a meeting at the US embassy in London in the late 1980s.

The United States Congress was about to decide whether to give more money to the Contras in their campaign against the state of Nicaragua. I was a member of a delegation speaking on behalf of Nicaragua but the most important member of this delegation was a Father John Metcalf. The leader of the US body was Raymond Seitz (then number two to the ambassador, later ambassador himself). Father Metcalf said:

'Sir, I am in charge of a parish in the north of Nicaragua. My parishioners built a school, a health center, a cultural center. We have lived in peace. A few months ago a Contra force attacked the parish. They destroyed everything: the school, the health center, the cultural center. They raped nurses and teachers, slaughtered doctors, in the most brutal manner. They behaved like savages. Please demand that the US government withdraw its support from this shocking terrorist activity.'

Raymond Seitz had a very good reputation as a rational, responsible and highly sophisticated man. He was greatly respected in diplomatic circles. He listened, paused and then spoke with some gravity. 'Father,' he said, 'let me tell you something. In war, innocent people always suffer.' There was a frozen silence. We stared at him. He did not flinch.

Innocent people, indeed, always suffer.

Finally somebody said: 'But in this case "innocent people" were the victims of a gruesome atrocity subsidized by your government, one among many. If Congress allows the Contras more money further atrocities of this kind will take place. Is this not the case? Is your government not therefore guilty of supporting acts of murder and destruction upon the citizens of a sovereign state?'

Seitz was imperturbable. 'I don't agree that the facts as presented support your assertions,' he said.

As we were leaving the embassy a US aide told me that he enjoyed my plays. I did not reply.

I should remind you that at the time President Reagan made the following statement: 'The Contras are the moral equivalent of our Founding Fathers.'

The United States supported the brutal Somoza dictatorship in Nicaragua for over 40 years. The Nicaraguan people, led by the Sandinistas, overthrew this regime in 1979, a breathtaking popular revolution.

The Sandinistas weren't perfect. They possessed their fair share of arrogance and their political philosophy contained a number of contradictory elements. But they were intelligent, rational and civilized. They set out to establish a stable, decent, pluralistic society. The death penalty was abolished. Hundreds of thousands of poverty-stricken peasants were brought back from the dead. Over 100,000 families were given title to land. Two thousand schools were built. A quite remarkable literacy campaign reduced illiteracy in the country to less than one-seventh. Free education was established and a free health service. Infant mortality was reduced by a third. Polio was eradicated.

The United States denounced these achievements as Marxist/Leninist subversion. In the view of the US government, a dangerous example was being set. If Nicaragua was allowed to establish basic norms of social and economic justice, if it was allowed to raise the standards of health care and education and achieve social unity and national self respect, neighbouring countries would ask the same questions and do the same things. There was of course at the time fierce resistance to the status quo in El Salvador.

I spoke earlier about 'a tapestry of lies' which surrounds us. President Reagan commonly described Nicaragua as a 'totalitarian dungeon'. This was taken generally by the media, and certainly by the British government, as accurate and fair comment. But there was in fact no record of death squads under the Sandinista government. There was no record of torture. There was no record of systematic or official military brutality. No priests were ever murdered in Nicaragua. There were in fact three priests in the government, two Jesuits and a Maryknoll missionary. The totalitarian dungeons were actually next door, in El Salvador and Guatemala. The United States had brought down the democratically elected government of Guatemala in

1954 and it is estimated that over 200,000 people had been victims of successive military dictatorships.

Six of the most distinguished Jesuits in the world were viciously murdered at the Central American University in San Salvador in 1989 by a battalion of the Alcatl regiment trained at Fort Benning, Georgia, USA. That extremely brave man Archbishop Romero was assassinated while saying mass. It is estimated that 75,000 people died. Why were they killed? They were killed because they believed a better life was possible and should be achieved. That belief immediately qualified them as communists. They died because they dared to question the status quo, the endless plateau of poverty, disease, degradation and oppression, which had been their birthright.

The United States finally brought down the Sandinista government. It took some years and considerable resistance but relentless economic persecution and 30,000 dead finally undermined the spirit of the Nicaraguan people. They were exhausted and poverty stricken once again. The casinos moved back into the country. Free health and free education were over. Big business returned with a vengeance. 'Democracy' had prevailed.

But this 'policy' was by no means restricted to Central America. It was conducted throughout the world. It was neverending. And it is as if it never happened.

The United States supported and in many cases engendered every right-wing military dictatorship in the world after the end of the Second World War. I refer to Indonesia, Greece, Uruguay, Brazil, Paraguay, Haiti, Turkey, the Philippines, Guatemala, El Salvador and, of course, Chile. The horror the United States inflicted upon Chile in 1973 can never be purged and can never be forgiven.

Hundreds of thousands of deaths took place throughout these countries. Did they take place? And are they in all cases attributable to US foreign policy? The answer is yes they did take place and they are attributable to American foreign policy. But you wouldn't know it.

It never happened. Nothing ever happened. Even while it was happening it wasn't happening. It didn't matter. It was of no interest. The crimes of the United States have been systematic, constant, vicious, remorseless, but very few people have actually talked about them. You have to hand it to America. It has exercised a quite clinical manipulation of power worldwide while masquerading as a force for universal good. It's a brilliant, even witty, highly successful act of hypnosis.

I put to you that the United States is without doubt the greatest show on the road. Brutal, indifferent, scornful and ruthless it may be but it is also very clever. As a salesman it is out on its own and its most saleable commodity is self-love. It's a winner. Listen to all American presidents on television say the words, 'the American people', as in the sentence, 'I say to the American people it is time to pray and to defend the rights of the American people and I ask the American people to trust their president in the action he is about to take on behalf of the American people.'

It's a scintillating stratagem. Language is actually employed to keep thought at bay. The words 'the American people' provide a truly voluptuous cushion of reassurance. You don't need to think. Just lie back on the cushion. The cushion may be suffocating your intelligence and your critical faculties but it's very comfortable. This does not apply of course to the 40 million people living below the poverty line and the 2 million men and women imprisoned in the vast gulag of prisons, which extends across the US.

The United States no longer bothers about low intensity conflict. It no longer sees any point in being reticent or even devious. It puts its cards on the table without fear or favour. It quite simply doesn't give a damn about the United Nations, international law or critical dissent, which it regards as impotent and irrelevant. It also has its own bleating little lamb tagging behind it on a lead, the pathetic and supine Great Britain.

What has happened to our moral sensibility? Did we ever have any? What do these words mean? Do they refer to a term very rarely employed these days—conscience? A conscience to do not only with our own acts but to do with our shared responsibility in the acts of others? Is all this dead? Look at Guantanamo Bay. Hundreds of people detained without charge for over three years, with no legal representation or due process, technically detained forever. This totally illegitimate structure is maintained in defiance of the Geneva Convention. It is not only tolerated but hardly thought about by what's called the 'international community'. This criminal outrage is being committed by a country which declares itself to be 'the leader of the free world'. Do we think about the inhabitants of Guantanamo Bay? What does the media say about them? They pop up occasionally—a small item on page six. They have been consigned to a no-man's-land from which indeed they may never return. At present many are on hunger strike, being force-fed, including British residents. No niceties in these force-feeding procedures. No sedative or anesthetic. Just a tube stuck up your nose and into your throat. You vomit blood. This is torture. What has the British Foreign Secretary said about this? Nothing. What has the British Prime Minister said about this? Nothing. Why not? Because the United States has said: to criticize our conduct in Guantanamo Bay constitutes an unfriendly act. You're either with us or against us. So Blair shuts up.

The invasion of Iraq was a bandit act, an act of blatant state terrorism, demonstrating absolute contempt for the concept of international law. The invasion was an arbitrary military action inspired by a series of lies upon lies and gross manipulation of the media and therefore of the public; an act intended to consolidate American military and economic control of the

Middle East masquerading—as a last resort—all other justifications having failed to justify themselves—as liberation. A formidable assertion of military force responsible for the death and mutilation of thousands and thousands of innocent people.

We have brought torture, cluster bombs, depleted uranium, innumerable acts of random murder, misery, degradation and death to the Iraqi people and call it 'bringing freedom and democracy to the Middle East'.

How many people do you have to kill before you qualify to be described as a mass murderer and a war criminal? One hundred thousand? More than enough, I would have thought. Therefore it is just that Bush and Blair be arraigned before the International Criminal Court of Justice. But Bush has been clever. He has not ratified the International Criminal Court of Justice. Therefore if any American soldier or for that matter politician finds himself in the dock Bush has warned that he will send in the marines. But Tony Blair has ratified the Court and is therefore available for prosecution. We can let the Court have his address if they're interested. It is Number 10, Downing Street, London.

Death in this context is irrelevant. Both Bush and Blair place death well away on the back burner. At least 100,000 Iraqis were killed by American bombs and missiles before the Iraq insurgency began. These people are of no moment. Their deaths don't exist. They are blank. They are not even recorded as being dead. 'We don't do body counts,' said the American general Tommy Franks.

Early in the invasion there was a photograph published on the front page of British newspapers of Tony Blair kissing the cheek of a little Iraqi boy. 'A grateful child,' said the caption. A few days later there was a story and photograph, on an inside page, of another four-year-old boy with no arms. His family had been blown up by a missile. He was the only survivor. 'When do I get my arms back?' he asked. The story was dropped. Well, Tony Blair wasn't holding him in his arms, nor the body of any other mutilated child, nor the body of any bloody corpse. Blood is dirty. It dirties your shirt and tie when you're making a sincere speech on television.

The 2,000 American dead are an embarrassment. They are transported to their graves in the dark. Funerals are unobtrusive, out of harm's way. The mutilated rot in their beds, some for the rest of their lives. So the dead and the mutilated both rot, in different kinds of graves.

Here is an extract from a poem by Pablo Neruda, 'I'm Explaining a Few Things':

> And one morning all that was burning,
> one morning the bonfires
> leapt out of the earth
> devouring human beings
> and from then on fire,
> gunpowder from then on,
> and from then on blood.
> Bandits with planes and Moors,
> bandits with finger-rings and duchesses,
> bandits with black friars spattering blessings
> came through the sky to kill children
> and the blood of children ran through the streets
> without fuss, like children's blood.
>
> Jackals that the jackals would despise
> stones that the dry thistle would bite on and spit out,
> vipers that the vipers would abominate.
> Face to face with you I have seen the blood
> of Spain tower like a tide
> to drown you in one wave
> of pride and knives.

Treacherous
generals:
see my dead house,
look at broken Spain:
from every house burning metal flows
instead of flowers
from every socket of Spain
Spain emerges and from every dead child a rifle with eyes
and from every crime bullets are born
which will one day find
the bull's eye of your hearts.

And you will ask: why doesn't his poetry
speak of dreams and leaves
and the great volcanoes of his native land.

Come and see the blood in the streets.
Come and see
the blood in the streets.
Come and see the blood
in the streets![1]

Let me make it quite clear that in quoting from Neruda's poem I am in no way comparing Republican Spain to Saddam Hussein's Iraq. I quote Neruda because nowhere in contemporary poetry have I read such a powerful visceral description of the bombing of civilians.

I have said earlier that the United States is now totally frank about putting its cards on the table. That is the case. Its official declared policy is now defined as 'full spectrum dominance'. That is not my term, it is theirs. 'Full spectrum dominance' means control of land, sea, air and space and all attendant resources.

The United States now occupies 702 military installations throughout the world in 132 countries, with the honourable exception of Sweden, of course. We don't quite know how they got there but they are there all right.

The United States possesses 8,000 active and operational nuclear warheads. Two thousand are on hair trigger alert, ready to be launched with fifteen minutes' warning. It is developing new systems of nuclear force, known as bunker busters. The British, ever cooperative, are intending to replace their own nuclear missile, Trident. Who, I wonder, are they aiming at? Osama bin Laden? You? Me? Joe Dokes? China? Paris? Who knows? What we do know is that this infantile insanity—the possession and threatened use of nuclear weapons—is at the heart of present American political philosophy. We must remind ourselves that the United States is on a permanent military footing and shows no sign of relaxing it.

Many thousands, if not millions, of people in the United States itself are demonstrably sickened, shamed and angered by their government's actions, but as things stand they are not a coherent political force—yet. But the anxiety, uncertainty and fear which we can see growing daily in the United States is unlikely to diminish.

I know that President Bush has many extremely competent speech writers but I would like to volunteer for the job myself. I propose the following short address which he can make on television to the nation. I see him grave, hair carefully combed, serious, winning, sincere, often beguiling, sometimes employing a wry smile, curiously attractive, a man's man.

'God is good. God is great. God is good. My God is good. Bin Laden's God is bad. His is a bad God. Saddam's God was bad, except he didn't have one. He was a barbarian. We are not barbarians. We don't chop people's heads off. We believe in freedom. So does God. I am not a barbarian. I am the democratically elected leader of a freedom-loving democracy. We are a compassionate society. We give compassionate electrocution and compassionate lethal injection. We are a great nation. I am not a dictator. He is. I am not a barbarian. He is. And he is. They all are. I possess moral authority. You see this fist? This is my moral authority. And don't you forget it.'

A writer's life is a highly vulnerable, almost naked activity. We don't have to weep about that. The writer makes his choice and is stuck with it. But it is true to say that you are open to all the winds, some of them icy indeed. You are out on your own, out on a limb. You find no shelter, no protection—unless you lie—in which case of course you have constructed your own protection and, it could be argued, become a politician.

I have referred to death quite a few times this evening. I shall now quote a poem of my own called 'Death'.

> Where was the dead body found?
> Who found the dead body?
> Was the dead body dead when found?
> How was the dead body found?
>
> Who was the dead body?
>
> Who was the father or daughter or brother
> Or uncle or sister or mother or son
> Of the dead and abandoned body?
>
> Was the body dead when abandoned?
> Was the body abandoned?
> By whom had it been abandoned?
>
> Was the dead body naked or dressed for a journey?
>
> What made you declare the dead body dead?
> Did you declare the dead body dead?
> How well did you know the dead body?
> How did you know the dead body was dead?
>
> Did you wash the dead body
> Did you close both its eyes

> Did you bury the body
> Did you leave it abandoned
> Did you kiss the dead body

When we look into a mirror we think the image that confronts us is accurate. But move a millimetre and the image changes. We are actually looking at a never-ending range of reflections. But sometimes a writer has to smash the mirror—for it is on the other side of that mirror that the truth stares at us.

I believe that despite the enormous odds which exist, unflinching, unswerving, fierce intellectual determination, as citizens, to define the *real* truth of our lives and our societies is a crucial obligation which devolves upon us all. It is in fact mandatory.

If such a determination is not embodied in our political vision we have no hope of restoring what is so nearly lost to us—the dignity of man.

---

1 'I'm Explaining a Few Things' translated by Nathaniel Tarn, from *Pablo Neruda: Selected Poems*, published by Jonathan Cape. Reprinted by permission of The Random House Group Ltd.

Elfriede Jelinek

Sidelined
2004

Elfriede Jelinek spent her childhood in Vienna, where she went to school and later studied composition and organ at the Vienna Conservatory. She began writing poetry when still young, and her first collection, Lisas Schatten, *was published in 1967 when she was 21.*

Jelinek's writing has been described as a combination of purposeful political writing and self-therapy. Her multi-faceted, stream-of-consciousness texts are acclaimed by some, and criticized by others. She has produced many novels and plays, and much of her work has focused on female sexuality and its abuse, and the dominance of power and aggression in human relations. Jelinek's latter work has broadened to encompass social criticism in general and Austria's Nazi past in particular. Her novels include Wir sind Lockvögel, Baby! *(*We are Decoys, Baby!*),* Die Liebhaberinnen *(*Women as Lovers*) and* Die Klavierspielerin *(*The Piano Teacher*), which was made into an award-winning film in 2001.*

Over the past two decades, the focus of Jelinek's writing has shifted from prose to theatre. Moving away from the use of traditional dialogue in her plays, Jelinek has instead placed an emphasis on choreography and employs a series of polyphonic monologues that serve to remove the delineation of roles, thus allowing many voices to be heard simultaneously. Her experimental style has led to some dubbing her plays a new form of theatre. Jelinek's plays include The Wall, Rosamunde *and* Ein Sportstück *(*A Piece of Sport*), the latter an exploration of violence and fascism in the sporting world.*

Jelinek was awarded the Nobel Prize 'for her musical flow of voices and counter-voices in novels and plays that with extraordinary linguistic zeal reveal the absurdity of society's clichés and their subjugating power'.

Is writing the gift of curling up, of curling up with reality? One would so love to curl up, of course, but what happens to me then? What happens to those, who don't really know reality at all? It's so very dishevelled. No comb, that could smooth it down. The writers run through it and despairingly gather together their hair into a style, which promptly haunts them at night. Something's wrong with the way one looks. The beautifully piled up hair can be chased out of its home of dreams again, but can anyway no longer be tamed. Or hangs limp once more, a veil before a face, no sooner than it could finally be subdued. Or stands involuntarily on end in horror at what is constantly happening. It simply won't be tidied up. It doesn't want to. No matter how often one runs the comb with the couple of broken-off teeth through it—it just doesn't. Something is even less right than before. The writing, that deals with what happens, runs through one's fingers like the time, and not only the time, during which it was written, during which life stopped. No one has missed anything, if life stopped. Not the one living and not dead time, and the one who is dead not at all. When one was still writing, time found its way into the work of other writers. Since it is time, it can do everything at once: find its way into one's own work and simultaneously into the work of others, blow into the tousled hairstyles of others like a fresh, even if malign wind, which has risen suddenly and unexpectedly from the direction of reality. Once something has risen, then perhaps it doesn't lie down again so quickly. The angry wind blows and sweeps everything with it. And it sweeps everything away, no matter where, but never back to this reality, which is supposed to be represented. Everywhere, except there. Reality is what gets under the hair, under the skirts and just that: sweeps them away and into something else. How can the writer know reality, if it is that which gets into him and sweeps him away, forever onto the sidelines.

From there, on the one hand, he can see better, on the other he himself cannot remain on the way of reality. There is no place for him there. His place is always outside. Only what he says from the outside can be taken up inside, and that because he speaks ambiguities. And then there are already two who fit, two whose faces are right, who warn, that nothing is happening, two who construe it in different directions, reach out to the inadequate grounds, which have long ago broken off like the fangs of the comb. Either or. True or false. It had to happen sooner or later, since the ground as building ground was quite inadequate. And how could one build on a bottomless pit anyway? But the inadequacy that enters the writers' field of vision, is still adequate enough for something, that they could also take or leave. They could take or leave it, and they do leave it. They don't kill it. They merely look at it with their bleary eyes, but it does not become arbitrary because of this bleary gaze. The gaze is well aimed. Whatever is struck by this gaze says, even as it sinks down, although it has hardly been looked at, although it has not even been exposed to the sharp gaze of the public, whatever has been struck never says, that it could also have been something else, before it fell victim to this one description. It says exactly what had been better left unsaid (because it could have been better said?), what always had to remain unclear and groundless. Too many have already sunk into it up to their stomachs. It's quicksand, but it doesn't quicken anything. It is groundless, but not without grounds. It is as you like, but it is not liked.

The sidelines are at the service of the life, that precisely does not take place there, otherwise we would not all be in the thick of it, in the fullness, the fullness of human life, and it is at the service of the observation of the life, which is always taking place somewhere else. Where one is not. Why insult someone, because he cannot find his way back to the path of journeying, of life, of life's journey, if he has borne it—and this bearing is no bearing someone, but nor is it any kind of bearing on—has simply fortuitously borne it, like the dust on a pair of shoes, which is pitilessly hunted down by the housewife, if a little less pitilessly than the stranger is hunted down by the locals. What kind of dust is it? Is it radioactive or active by itself, just like that, I'm only asking, because it leaves this strange trail of light on the way? Is what is running alongside and never meeting up with the writer again, the way, or is the writer the one who is running alongside, onto the sidelines? He has not yet passed away, but he's already passed the line nevertheless. From there he sees those who have parted from him, but from one another too, in all their variety, in order to represent them in all their credulity, in order to get them on form, because form is the most important thing, anyway he sees them better from there. But that, too, is chalked up against him, so are those chalk marks and not particles of luminous matter, which mark the way of writing? At any rate it's a marking out, which simultaneously shows and obscures and afterwards carefully covers up again the trail he himself laid. One was never there at all. But nevertheless one knows what's up. The words have come down from a screen, from blood-smeared faces distorted with pain, from laughing, made-up faces, with lips pumped up beforehand just for the make-up or from others, who gave the right answer to a question in a quiz, or born mouthers, women, who have nothing for and nothing against, who stood up and took off a jacket to point their freshly hardened breasts, which were once steeled and belonged to men, at the camera. In addition any amount of throats, out of which singing comes like bad breath, only louder. That is what could be seen on the way, if one were still on it. One goes out of the way of the way. Perhaps one sees it from a distance, where one remains alone, and how gladly, because one wants to see the way, but not walk it. Did this path make a noise just now? Does it want to draw attention to itself with noises now and not just with lights, loud people, loud lights? Is the way, which one cannot walk, afraid of not being walked at all, when so many sins are being constantly committed after all, torture, outrages, theft, threatening behavior, necessary threat in the manufacture of significant world fates? It makes no difference to the way. It bears everything, firmly, even if groundlessly. Without ground. On lost ground. My hair, as already mentioned, is standing on end, and no setting lotion there, which could force it to firm up again. No firmness in myself either. Not on me, not in me. When one's on the sidelines, one always has to be ready to jump a bit and then another bit to the side, into the empty space, which is right next to the sidelines. And the sidelines have brought their sideline pitfall along with them, it's ready at any time, it gapes wide, to lure one even further out. Luring out is luring in. Please, I don't want to lose sight now of the way, which I'm not on. I would so like to describe it honestly and above all truly and accurately. If I'm actually looking at it, it should also do something for me. But this way spares me nothing. It leaves me nothing. What else is there left for me? I am prevented from being on my way, I can hardly make my way at all. I am out, while not going out. And there, too, I should certainly like to have protection against my own uncertainty, but also against the uncertainty of the ground, on which I'm standing. It runs to make certain, not only to protect me, my language right beside me, and checks, whether I am doing it properly, describing reality properly wrongly, because it always has to be described wrongly, there's no other way, but so wrongly, that anyone who reads or hears it, notices the falseness immediately. Those are lies! And this dog, language, which is supposed to protect me, that's why I have him, after all, is now snapping at my heels. My protector wants to bite me. My only protector against being described, language, which, conversely, exists to describe something else, that I am not—that is why I cover so much paper—my only protector is turning against me. Perhaps I only keep him at all, so that he, while pretending to protect me, pounces on me. Because I sought protection in writing, this being on my way, language, which in motion, in speaking, appeared to be a safe shelter, turns against me. No wonder. I mistrusted it immediately, after all. What kind of camouflage is that, which exists, not to make one invisible, but ever more distinct?

Sometimes language finds itself on the way by mistake, but it doesn't go out of the way. It is no arbitrary process, speaking with language, it is one that is involuntarily arbitrary, whether one likes it or not. Language knows what it wants. Good for it, because I don't know, no not at all. Talk, talking in general keeps on talking over there now, because there's always talking, talking, without beginning or end, but there's no speaking. So there's talking over there, wherever the others are staying, because they don't want to linger, they're very occupied. Only them over there. Not me. Only the language, which sometimes moves away from me, to the people, not the other people, but moves away over to the real, genuine, on the well-signposted way (who can go astray here?), following their every movement like a camera, so that it at least, the language, finds out, how and what life is, because then it is precisely not that, and afterwards all of it must be described, even in what it precisely is not. Let's talk about the fact, that we are supposed to go for a medical check-up once again. Yet all at once we suddenly speak, with due rigour, like someone who has a choice, whether or not to speak. Whatever happens, only the language goes away from me, I myself, I stay away. The language goes. I stay, but away. Not on the way. And I'm speechless.

No, it's still there. Has it perhaps been there all the time, did it weigh up, whom it could weigh down? It has noticed me now and immediately snaps at me, this language. It dares to adopt this tone of command to me, it raises its hand against me, it doesn't like me. It would gladly like the nice people on the way, alongside whom it runs, like the dog it is, feigning obedience. In reality it not only disobeys me, but everyone else, too. It is for no one but itself. It cries out through the night, because no one has remembered to put up lights beside this way, which are supplied by nothing but the sun and no longer need any current at all from the socket, or to find the path a proper path name. But it has so many names, that it would be impossible to keep up with all the naming, if one tried. I shout across, in my loneliness, stamping across these graves of the departed, because since I am already running alongside, I cannot pay attention as well to what I'm treading on, whom I'm treading down, I would only somehow like to get to the place where my language already is, and where it smirks mockingly across at me. Because it knows, that, if I ever tried to live, it would soon trip me up, then rub salt in my wounds. Good. So I will scatter salt on the way of the others, I throw it down, so that their ice melts, coarse salt, so that their language loses its firm ground. And yet it has long been groundless. What bottomless cheek on its part! If I do not have solid ground under my feet, then my language can't either. Serve it right! Why did it not stay with me, on the sidelines, why did it part from me? It wanted to see more than me? On the highway over there, where there are more people, above all more likeable ones, chatting nicely to each other? It wanted to know more than me? It has always known more than me, it's true, but it has to know even more than that. It will end up killing itself by eating into itself, my language. It will overindulge on reality. Serve it right! I spat it out, but it spits nothing out, it's good at keeping it down. My language calls over to me, over on the sidelines, it likes best of all to call over to the sidelines, it doesn't have to take such careful aim, but it doesn't have to, because it always hits the target, not by saying something or other, but by speaking with the 'austerity of letting be', as Heidegger says about Trakl. It calls me, language does, today anyone can do it, because everyone always carries their language around with them in a small gadget, so that they can speak, why would they have learned it?, so it calls me where I am caught in the trap and cry out and thrash about, but no, it's not true, my language isn't calling, it's gone, too, my language has gone from me, that's why it has to call, it shouts in my ear, no matter out of which gadget, a computer or a mobile phone, a phone booth, from where it roars in my ear, that there's no point in saying something out loud, it already does that anyway, I should simply say what it tells me; because there would be even less point in for once speaking what was on one's mind to a dear person, who has fallen down on the case and whom one can trust, because he has fallen and won't get up again so quickly, in order to pursue one and, yes, to chat a little. There's no point. The words of my language over there on the pleasant way (I know it's more pleasant than mine, which is actually no way at all, but I can't see it clearly, but I know, that I too would like to be there), the words of my language have, therefore, in parting from me, immediately become a speaking out. No, no talking it out with someone. A speaking out. It listens to itself speaking out, my language, it corrects itself, because speaking can still be improved at any time; yes, it can always be improved, it is even entirely there to be improved and then to make a new linguistic ruling, but then only to be able immediately to overturn the rules again. That will then be the new way to salvation, of course I mean solution. A quick fix. Please, dear language, don't you for once want to listen first? So that you learn something, so that you at last learn the rules of speaking ... What are you shouting and grumbling about over there? Are you doing it, language, so that I graciously take you in you again? I thought, you didn't want to come back to me at all! There was no sign, that you wanted to come back to me, it would have been pointless anyway, I wouldn't have understood the sign. You only became language to get away from me and to ensure that I got on? But nothing is ensured. And by you not at all, as well as I know you. I don't even recognise you again. You want to come back to me of your own accord? I won't take you in any more, what do you say to that? Away is away. Away is no way. So if my loneliness, if my constant absence, my uninterrupted existence on the sidelines came in person to fetch back language, so that it, well-looked-after by me, at last came home, to a beautiful sound, which it could utter, then it would only happen, so that with this sound, this penetrating, piercing howling of a siren, blown by the wind, it could drive me further, ever further back from the sidelines. Because of the recoil of this language, which I myself produced and which has run away from me (or did I produce it for that purpose? So that it immediately runs away from me, because I have not managed to run away from myself in time?), I am chased ever deeper into this space beyond the sidelines. My language is already wallowing blissfully in its muddy pool, the little provisional grave on the way, and it looks up at the grave in the air, it wallows on its back, a friendly creature, which would like to please human beings like any respectable language, it wallows, opens its legs, presumably to let itself be stroked, why else. It's greedy for caresses, after all. That stops it from gazing after the dead, so that I must gaze after them instead, and of course in the end it's down to me. So I had no time to curb my language, which now shamelessly rolls around under the hands of the caressers. There are simply too many dead, whom I have to see to, that's an Austrian technical term for: whom I have to look after, whom I have to treat well, but then we're famous for that, for always treating everyone well. The world is looking to us, no need to worry. We don't have to take care of that. Yet the more clearly this demand, to gaze at the dead, sounds in me, the less am I able to pay attention to my words. I must gaze at the dead, while meanwhile the strollers are stroking the good old language and chucking it under the chin, which doesn't make the dead any more alive. No one is to blame. Even I, disheveled as I and my hair are, am not to blame for the dead staying dead. I want the language over there to finally stop making itself the slave of strangers' hands, no matter how good it feels, I want it to begin by stopping making demands, but itself become a demand, to finally face up to, not the caresses, but a demand to come back to me, because language always has to face up, only doesn't always know it and doesn't listen to me. It has to face up, because the people who want to adopt it instead of a child, it's so lovable, if one loves it, people therefore never face up, they decide, they don't answer calls, many of them even immediately destroyed, tore up, burnt their call-up order to sociability, and the flag along with it. So the more people who take up the invitation of my language to scratch its stomach, to ruffle something, to affectionately accept its friendliness, the further I stumble away, I have finally lost my language to those who treat it better, I'm almost flying, where on earth was this way, that I need in order to hurry down? How do I get where to do what? How do I get to the place, where I can unpack my tools, but in reality can right away pack them up again? Over there something bright is gleaming under the branches, is that the place, where my language first of all flatters the others, rocks them into a sense of security, only in order for itself to be lovingly rocked in the end for once? Or does it want to snap again? It always wants to do nothing but bite, only the others don't know it yet, but I know it very well, it was with me for a long time. Beforehand there's first of all cuddles and whispering sweet nothings to this seemingly tame creature, which everyone has at home anyway, why should they bring a strange animal into the house? So why should this language be any different from what they already know? And if it were different, then perhaps it might be dangerous to take it in. Perhaps it won't get on with the one they already have. The more friendly strangers there are, who know how to live, but are nevertheless very far from knowing their life, since they pursue their caressing intents, because they always have to pursue something, the more my seeing no longer clearly sees the way through to the language any more. Miles and more. Who else should be able to see through things, if not seeing? Speaking wants to take over seeing as well? It wants to speak, before it has even seen? It wallows there, is groped by hands, buffeted by winds, caressed by storms, insulted by listening, until it stops listening altogether. Well, then: all listen here for once! Whoever doesn't want to listen, must speak without being listened to. Almost everyone is not listened to, although they speak. I am listened to, although my language does not belong to me, although I can hardly see it any more. Much is said against it. So it no longer has much to say for itself, that's fine. It's listened to, as it slowly repeats, while somewhere a red button is pressed, which sets off a terrible explosion. There's nothing left to say except: Our Father, which art. It cannot mean me, although after all I am father, that is: mother, of my language. I am the father of my mother tongue. The mother tongue was there from the beginning, it was in me, but no father was there, who might have belonged to it. My language was often unbecoming, that was often made clear enough to me, but I didn't want to take the hint. My fault. The father left this nuclear family along with the mother tongue. Right he was. In his place I would not have stayed either. My mother tongue has followed my father now, it's gone. It is, as already mentioned, over there. It listens to the people on the way. On the father's way, who went too soon. Now the language knows something, that you don't know, that he didn't know. But the more it knows, the less it says. Of course, it's constantly saying something, but it's saying nothing. And already the loneliness is taking its leave. It's no longer needed. No one sees, that I am still inside, in the loneliness. I am not heeded. Perhaps I am honoured, but I am not heeded. How do

I ensure that all these words of mine say something, that could say something to us? I cannot do it by speaking. In fact I cannot even speak, because my language is unfortunately not at home just now. Over there it says something else, which I didn't ask it to either, but it has already forgotten my command from the start. It doesn't tell me, although it belongs to me, after all. My language doesn't tell me anything, how should it then tell others something? But nor is it saying nothing, you must admit that! It says all the more, the further away from me it is, indeed, only then does it dare say something, that it wants to say itself, then it dares to disobey me, to resist me. When one looks, one moves further away from the object, the longer one looks at it. When one speaks, one catches hold of it again, but one cannot hold onto it. It tears itself away and hurries after its own naming, the many words I have made and I have lost. Words have been exchanged often enough, the exchange rate is incredibly bad, and then it's no more than: incredible. I say something, and then it's already been forgotten from the start. That's what it strove for, it wanted to get away from me. The unspeakable is spoken every day, but what I say, that isn't to be allowed. That's mean of what has been spoken. That is incredibly mean. The spoken doesn't even want to belong to me. It wants to be done, so that one can say: said and done. I would even be satisfied, if it denied belonging to me, my language, but it should belong to me nevertheless. How can I ensure, that it is at least a little attached to me? Nothing sticks to the others after all, so I offer myself to it. Come back! Come back, please! But no. Over there on the path it's listening to secrets, that I'm not supposed to know, my language, and it passes them on, these secrets, to others who don't want to hear them. I would want to, it would be my right, indeed, it would go down well, if you like, but it doesn't stand still, and speak to me, it doesn't do that either. It is in the empty space which is distinguished and differentiates itself from me, in that there are very many there. Emptiness is the way. I am even on the sidelines of emptiness. I have left the way. I have only said things after another. Much has been said about me, but hardly any of it is true. I myself have only said what others have said, and I say: that is now what is really said. As I said—simply incredible! It's a long time since so much has been said. One's listening can't keep up any more, although one must listen, in order to be able to do something. In this respect, which in reality is a looking away, even a looking away from myself, there's nothing to be said about me, there's nothing to be said, nothing more to be said. I'm always only gazing after life, my language turns its back on me, so that it can present its stomach to strangers to caress, shameless, to me it only shows its back, if anything at all. Too often it doesn't give me a sign and doesn't say anything either. Sometimes I don't even see it over there any more, and now I can't even say 'as has already been said', because while I've already said it often enough, I cannot say it any more, I'm lost for words. Sometimes I see the back or the soles of the feet, on which they can't really walk, the words, but faster than I have been able to for a long time and even now. What am I doing there? Is that why my dear language has lain down some distance away from me? That way it will, of course, always be faster than me, jump up and run away, when I go across to it from my place of work, to fetch it. I don't know, why I should fetch it. So that it doesn't fetch me? Perhaps it, who ran away from me, knows? Who doesn't follow me? Who now follows the looking and speaking of others, and really can't mix up them with me. They are other, because they are the others. For no other reason, except that they are the others. That's good enough for my speaking. The main thing is, I don't do it: speaking. The others, always the others, so that it's not me, who belongs to it, sweet language. I would so much like to stroke it, like the others over there, if I could only catch hold of it. But then it's over there, so that I can't catch hold of it.

When will it silently make off? When will something make off, so there's silence? The more the language over there makes off, the louder it can be heard. It's on everyone's lips, only not on my lips. My mind is clouded. I have not passed out, but my mind is clouded. I am worn out from gazing after my language like a lighthouse by the sea, which is supposed to light someone home and so has itself been lit up, and which as it revolves always reveals something else from the darkness, but is there anyway, whether it is lit up or not, it's a lighthouse, which doesn't help anyone, no matter how hard that man wishes it would, so as not to have to die in the water. The harder I try to make it out, the more obstinately it doesn't go out, language. I now put out this language light mechanically, I switch to the pilot light, but the more I try to clap myself over it, a snuffer on the end of a long pole, with which in my childhood the candles in the church were extinguished, the more I try to snuff out this flame, the more air it seems to have. And all the more loudly it cries out, rolling around under thousands of hands, which do it good, which unfortunately I have never done, I don't know myself, what would do me good, so it's crying out now, so it can keep away from me. It shouts at the others, so that they too join in and cry out like it, so that the noise grows louder. It shouts, that I shouldn't come too close. No one should come too close to anyone at all. And what has been said should also not come too close to what one wants to say. One shouldn't get too close to one's own language, that is an insult, it is quite capable of repeating something after itself, piercingly loud, so that no one hears, that what it says, was earlier recited to it. It even makes me promises, so that I will stay away from it. It promises me everything, if I just don't come close to it. Millions are allowed to get close to it, except me! Yet it's mine!

What do you think of that? I just can't tell you, what I think of that. This language must have forgotten its beginnings, I've got no other explanation. With me it started small. No, how big it's grown, I can't tell you! Like this I don't even recognize it. I knew it, when it was just so high. When it was so quiet, when the language was still my child. Now it has all at once become gigantic. That's not my child any more. The child has not grown up, only big, it doesn't know that it has not yet outgrown me, but it's wide awake nevertheless. It is so wide awake, that it drowns itself out with its crying, and anyone else who cries louder than it. Then it spirals up to an incredible pitch. Believe me, you really don't want to hear it! Also, please don't believe that I'm proud of this child! At its beginning I wanted it to remain as quiet as when it was still speechless. Even now, I don't want it to sweep over something like a storm, causing others to roar even louder and to raise their arms and throw hard objects, which my language can no longer even grasp and catch, it has, my fault, too, always been so unathletic. It doesn't catch. It can throw, but it can't catch. I remain imprisoned in it, even when it's away. I am the prisoner of my language, which is my prison warder. Funny—it's not even keeping an eye on me! Because it is so certain of me? Because it is so certain, that I won't run away, is that why it believes, it can leave me? Here comes someone, who has already died, and he talks to me, although that is not planned for him. He's allowed to, many dead are speaking now in their choked voices, now they dare to, because my own language is not keeping any eye on me. Because it knows, it isn't necessary. Even if it runs away from me, I won't slip through its hands. I am at hand for it, but it has slipped through my hands. But I remain. But what remains, the writers do not make. What remains is gone. The flight of fancy was cut. Nothing and no one has come. And if nevertheless, against all reason, something that has not come at all, a little would like to remain, then what does remain, language, the most fleeting of all, has disappeared. It has replied to a new situations vacant advert. What should remain, is always gone. It is at any rate not there. So what is left to one?

Translated from German by Martin Chalmers

J.M. Coetzee

He and His Man
2003

J.M. Coetzee was born in Cape Town, South Africa, and spent his childhood there and in the town of Worcester on the Western Cape. Although his parents were not British descendants, English was the language spoken in the family home. In the early 1960s Coetzee worked as a computer programmer for IBM in London while completing a thesis on Ford Madox Ford. He returned to South Africa in 1971, after an application for US residency was denied due to his involvement in protests against US military intervention in Vietnam.

In 1974, his first book, Dusklands, *was published in South Africa. Other works include* In the Heart of the Country, Waiting for the Barbarians, Foe, Age of Iron, The Master of St Petersburg *and* Elizabeth Costello. *He has twice won the Man Booker Prize, first with* Life & Times of Michael K *in 1983 and again in 1999 with the novel* Disgrace. *Coetzee's writing is characterized by anti-imperialist attitudes, and the problems faced by modern-day Africa—racial divides, crime, land ownership—are all touched on in his writing, feeding into an exploration of the alienation of the individual that these problems cause.*

In 2002 Coetzee emigrated to Australia, where he now lives in Adelaide. In 2003, the Academy awarded its highest honor to Coetzee, 'who in innumerable guises portrays the surprising involvement of the outsider'.

> But to return to my new companion. I was greatly delighted with him, and made it my business to teach him everything that was proper to make him useful, handy, and helpful; but especially to make him speak, and understand me when I spoke; and he was the aptest scholar there ever was.
>
> —Daniel Defoe, *Robinson Crusoe*

Boston, on the coast of Lincolnshire, is a handsome town, writes his man. The tallest church steeple in all of England is to be found there; sea-pilots use it to navigate by. Around Boston is fen country. Bitterns abound, ominous birds who give a heavy, groaning call loud enough to be heard two miles away, like the report of a gun.

The fens are home to many other kinds of birds too, writes his man, duck and mallard, teal and widgeon, to capture which the men of the fens, the fen men, raise tame ducks, which they call decoy ducks or duckoys.

Fens are tracts of wetland. There are tracts of wetland all over Europe, all over the world, but they are not named fens; *fen* is an English word, it will not migrate.

These Lincolnshire duckoys, writes his man, are bred up in decoy ponds, and kept tame by being fed by hand. Then when the season comes they are sent abroad to Holland and Germany. In Holland and Germany they meet with others of their kind, and, seeing how miserably these Dutch and German ducks live, how their rivers freeze in winter and their lands are covered in snow, fail not to let them know, in a form of language which they make them understand, that in England from where they come the case is quite otherwise: English ducks have sea shores full of nourishing food, tides that flow freely up the creeks; they have lakes, springs, open ponds and sheltered ponds; also lands full of corn left behind by the gleaners; and no frost or snow, or very light.

By these representations, he writes, which are made all in duck language, they, the decoy ducks or duckoys, draw together vast numbers of fowl and, so to say, kidnap them. They guide them back across the seas from Holland and Germany and settle them down in their decoy ponds on the fens of Lincolnshire, chattering and gabbling to them all the time in their own language, telling them these are the ponds they told them of, where they shall live safely and securely.

And while they are so occupied the decoy men, the masters of the decoy ducks, creep into covers or coverts they have built of reeds upon the fens, and all unseen toss handfuls of corn upon the water; and the decoy ducks or duckoys follow them, bringing their foreign guests behind. And so over two or three days they lead their guests up narrower and narrower waterways, calling to them all the time to see how well we live in England, to a place where nets have been spanned.

Then the decoy men send out their decoy dog, which has been perfectly trained to swim after fowl, barking as he swims. Being alarmed to the last degree by this terrible creature, the ducks take to the wing, but are forced down again into the water by the arched nets above, and so must swim or perish, under the net. But the net grows narrower and narrower, like a purse, and at the end stand the decoy men, who take their captives out one by one. The decoy ducks are stroked and made much of, but as for their guests, these are clubbed on the spot and plucked and sold by the hundred and by the thousand.

All of this news of Lincolnshire his man writes in a neat, quick hand, with quills that he sharpens with his little penknife each day before a new bout with the page.

In Halifax, writes his man, there stood, until it was removed in the reign of King James the First, an engine of execution, which worked thus. The condemned man was laid with his head on the cross-base or cup of the scaffold; then the executioner knocked out a pin which held up the heavy blade. The blade descended down a frame as tall as a church door and beheaded the man as clean as a butcher's knife.

Custom had it in Halifax, though, that if between the knocking out of the pin and the descent of the blade the condemned man could leap to his feet, run down the hill and swim across the river without being seized again by the executioner, he would be let free. But in all the years the engine stood in Halifax this never happened.

He (not his man now but he) sits in his room by the waterside in Bristol and reads this. He is getting on in years, almost it might be said he is an old man by now. The skin of his face, that had been almost blackened by the tropic sun before he made a parasol out of palm or palmetto leaves to shade himself, is paler now, but still leathery like parchment; on his nose is a sore from the sun that will not heal.

The parasol he has still with him in his room, standing in a corner, but the parrot that came back with him has passed away. *Poor Robin!* the parrot would squawk from its perch on his shoulder, *Poor Robin Crusoe! Who shall save poor Robin?* His wife could not abide the lamenting of the parrot, *Poor Robin* day in, day out. *I shall wring its neck*, said she, but she had not the courage to do so.

When he came back to England from his island with his parrot and his parasol and his chest full of treasure, he lived for a while tranquilly enough with his old wife on the estate he bought in Huntingdon, for he had become a wealthy man, and wealthier still after the printing of the book of his adventures. But the years in the island, and then the years travelling with his serving-man Friday (poor Friday, he laments to himself, squawk-squawk, for the parrot would never speak Friday's name, only his), had made the life of a landed gentleman dull for him. And, if the truth be told, married life was a sore disappointment too. He found himself retreating more and more to the stables, to his horses, which blessedly did not chatter, but whinnied softly when he came, to show that they knew who he was, and then held their peace.

It seemed to him, coming from his island, where until Friday arrived he lived a silent life, that there was too much speech in the world. In bed beside his wife he felt as if a shower of pebbles were being poured upon his head, in an unending rustle and clatter, when all he desired was to sleep.

So when his old wife gave up the ghost he mourned but was not sorry. He buried her and after a decent while took this room in the Jolly Tar on the Bristol waterfront, leaving the direction of the estate in Huntingdon to his son, bringing with him only the parasol from the island that made him famous and the dead parrot fixed to its perch and a few necessaries, and has lived here alone ever since, strolling by day about the wharves and quays, staring out west over the sea, for his sight is still keen, smoking his pipes. As to his meals, he has these brought up to his room; for he finds no joy in society, having grown used to solitude on the island.

He does not read, he has lost the taste for it; but the writing of his adventures has put him in the habit of writing, it is a pleasant enough recreation. In the evening by candlelight he will take out his papers and sharpen his quills and write a page or two of his man, the man who sends report of the duckoys of Lincolnshire, and of the great engine of death in Halifax, that one can escape if before the awful blade can descend one can leap to one's feet and dash down the hill, and of numbers of other things. Every place he goes he sends report of, that is his first business, this busy man of his.

Strolling along the harbour wall, reflecting upon the engine from Halifax, he, Robin, whom the parrot used to call poor Robin, drops a pebble and listens. A second, less than a second, before it strikes the water. God's grace is swift, but might not the great blade of tempered steel, being heavier than a pebble and being greased with tallow, be swifter? How will we ever escape it? And what species of man can it be who will dash so busily hither and thither across the kingdom, from one spectacle of death to another (clubbings, beheadings), sending in report after report?

A man of business, he thinks to himself. Let him be a man of business, a grain merchant or a leather merchant, let us say; or a manufacturer and purveyor of roof tiles somewhere where clay is plentiful, Wapping let us say, who must travel much in the interest of his trade. Make him prosperous, give him a wife who loves him and does not chatter too much and bears him children, daughters mainly; give him a reasonable happiness; then bring his happiness suddenly to an end. The Thames rises one winter, the kilns in which the tiles are baked are washed away, or the grain stores, or the leather works; he is ruined, this man of his, debtors descend upon him like flies or like crows, he has to flee his home, his wife, his children and seek hiding in the most wretched of quarters in Beggars Lane under a false name and in disguise. And all of this—the wave of water, the ruin, the flight, the pennilessness, the tatters, the solitude—let all of this be a figure of the shipwreck and the island where he, poor Robin, was secluded from the world for 26 years, till he almost went mad (and indeed, who is to say he did not, in some measure?).

Or else let the man be a saddler with a home and a shop and a warehouse in Whitechapel and a mole on his chin and a wife who loves him and does not chatter and bears him children, daughters mainly, and gives him much happiness, until the plague descends upon the city, it is the year 1665, the great fire of London has not yet come. The plague descends upon London: daily, parish by parish, the count of the dead mounts, rich and poor, for the plague makes no distinction among stations, all this saddler's worldly wealth will not save him. He sends his wife and daughters into the countryside and makes plans to flee himself, but then does not. *Thou shalt not be afraid for the terror at night*, he reads, opening the Bible at hazard, *not for the arrow that flieth by day; not for the pestilence that walketh in darkness; nor for the destruction that wasteth at noon-day. A thousand shall fall at thy side, and ten thousand at thy right hand, but it shall not come nigh thee.*

Taking heart from this sign, a sign of safe passage, he remains in afflicted London and sets about writing reports. I came upon a crowd in the street, he writes, and a woman in their midst pointing to the heavens. *See*, she cries, *an angel in white brandishing a flaming sword!* And the crowd all nod among themselves, *Indeed it is so*, they say: *an angel with a sword!* But he, the saddler, can see no angel, no sword. All he can see is a strange-shaped cloud brighter on the one side than the other, from the shining of the sun.

It is an allegory! cries the woman in the street; but he can see no allegory for the life of him. Thus in his report.

On another day, walking by the riverside in Wapping, his man that used to be a saddler but now has no occupation observes how a woman from the door of her house calls out to a man rowing in a dory: *Robert! Robert!* she calls; and how the man then rows ashore, and from the dory takes up a sack which he lays upon a stone by the riverside, and rows away again; and how the woman comes down to the riverside and picks up the sack and bears it home, very sorrowful-looking.

He accosts the man Robert and speaks to him. Robert informs him that the woman is his wife and the sack holds a week's supplies for her and their children, meat and meal and butter; but that he dare not approach nearer, for all of them, wife and children, have the plague upon them; and that it breaks his heart. And all of this—the man Robert and wife keeping communion through calls across the water, the sack left by the waterside—stands for itself certainly, but stands also as a figure of his, Robinson's, solitude on his island, where in his hour of darkest despair he called out across the waves to his loved ones in England to save him, and at other times swam out to the wreck in search of supplies.

Further report from that time of woe. Able no longer to bear the pain from the swellings in the groin and armpit that are the signs of the plague, a man runs out howling, stark naked, into the street, into Harrow Alley in Whitechapel, where his man the saddler witnesses him as he leaps and prances and makes a thousand strange gestures, his wife and children running after him crying out, calling to him to come back. And this leaping and prancing is allegoric of his own leaping and prancing when, after the calamity of the shipwreck and after he had scoured the strand for sign of his shipboard companions and found none, save a pair of shoes that were not mates, he had understood he was cast up all alone on a savage island, likely to perish and with no hope of salvation.

(But of what else does he secretly sing, he wonders to himself, this poor afflicted man of whom he reads, besides his desolation? What is he calling, across the waters and across the years, out of his private fire?)

A year ago he, Robinson, paid two guineas to a sailor for a parrot the sailor had brought back from, he said, Brazil— a bird not so magnificent as his own well-beloved creature but splendid nonetheless, with green feathers and a scarlet crest and a great talker too, if the sailor was to be believed. And indeed the bird would sit on its perch in his room in the inn, with a little chain on its leg in case it should try to fly away, and say the words *Poor Poll! Poor Poll!* over and over till he was forced to hood it; but could not be taught to say any other word, *Poor Robin!* for instance, being perhaps too old for that.

Poor Poll, gazing out through the narrow window over the mast-tops and, beyond the mast-tops, over the grey Atlantic swell: *What island is this*, asks Poor Poll, *that I am cast up on, so cold, so dreary? Where were you, my Saviour, in my hour of great need?*

A man, being drunk and it being late at night (another of his man's reports), falls asleep in a doorway in Cripplegate. The dead-cart comes on its way (we are still in the year of the plague), and the neighbours, thinking the man dead, place him on the dead-cart among the corpses. By and by the cart comes to the dead pit at Mountmill and the carter, his face all muffled against the effluvium, lays hold of him to throw him in; and he wakes up and struggles in his bewilderment. *Where am I?* he says. *You are about to be buried among the dead*, says the carter. *But am I dead then?* says the man. And this too is a figure of him on his island.

Some London-folk continue to go about their business, thinking they are healthy and will be passed over. But secretly they have the plague in their blood: when the infection reaches their heart they fall dead upon the spot, so reports his man, as if struck by lightning. And this is a figure for life itself, the whole of life. Due preparation. We should make due preparation for death, or else be struck down where we stand. As he, Robinson, was made to see when of a sudden, on his island, he came one day upon the footprint of a man in the sand. It was a print, and therefore a sign: of a foot, of a man. But it was a sign of much else too. *You are not alone*, said the sign; and also, *No matter how far you sail, no matter where you hide, you will be searched out.*

In the year of the plague, writes his man, others, out of terror, abandoned all, their homes, their wives and children, and fled as far from London as they could. When the plague had passed, their flight was condemned as cowardice on all sides. But, writes his man, we forget what kind of courage was called on to confront the plague. It was not a mere soldier's courage, like gripping a weapon and charging the foe: it was like charging Death itself on his pale horse.

Even at his best, his island parrot, the better loved of the two, spoke no word he was not taught to speak by his master.

How then has it come about that this man of his, who is a kind of parrot and not much loved, writes as well as or better than his master? For he wields an able pen, this man of his, no doubt of that. *Like charging Death himself on his pale horse.* His own skill, learned in the counting house, was in making tallies and accounts, not in turning phrases. *Death himself on his pale horse*: those are words he would not think of. Only when he yields himself up to this man of his do such words come.

And decoy ducks, or duckoys: What did he, Robinson, know of decoy ducks? Nothing at all, until this man of his began sending in reports.

The duckoys of the Lincolnshire fens, the great engine of execution in Halifax: reports from a great tour this man of his seems to be making of the island of Britain, which is a figure of the tour he made of his own island in the skiff he built, the tour that showed there was a farther side to the island, craggy and dark and inhospitable, which he ever afterwards avoided, though if in the future colonists shall arrive upon the island they will perhaps explore it and settle it; that too being a figure, of the dark side of the soul and the light.

When the first bands of plagiarists and imitators descended upon his island history and foisted on the public their own feigned stories of the castaway life, they seemed to him no more or less than a horde of cannibals falling upon his own flesh, that is to say, his life; and he did not scruple to say so. *When I defended myself against the cannibals, who sought to strike me down and roast me and devour me*, he wrote, *I thought I defended myself against the thing itself. Little did I guess*, he wrote, *that these cannibals were but figures of a more devilish voracity, that would gnaw at the very substance of truth*.

But now, reflecting further, there begins to creep into his breast a touch of fellow feeling for his imitators. For it seems to him now that there are but a handful of stories in the world;

and if the young are to be forbidden to prey upon the old then they must sit for ever in silence.

Thus in the narrative of his island adventures he tells of how he awoke in terror one night convinced the devil lay upon him in his bed in the shape of a huge dog. So he leapt to his feet and grasped a cutlass and slashed left and right to defend himself while the poor parrot that slept by his bedside shrieked in alarm. Only many days later did he understand that neither dog nor devil had lain upon him, but rather that he had suffered a palsy of a passing kind, and being unable to move his leg had concluded there was some creature stretched out upon it. Of which event the lesson would seem to be that all afflictions, including the palsy, come from the devil and are the very devil; that a visitation by illness may be figured as a visitation by the devil, or by a dog figuring the devil, and vice versa, the visitation figured as an illness, as in the saddler's history of the plague; and therefore that no one who writes stories of either, the devil or the plague, should forthwith be dismissed as a forger or a thief.

WHEN, YEARS AGO, he resolved to set down on paper the story of his island, he found that the words would not come, the pen would not flow, his very fingers were stiff and reluctant. But day by day, step by step, he mastered the writing business, until by the time of his adventures with Friday in the frozen north the pages were rolling off easily, even thoughtlessly.

That old ease of composition has, alas, deserted him. When he seats himself at the little writing-desk before the window looking over Bristol Harbour, his hand feels as clumsy and the pen as foreign an instrument as ever before.

Does he, the other one, that man of his, find the writing business easier? The stories he writes of ducks and machines of death and London under the plague flow prettily enough;

but then so did his own stories once. Perhaps he misjudges him, that dapper little man with the quick step and the mole upon his chin. Perhaps at this very moment he sits alone in a hired room somewhere in this wide kingdom dipping the pen and dipping it again, full of doubts and hesitations and second thoughts.

How are they to be figured, this man and he? As master and slave? As brothers, twin brothers? As comrades in arms? Or as enemies, foes? What name shall he give this nameless fellow with whom he shares his evenings and sometimes his nights too, who is absent only in the daytime, when he, Robin, walks the quays inspecting the new arrivals and his man gallops about the kingdom making his inspections?

Will this man, in the course of his travels, ever come to Bristol? He yearns to meet the fellow in the flesh, shake his hand, take a stroll with him along the quayside and hearken as he tells of his visit to the dark north of the island, or of his adventures in the writing business. But he fears there will be no meeting, not in this life. If he must settle on a likeness for the pair of them, his man and he, he would write that they are like two ships sailing in contrary directions, one west, the other east. Or better, that they are deckhands toiling in the rigging, the one on a ship sailing west, the other on a ship sailing east. Their ships pass close, close enough to hail. But the seas are rough, the weather is stormy: their eyes lashed by the spray, their hands burned by the cordage, they pass each other by, too busy even to wave.

Imre Kertész

Heureka!
2002

Imre Kertész was born in Budapest in 1929 and spent the last two years of the Second World War as an inmate of Auschwitz and then Buchenwald. It is this experience that dominates his writing. On his return to Hungary after the war, Kertész established himself as an independent writer and translator of German authors such as Nietzsche, Freud, Roth and Wittgenstein.

Based on his experiences in the camps, Kertész's first novel, Sorstalanság *(Fateless), was published in 1975. It forms the first in what is regarded as a trilogy of autobiographical novels, and was followed by* A kudarc *(The Failure) in 1988 and* Kaddis a meg nem született gyermekért *(Kaddish for a Child Not Born) in 1990. 'Kaddish' is the name given to the Jewish prayer for the dead, and in this work the prayer is for the child that Kertész refuses to bring into the world that permitted the horrors of Auschwitz. Other novels include* A nyomkeresö *(The Pathfinder) and* Az angol labogó *(The English Flag). His lectures and essays have been collected in* A holocaust mint kultúra *(The Holocaust as Culture) and* A gondolatnyi csend, amíg kivégzöoztag újratölt *(Moments of Silence While the Execution Squad Reloads).*

The Academy praised Kertész's work as 'writing that upholds the fragile experience of the individual against the barbaric arbitrariness of history'.

I must begin with a confession, a strange confession perhaps, but a candid one. From the moment I stepped on the airplane to make the journey here and accept this year's Nobel Prize in Literature, I have been feeling the steady, searching gaze of a dispassionate observer on my back. Even at this special moment, when I find myself being the center of attention, I feel I am closer to this cool and detached observer than to the writer whose work, of a sudden, is read around the world. I can only hope that the speech I have the honor to deliver on this occasion will help me dissolve the duality and fuse the two selves within me.

For now, though, I still have trouble understanding the gap that I sense between the high honor and my life and work. Perhaps I lived too long under dictatorships, in a hostile, relentlessly alien intellectual environment, to have developed a distinct literary consciousness; even to contemplate such a thing would have been useless. Besides, all I heard from all sides was that what I gave so much thought to, the 'topic' that forever preoccupied me, was neither timely nor very attractive. For this reason, and also because I happen to believe it, I have always considered writing a highly personal, private matter.

Not that such a matter necessarily precludes seriousness—even if this seriousness did seem somewhat ludicrous in a world where only lies were taken seriously. Here the notion that the world is an objective reality existing independently of us was an axiomatic philosophical truth. Whereas I, on a lovely spring day in 1955, suddenly came to the realization that there exists only one reality, and that is me, my own life, this fragile gift bestowed for an uncertain time, which had been seized, expropriated by alien forces and circumscribed, marked up, branded—and which I had to take back from 'History', this dreadful Moloch, because it was mine and mine alone, and I had to manage it accordingly.

Needless to say, all this turned me sharply against everything in that world, which, though not objective, was undeniably a reality. I am speaking of communist Hungary, of 'thriving and flourishing' socialism. If the world is an objective reality that exists independently of us, then humans themselves, even in their own eyes, are nothing more than objects, and their life stories merely a series of disconnected historical accidents, which they may wonder at, but which they themselves have nothing to do with. It would make no sense to arrange the fragments in a coherent whole, because some of it may be far too objective for the subjective Self to be held responsible for it.

A year later, in 1956, the Hungarian Revolution broke out. For a single moment the country turned subjective. Soviet tanks, however, restored objectivity before long.

I do not mean to be facetious. Consider what happened to language in the twentieth century, what became of words. I daresay that the first and most shocking discovery made by writers in our time was that language, in the form it came down to us, a legacy of some primordial culture, had simply become unsuitable to convey concepts and processes that had once been unambiguous and real. Think of Kafka, think of Orwell, in whose hands the old language simply disintegrated. It was as if they were turning it round and round in an open fire, only to display its ashes afterward, in which new and previously unknown patterns emerged.

But I should like to return to what for me is strictly private —writing. There are a few questions, which someone in my situation will not even ask. Jean-Paul Sartre, for instance, devoted an entire little book to the question: For whom do we write? It is an interesting question, but it can also be dangerous, and I thank my lucky stars that I never had to deal with it. Let us see what the danger consists of. If a writer were to pick a social class or group that he would like, not only to delight but also influence, he would first have to examine his style to see whether it is a suitable means by which to exert influence. He will soon be assailed by doubts, and spend his time watching himself. How can he know for sure what his readers want, what they really like? He cannot very well ask each and every one. And even if he did, it wouldn't do any good. He would have to rely on *his* image of his would-be readers, the expectations *he* ascribed to them, and imagine what would have the effect on *him* that *he* would like to achieve.

For whom does a writer write, then? The answer is obvious: he writes for himself.

At least I can say that I have arrived at this answer fairly straightforwardly. Granted, I had it easier—I had no readers and no desire to influence anyone. I did not begin writing for a specific reason, and what I wrote was not addressed to anyone. If I had an aim at all, it was to be faithful, in language and form, to the subject at hand, and nothing more. It was important to make this clear during the ridiculous and sad period when literature was state-controlled and 'engagé'.

It would be more difficult to answer another, perfectly legitimate though still rather more dubious question: *Why* do we write? Here, too, I was lucky, for it never occurred to me that when it came to this question, one had a choice. I described a relevant incident in my novel *Failure*. I stood in the empty corridor of an office building, and all that happened was that from the direction of another, intersecting corridor I heard echoing footsteps. A strange excitement took hold of me. The sound grew louder and louder, and though they were clearly the steps of a single, unseen person, I suddenly had the feeling that I was hearing the footsteps of thousands. It was as if a huge procession was pounding its way down that corridor. And at that point I perceived the irresistible attraction of those footfalls, that marching multitude. In a single moment I understood the ecstasy of self-abandonment, the intoxicating pleasure of melting into the crowd—what Nietzsche called, in a different context though relevantly for this moment too, a Dionysian experience. It was almost as though some physical force were pushing me, pulling me toward the unseen marching columns. I felt I had to stand back and press against the wall, to keep me from yielding to this magnetic, seductive force.

I have related this intense moment as I (had) experienced it. The source from which it sprang, like a vision, seemed somewhere outside of me, not in me. Every artist is familiar with such moments. At one time they were called sudden inspirations. Still, I wouldn't classify the experience as an artistic revelation, but rather as an existential self-discovery. What I gained from it was not my art—its tools would not be mine for some time—but my life, which I had almost lost. The experience was about solitude, a more difficult life, and the things I have already mentioned—the need to step out of the mesmerizing crowd, out of History, which renders you faceless and fateless. To my horror, I realized that ten years after I had returned from the Nazi concentration camps, and halfway still under the awful spell of Stalinist terror, all that remained of the whole experience were a few muddled impressions, a few anecdotes. Like it didn't even happen to me, as people are wont to say.

It is clear that such visionary moments have a long prehistory. Sigmund Freud would trace them back to a repressed traumatic experience. And he may well be right. I, too, am inclined toward the rational approach; mysticism and unreasoning rapture of all kinds are alien to me. So when I speak of a vision, I must mean something real that assumes a supernatural guise—the sudden, almost violent eruption of a slowly ripening thought within me. Something conveyed in the ancient cry, 'Eureka!'—'I've got it!' But what?

I once said that so-called socialism for me was the petite madeleine cake that, dipped into Proust's tea, evoked in him the flavor of bygone years. For reasons having to do with the language I spoke, I decided, after the suppression of the 1956 revolt, to remain in Hungary. Thus I was able to observe, not as a child this time but as an adult, how a dictatorship functions. I saw how an entire nation could be made to deny its ideals, and watched the early, cautious moves toward accommodation. I understood that hope is an instrument of evil, and the Kantian categorical imperative—ethics in general—is but the pliable handmaiden of self-preservation.

Can one imagine greater freedom than that enjoyed by a writer in a relatively limited, rather tired, even decadent dictatorship? By the 1960s, the dictatorship in Hungary had reached a state of consolidation that could almost be called a societal consensus. The West later dubbed it, with good-humored forbearance, 'goulash communism'. It seemed that after the initial foreign disapproval, Hungary's own version quickly turned into the West's favorite brand of communism. In the miry depths of this consensus, one either gave up the struggle or found the winding paths to inner freedom. A writer's overhead, after all, is very low; to practice his profession, all he needs are paper and pencil. The nausea and depression to which I awoke each morning led me at once into the world I intended to describe. I had to discover that I had placed a man groaning under the logic of one type of totalitarianism in another totalitarian system, and this turned the language of my novel into a highly allusive medium. If I look back now and size up honestly the situation I was in at the time, I have to conclude that in the West, in a free society, I probably would not have been able to write the novel known by readers today as *Fateless*, the novel singled out by the Swedish Academy for the highest honour.

No, I probably would have aimed at something different. Which is not to say that I would not have tried to get at the truth, but perhaps at a different kind of truth. In the free marketplace of books and ideas, I, too, might have wanted to produce a showier fiction. For example, I might have tried to break up time in my novel, and narrate only the most powerful scenes. But the hero of my novel does not live his own time in the concentration camps, for neither his time nor his language, not even his own person, is really his. He doesn't remember; he exists. So he has to languish, poor boy, in the dreary trap of linearity, and cannot shake off the painful details. Instead of a spectacular series of great and tragic moments, he has to live through everything, which is oppressive and offers little variety, like life itself.

But the method led to remarkable insights. Linearity demanded that each situation that arose be completely filled out. It did not allow me, say, to skip cavalierly over twenty minutes of time, if only because those twenty minutes were there before me, like a gaping, terrifying black hole, like a mass grave. I am speaking of the twenty minutes spent on the arrival platform of the Birkenau extermination camp—the time it took people clambering down from the train to reach the officer doing the selecting. I more or less remembered the twenty minutes, but the novel demanded that I distrust my memory. No matter how many survivors' accounts, reminiscences and confessions I had read, they all agreed that everything proceeded all too quickly and unnoticeably. The doors of the railroad cars were flung open, they heard shouts, the barking of dogs, men and women were abruptly separated, and in the midst of the hubbub, they found themselves in front of an officer. He cast a fleeting glance at them, pointed to something with his outstretched arm, and before they knew it they were wearing prison clothes.

I remembered these twenty minutes differently. Turning to authentic sources, I first read Tadeusz Borowski's stark, unsparing and self-tormenting narratives, among them the story entitled 'This Way for the Gas, Ladies and Gentlemen'. Later, I came upon a series of photographs of human cargo arriving at the Birkenau railroad platform—photographs taken by an SS soldier and found by American soldiers in a former SS barracks in the already liberated camp at Dachau. I looked at these photographs in utter amazement. I saw lovely, smiling women and bright-eyed young men, all of them well-intentioned, eager to cooperate. Now I understood how and why those humiliating twenty minutes of idleness and helplessness faded from their memories. And when I thought how all this was repeated the same way for days, weeks, months and years on end, I gained an insight into the mechanism of horror; I learned how it became possible to turn human nature against one's own life.

So I proceeded, step by step, on the linear path of discovery; this was my heuristic method, if you will. I realized soon enough that I was not the least bit interested in whom I was writing for and why. One question interested me: What have I still got to do with literature? For it was clear to me that an uncrossable line separated me from literature and the ideals, the spirit associated with the concept of literature. The name of this demarcation line, as of many other things, is Auschwitz. When we write about Auschwitz, we must know that Auschwitz, in a certain sense at least, suspended literature. One can only write a black novel about Auschwitz, or—you should excuse the expression—a cheap serial, which begins in Auschwitz and is still not over. By which I mean that nothing has happened since Auschwitz that could reverse or refute Auschwitz. In my writings the Holocaust could never be present in the past tense.

It is often said of me—some intend it as a compliment, others as a complaint—that I write about a single subject: the Holocaust. I have no quarrel with that. Why shouldn't I accept, with certain qualifications, the place assigned to me on the shelves of libraries? Which writer today is not a writer of the Holocaust? One does not have to choose the Holocaust as one's subject to detect the broken voice that has dominated modern European art for decades. I will go so far as to say that I know of no genuine work of art that does not reflect this break. It is as if, after a night of terrible dreams, one looked around the world, defeated, helpless. I have never tried to see the complex of problems referred to as the Holocaust merely as the insolvable conflict between Germans and Jews. I never believed that it was the latest chapter in the history of Jewish suffering, which followed logically from their earlier trials and tribulations. I never saw it as a one-time aberration, a large-scale pogrom, a precondition for the creation of Israel. What I discovered in Auschwitz is the human condition, the end point of a great adventure, where the European traveller arrived after his two-thousand-year-old moral and cultural history.

Now the only thing to reflect on is where we go from here. The problem of Auschwitz is not whether to draw a line under it, as it were; whether to preserve its memory or slip it into the appropriate pigeonhole of history; whether to erect a monument to the murdered millions, and if so, what kind. The real problem with Auschwitz is that it happened, and this cannot be altered—not with the best, or worst, will in the world. This gravest of situations was characterized most accurately by the Hungarian Catholic poet János Pilinszky when he called it a 'scandal'. What he meant by it, clearly, is that Auschwitz occurred in a Christian cultural environment, so for those with a metaphysical turn of mind it can never be overcome.

Old prophecies speak of the death of God. Since Auschwitz we are more alone, that much is certain. We must create our values ourselves, day by day, with that persistent though invisible ethical work that will give them life, and perhaps turn them into the foundation of a new European culture. I consider the prize with which the Swedish Academy has seen fit to honor my work as an indication that Europe again needs the experience that witnesses to Auschwitz, to the Holocaust were forced to acquire. The decision—permit me to say this—bespeaks courage, firm resolve even—for those who made it wished me to come here, though they could have easily guessed what they would hear from me. What was revealed in the Final Solution, in *l'univers concentrationnaire*, cannot be misunderstood, and the only way survival is possible, and the preservation of creative power, is if we recognize the zero point that is Auschwitz. Why couldn't this clarity of vision be fruitful? At the bottom of all great realizations, even if they are born of unsurpassed tragedies, there lies the greatest European value of all, the longing for liberty, which suffuses our lives with something more, a richness, making us aware of the positive fact of our existence, and the responsibility we all bear for-it.

It makes me especially happy to be expressing these thoughts in my native language: Hungarian. I was born in Budapest, in a Jewish family, whose maternal branch hailed from the Transylvanian city of Kolozsvár (Cluj) and the paternal side from the south-western corner of the Lake Balaton region. My grandparents still lit the Sabbath candles every Friday night, but they changed their name to a Hungarian one, and it was natural for them to consider Judaism their religion and Hungary their homeland. My maternal grandparents perished in the Holocaust; my paternal grandparents' lives were destroyed by Mátyás Rákosi's communist rule, when Budapest's Jewish old-age home was relocated to the northern border region of the country. I think this brief family history encapsulates and symbolizes this country's modern-day travails. What it teaches me, though, is that there is not only bitterness in grief, but also extraordinary moral potential. Being a Jew to me is once again, first and foremost, a moral challenge. If the Holocaust has by now created a culture, as it undeniably has, its aim must be that an irredeemable reality give rise by way of the spirit to restoration—a catharsis. This desire has inspired me in all my creative endeavors.

I must confess I still have not found the reassuring balance between my life, my works and the Nobel Prize. For now I feel profound gratitude—gratitude for the love that saved me and sustains me still. But let us consider that in this difficult-to-follow life journey, in this 'career' of mine, if I could so put it, there is something stirring, something absurd, something which cannot be pondered without one being touched by a belief in an otherworldly order, in providence, in metaphysical justice—in other words, without falling into the trap of self-deception, and thus running aground, going under, severing the deep and tortuous ties with the millions who perished and who never knew mercy. It is not so easy to be an exception. But if we were destined to be exceptions, we must make our peace with the absurd order of chance, which reigns over our lives with the whim of a death squad, exposing us to inhuman powers, monstrous tyrannies.

And yet something very special happened while I was preparing this lecture, which in a way reassured me. One day I received a large brown envelope in the mail. It was sent to me by Doctor Volkhard Knigge, the director of the Buchenwald Memorial Center. He enclosed a small envelope with his congratulatory note, and described what was in the envelope, so, in case I didn't have the strength to look, I wouldn't have to. The envelope contained a copy of the original daily report on the camp's prisoners for February 18, 1945. In the 'Abgänge', that is, the 'Decrement' column, I learned about the death of Prisoner #64,921—Imre Kertész, factory worker, born in 1927. The two false data: the year of my birth and my occupation were entered in the official registry when I was brought to Buchenwald. I had made myself two years older so I wouldn't be classified as a child, and had said worker rather than student to appear more useful to them.

In short, I died once, so I could live. Perhaps that is my real story. If it is, I dedicate this work, born of a child's death, to the millions who died and to those who still remember them. But, since we are talking about literature, after all, the kind of literature that, in the view of your Academy, is also a testimony, my work may yet serve a useful purpose in the future, and—this is my heart's desire—may even speak to the future. Whenever I think of the traumatic impact of Auschwitz, I end up dwelling on the vitality and creativity of those living today. Thus, in thinking about Auschwitz, I reflect, paradoxically, not on the past but the future.

Translated from Hungarian by Ivan Sanders

V.S. Naipaul

Two Worlds
2001

V.S. Naipaul is a descendant of indentured labourers sent from northern India to Trinidad. He received a scholarship to study at University College in Oxford at the age of eighteen, and after completing his studies, remained in England. Apart from a short stint as a freelance journalist for the BBC in the mid-1950s, Naipaul has supported himself solely through his writing.

Described as a 'universal' writer, Naipaul's work can be viewed as the accretion of his lived experience. He has travelled widely through Asia, Africa and America, and this, coupled with what he considers his dispossession or lack of roots, contributes to the cosmopolitan and profoundly humanistic nature of his writing. His work explores history, culture and society through examinations of revolution, slavery, decolonization and emerging nationalism in the third world. His earliest work is set in the West Indies, such as the novels The Mystic Masseur *and* A House for Mr Biswas. *Other novels include* Guerillas, A Bend in the River, The Enigma of Arrival *and* Magic Seeds. *His non-fiction works include* India: A Million Mutinies Now, Among the Believers *and* Beyond Belief.

The Academy describes Naipaul as 'having united perceptive narrative and incorruptible scrutiny in works that compel us to see the presence of suppressed histories'.

This is unusual for me. I have given readings and not lectures. I have told people who ask for lectures that I have no lecture to give. And that is true. It might seem strange that a man who has dealt in words and emotions and ideas for nearly 50 years shouldn't have a few to spare, so to speak. But everything of value about me is in my books. Whatever extra there is in me at any given moment isn't fully formed. I am hardly aware of it; it awaits the next book. It will—with luck—come to me during the actual writing, and it will take me by surprise. That element of surprise is what I look for when I am writing. It is my way of judging what I am doing—which is never an easy thing to do.

Proust has written with great penetration of the difference between the writer as writer and the writer as a social being. You will find his thoughts in some of his essays in *Against Sainte-Beuve*, a book reconstituted from his early papers.

The 19th-century French critic Sainte-Beuve believed that to understand a writer it was necessary to know as much as possible about the exterior man, the details of his life. It is a beguiling method, using the man to illuminate the work. It might seem unassailable. But Proust is able very convincingly to pick it apart. 'This method of Sainte-Beuve', Proust writes, 'ignores what a very slight degree of self-acquaintance teaches us: that a book is the product of a different self from the self we manifest in our habits, in our social life, in our vices. If we would try to understand that particular self, it is by searching our own bosoms, and trying to reconstruct it there, that we may arrive at it.'

Those words of Proust should be with us whenever we are reading the biography of a writer—or the biography of anyone who depends on what can be called inspiration. All the details of the life and the quirks and the friendships can be laid out for us, but the mystery of the writing will remain. No amount of documentation, however fascinating, can take us there. The biography of a writer—or even the autobiography—will always have this incompleteness.

Proust is a master of happy amplification, and I would like to go back to *Against Sainte-Beuve* just for a little. 'In fact', Proust writes, 'it is the secretions of one's innermost self, written in solitude and for oneself alone that one gives to the public. What one bestows on private life—in conversation ... or in those drawing-room essays that are scarcely more than conversation in print—is the product of a quite superficial self, not of the innermost self which one can only recover by putting aside the world and the self that frequents the world.'

When he wrote that, Proust had not yet found the subject that was to lead him to the happiness of his great literary labour. And you can tell from what I have quoted that he was a man trusting to his intuition and waiting for luck. I have quoted these words before in other places. The reason is that they define how I have gone about my business. I have trusted to intuition. I did it at the beginning. I do it even now. I have no idea how things might turn out, where in my writing I might go next. I have trusted to my intuition to find the subjects, and I have written intuitively. I have an idea when I start, I have a shape; but I will fully understand what I have written only after some years.

I said earlier that everything of value about me is in my books. I will go further now. I will say I am the sum of my books. Each book, intuitively sensed and, in the case of fiction, intuitively worked out, stands on what has gone before, and grows out of it. I feel that at any stage of my literary career it could have been said that the last book contained all the others.

It's been like this because of my background. My background is at once exceedingly simple and exceedingly confused. I was born in Trinidad. It is a small island in the mouth of the great Orinoco river of Venezuela. So Trinidad is not strictly of South America, and not strictly of the Caribbean. It was developed as a New World plantation colony, and when I was born in 1932 it had a population of about 400,000. Of this, about 150,000 were Indians, Hindus and Muslims, nearly all of peasant origin, and nearly all from the Gangetic plain.

This was my very small community. The bulk of this migration from India occurred after 1880. The deal was like this. People indentured themselves for five years to serve on the estates. At the end of this time they were given a small piece of land, perhaps five acres, or a passage back to India. In 1917, because of agitation by Gandhi and others, the indenture system was abolished. And perhaps because of this, or for some other reason, the pledge of land or repatriation was dishonoured for many of the later arrivals. These people were absolutely destitute. They slept in the streets of Port of Spain, the capital. When I was a child I saw them. I suppose I didn't know they were destitute—I suppose that idea came much later—and they made no impression on me. This was part of the cruelty of the plantation colony.

I was born in a small country town called Chaguanas, two or three miles inland from the Gulf of Paria. Chaguanas was a strange name, in spelling and pronunciation, and many of the Indian people—they were in the majority in the area—preferred to call it by the Indian caste name of Chauhan.

I was 34 when I found out about the name of my birthplace. I was living in London, had been living in England for sixteen years. I was writing my ninth book. This was a history of Trinidad, a human history, trying to re-create people and their stories. I used to go to the British Museum to read the Spanish documents about the region. These documents—recovered from the Spanish archives—were copied out for the British government in the 1890s at the time of a nasty boundary dispute with Venezuela. The documents begin in 1530 and end with the disappearance of the Spanish Empire.

I was reading about the foolish search for El Dorado, and the murderous interloping of the English hero, Sir Walter Raleigh. In 1595 he raided Trinidad, killed all the Spaniards he could, and went up the Orinoco looking for El Dorado. He found nothing, but when he went back to England he said he had. He had a piece of gold and some sand to show. He said he had hacked the gold out of a cliff on the bank of the Orinoco. The Royal Mint said that the sand he asked them to assay was worthless, and other people said that he had bought the gold beforehand from North Africa. He then published a book to prove his point, and for four centuries people have believed that Raleigh had found something. The magic of Raleigh's book, which is really quite difficult to read, lay in its very long title: *The Discovery of the Large, Rich, and Beautiful Empire of Guiana, with a relation of the great and golden city of Manoa (which the Spaniards call El Dorado) and the provinces of Emeria, Aromaia, Amapaia, and other countries, with their rivers adjoining.* How real it sounds! And he had hardly been on the main Orinoco.

And then, as sometimes happens with confidence men, Raleigh was caught by his own fantasies. Twenty-one years later, old and ill, he was let out of his London prison to go to Guiana and find the gold mines he said he had found. In this fraudulent venture his son died. The father, for the sake of his reputation, for the sake of his lies, had sent his son to his death. And then Raleigh, full of grief, with nothing left to live for, went back to London to be executed.

The story should have ended there. But Spanish memories were long—no doubt because their imperial correspondence was so slow: it might take up to two years for a letter from Trinidad to be read in Spain. Eight years afterwards the Spaniards of Trinidad and Guiana were still settling their scores with the Gulf Indians. One day in the British Museum I read a letter from the King of Spain to the governor of Trinidad. It was dated October 12, 1625.

'I asked you', the King wrote, 'to give me some information about a certain nation of Indians called Chaguanes, who you say number above one thousand, and are of such bad disposition that it was they who led the English when they captured the town. Their crime hasn't been punished because forces were not available for this purpose and because the Indians acknowledge no master save their own will. You have decided to give them a punishment. Follow the rules I have given you; and let me know how you get on.'

What the governor did I don't know. I could find no further reference to the Chaguanes in the documents in the museum. Perhaps there were other documents about the Chaguanes in the mountain of paper in the Spanish archives in Seville which the British government scholars missed or didn't think important enough to copy out. What is true is that the little tribe of over a thousand—who would have been living on both sides of the Gulf of Paria—disappeared so completely that no one in the town of Chaguanas or Chauhan knew anything about them. And the thought came to me in the museum that I was the first person since 1625 to whom that letter of the King of Spain had a real meaning. And that letter had been dug out of the archives only in 1896 or 1897. A disappearance, and then the silence of centuries.

We lived on the Chaguanes' land. Every day in term time—I was just beginning to go to school—I walked from my grandmother's house—past the two or three main-road stores, the Chinese parlor, the Jubilee Theatre and the high-smelling little Portuguese factory that made cheap blue soap and cheap yellow soap in long bars that were put out to dry and harden in the mornings—every day I walked past these eternal-seeming things—to the Chaguanas Government School. Beyond the school was sugar-cane, estate land, going up to the Gulf of Paria. The people who had been dispossessed would have had their own kind of agriculture, their own calendar, their own codes, their own sacred sites. They would have understood the Orinoco-fed currents in the Gulf of Paria. Now all their skills and everything else about them had been obliterated.

The world is always in movement. People have everywhere at some time been dispossessed. I suppose I was shocked by this discovery in 1967 about my birthplace because I had never had any idea about it. But that was the way most of us lived in the agricultural colony, blindly. There was no plot by the authorities to keep us in our darkness. I think it was more simply that the knowledge wasn't there. The kind of knowledge about the Chaguanes would not have been considered important, and it would not have been easy to recover. They were a small tribe, and they were aboriginal. Such people—on the mainland, in what was called B.-G., British Guiana—were known to us, and were a kind of joke. People who were loud and ill-behaved were known, to all groups in Trinidad, I think, as *warrahoons*. I used to think it was a made-up word, made up to suggest wildness. It was only when I began to travel in Venezuela, in my forties, that I understood that a word like that was the name of a rather large aboriginal tribe there.

There was a vague story when I was a child—and to me now it is an unbearably affecting story—that at certain times aboriginal people came across in canoes from the mainland, walked through the forest in the south of the island, and at a certain spot picked some kind of fruit or made some kind of offering, and then went back across the Gulf of Paria to the sodden estuary of the Orinoco. The rite must have been of enormous importance to have survived the upheavals of four hundred years, and the extinction of the aborigines in Trinidad. Or perhaps—though Trinidad and Venezuela have a common flora—they had come only to pick a particular kind of fruit. I don't know. I can't remember anyone inquiring. And now the memory is all lost; and that sacred site, if it existed, has become common ground.

What was past was past. I suppose that was the general attitude. And we Indians, immigrants from India, had that attitude to the island. We lived for the most part ritualized lives, and were not yet capable of self-assessment, which is where learning begins. Half of us on this land of the Chaguanes were pretending—perhaps not pretending, perhaps only feeling, never formulating it as an idea—that we had brought a kind of

India with us, which we could, as it were, unroll like a carpet on the flat land.

My grandmother's house in Chaguanas was in two parts. The front part, of bricks and plaster, was painted white. It was like a kind of Indian house, with a grand balustraded terrace on the upper floor, and a prayer-room on the floor above that. It was ambitious in its decorative detail, with lotus capitals on pillars, and sculptures of Hindu deities, all done by people working only from a memory of things in India. In Trinidad it was an architectural oddity. At the back of this house, and joined to it by an upper bridge room, was a timber building in the French Caribbean style. The entrance gate was at the side, between the two houses. It was a tall gate of corrugated iron on a wooden frame. It made for a fierce kind of privacy.

So as a child I had this sense of two worlds, the world outside that tall corrugated-iron gate, and the world at home—or, at any rate, the world of my grandmother's house. It was a remnant of our caste sense, the thing that excluded and shut out. In Trinidad, where as new arrivals we were a disadvantaged community, that excluding idea was a kind of protection; it enabled us—for the time being, and only for the time being—to live in our own way and according to our own rules, to live in our own fading India. It made for an extraordinary self-centeredness. We looked inwards; we lived out our days; the world outside existed in a kind of darkness; we inquired about nothing.

There was a Muslim shop next door. The little loggia of my grandmother's shop ended against his blank wall. The man's name was Mian. That was all that we knew of him and his family. I suppose we must have seen him, but I have no mental picture of him now. We knew nothing of Muslims. This idea of strangeness, of the thing to be kept outside, extended even to other Hindus. For example, we ate rice in the middle of the day, and wheat in the evenings. There were some extraordinary people who reversed this natural order and ate rice in the evenings. I thought of these people as strangers—you must imagine me at this time as under seven, because when I was seven all this life of my grandmother's house in Chaguanas came to an end for me. We moved to the capital, and then to the hills to the north-west.

But the habits of mind engendered by this shut-in and shutting-out life lingered for quite a while. If it were not for the short stories my father wrote I would have known almost nothing about the general life of our Indian community. Those stories gave me more than knowledge. They gave me a kind of solidity. They gave me something to stand on in the world. I cannot imagine what my mental picture would have been without those stories.

The world outside existed in a kind of darkness; and we inquired about nothing. I was just old enough to have some idea of the Indian epics, the Ramayana in particular. The children who came five years or so after me in our extended family didn't have this luck. No one taught us Hindi. Sometimes someone wrote out the alphabet for us to learn, and that was that; we were expected to do the rest ourselves. So, as English penetrated, we began to lose our language. My grandmother's house was full of religion; there were many ceremonies and readings, some of which went on for days. But no one explained or translated for us who could no longer follow the language. So our ancestral faith receded, became mysterious, not pertinent to our day-to-day life.

We made no inquiries about India or about the families people had left behind. When our ways of thinking had changed, and we wished to know, it was too late. I know nothing of the people on my father's side; I know only that some of them came from Nepal. Two years ago a kind Nepalese who liked my name sent me a copy of some pages from an 1872 gazetteer-like British work about India, *Hindu Castes and Tribes as Represented in Benares*; the pages listed—among a multitude of names—those groups of Nepalese in the holy city of Banaras who carried the name Naipal. That is all that I have.

Away from this world of my grandmother's house, where we ate rice in the middle of the day and wheat in the evenings, there was the great unknown—in this island of only 400,000 people. There were the African or African-derived people who were the majority. They were policemen; they were teachers. One of them was my very first teacher at the Chaguanas Government School; I remembered her with adoration for years. There was the capital, where very soon we would all have to go for education and jobs, and where we would settle permanently, among strangers. There were the white people, not all of them English; and the Portuguese and the Chinese, at one time also immigrants like us. And, more mysterious than these, were the people we called Spanish, *'pagnols*, mixed people of warm brown complexions who came from the Spanish time, before the island was detached from Venezuela and the Spanish Empire—a kind of history absolutely beyond my child's comprehension.

To give you this idea of my background, I have had to call on knowledge and ideas that came to me much later, principally from my writing. As a child I knew almost nothing, nothing beyond what I had picked up in my grandmother's house. All children, I suppose, come into the world like that, not knowing who they are. But for the French child, say, that knowledge is waiting. That knowledge will be all around them. It will come indirectly from the conversation of their elders. It will be in the newspapers and on the radio. And at school the work of generations of scholars, scaled down for school texts, will provide some idea of France and the French.

In Trinidad, bright boy though I was, I was surrounded by areas of darkness. School elucidated nothing for me. I was crammed with facts and formulas. Everything had to be learned by heart; everything was abstract for me. Again, I do not believe there was a plan or plot to make our courses like that. What we were getting was standard school learning. In another setting it would have made sense. And at least some of the failing would have lain in me. With my limited social background it was hard for me imaginatively to enter into other societies or societies that were far away. I loved the idea of books, but I found it hard to read them. I got on best with things like Andersen and Aesop, timeless, placeless, not excluding. And when at last in the sixth form, the highest form in the college, I got to like some of our literature texts—Moliere, Cyrano de Bergerac—I suppose it was because they had the quality of the fairytale.

When I became a writer those areas of darkness around me as a child became my subjects. The land; the aborigines; the New World; the colony; the history; India; the Muslim world, to which I also felt myself related; Africa; and then England, where I was doing my writing. That was what I meant when I said that my books stand one on the other, and that I am the sum of my books. That was what I meant when I said that my background, the source and prompting of my work, was at once exceedingly simple and exceedingly complicated. You will have seen how simple it was in the country town of Chaguanas. And I think you will understand how complicated it was for me as a writer. Especially in the beginning, when the literary models I had—the models given me by what I can only call my false learning—dealt with entirely different societies. But perhaps you might feel that the material was so rich it would have been no trouble at all to get started and to go on. What I have said about the background, however, comes from the knowledge I acquired with my writing. And you must believe me when I tell you that the pattern in my work has only become clear in the last two months or so. Passages from old books were read to me, and I saw the connections. Until then the greatest trouble for me was to describe my writing to people, to say what I had done.

I said I was an intuitive writer. That was so, and that remains so now, when I am nearly at the end. I never had a plan. I followed no system. I worked intuitively. My aim every time was do a book, to create something that would be easy and interesting to read. At every stage I could only work within my knowledge and sensibility and talent and world-view. Those things developed book by book. And I had to do the books I did because there were no books about those subjects to give me what I wanted. I had to clear up my world, elucidate it, for myself.

I had to go to the documents in the British Museum and elsewhere, to get the true feel of the history of the colony. I had to travel to India because there was no one to tell me what the India my grandparents had come from was like. There was the writing of Nehru and Gandhi; and strangely it was Gandhi, with his South African experience, who gave me more, but not enough. There was Kipling; there were British-Indian writers like John Masters (going very strong in the 1950s, with an announced plan, later abandoned, I fear, for 35 connected novels about British India); there were romances by women writers. The few Indian writers who had come up at that time were middle-class people, town-dwellers; they didn't know the India we had come from.

And when that Indian need was satisfied, others became apparent: Africa, South America, the Muslim world. The aim has always been to fill out my world picture, and the purpose comes from my childhood: to make me more at ease with myself. Kind people have sometimes written asking me to go and write about Germany, say, or China. But there is much good writing already about those places; I am willing to depend there on the writing that exists. And those subjects are for other people. Those were not the areas of darkness I felt about me as a child. So, just as there is a development in my work, a development in narrative skill and knowledge and sensibility, so there is a kind of unity, a focus, though I might appear to be going in many directions.

When I began I had no idea of the way ahead. I wished only to do a book. I was trying to write in England, where I stayed on after my years at the university, and it seemed to me that my experience was very thin, was not truly of the stuff of books. I could find in no book anything that came near my background. The young French or English person who wished to write would have found any number of models to set him on his way. I had none. My father's stories about our Indian community belonged to the past. My world was quite different. It was more urban, more mixed. The simple physical details of the chaotic life of our extended family—sleeping rooms or sleeping spaces, eating times, the sheer number of people—seemed impossible to handle. There was too much to be explained, both about my home life and about the world outside. And at the same time there was also too much about us—like our own ancestry and history—that I didn't know.

At last one day there came to me the idea of starting with the Port of Spain street to which we had moved from Chaguanas. There was no big corrugated-iron gate shutting out the world there. The life of the street was open to me. It was an intense pleasure for me to observe it from the verandah. This street life was what I began to write about. I wished to write fast, to avoid too much self-questioning, and so I simplified. I suppressed the child-narrator's background. I ignored the racial and social complexities of the street. I explained nothing. I stayed at ground level, so to speak. I presented people only as they appeared on the street. I wrote a story a day. The first stories were very short. I was worried about the material lasting long enough. But then the writing did its magic. The material began to present itself to me from many sources. The stories became longer; they couldn't be written in a day. And then the inspiration, which at one stage had seemed very easy, rolling me along, came to an end. But a book had been written, and I had in my own mind become a writer.

The distance between the writer and his material grew with the two later books; the vision was wider. And then intuition led me to a large book about our family life. During this book my writing ambition grew. But when it was over I felt I had done all that I could do with my island material. No matter how much I meditated on it, no further fiction would come.

Accident, then, rescued me. I became a traveler. I traveled in the Caribbean region and understood much more about the colonial set-up of which I had been part. I went to India, my ancestral land, for a year; it was a journey that broke my life in two. The books that I wrote about these two journeys took me to new realms of emotion, gave me a world-view I had never had, extended me technically. I was able in the fiction that then came to me to take in England as well as the Caribbean—and how hard that was to do. I was able also to take in all the racial groups of the island, which I had never before been able to do.

This new fiction was about colonial shame and fantasy, a book, in fact, about how the powerless lie about themselves, and lie to themselves, since it is their only resource. The book was called *The Mimic Men*. And it was not about mimics. It was about colonial men mimicking the condition of manhood, men who had grown to distrust everything about themselves. Some pages of this book were read to me the other day—I hadn't looked at it for more than 30 years—and it occurred to me that I had been writing about colonial schizophrenia. But I hadn't thought of it like that. I had never used abstract words to describe any writing purpose of mine. If I had, I would never have been able to do the book. The book was done intuitively, and only out of close observation.

I have done this little survey of the early part of my career to try to show the stages by which, in just ten years, my birthplace had altered or developed in my writing: from the comedy of street life to a study of a kind of widespread schizophrenia. What was simple had become complicated.

Both fiction and the travel-book form have given me my way of looking; and you will understand why for me all literary forms are equally valuable. It came to me, for instance, when I set out to write my third book about India—26 years after the first—that what was most important about a travel book were the people the writer traveled among. The people had to define themselves. A simple enough idea, but it required a new kind of book; it called for a new way of travelling. And it was the very method I used later when I went, for the second time, into the Muslim world.

I have always moved by intuition alone. I have no system, literary or political. I have no guiding political idea. I think that probably lies with my ancestry. The Indian writer R. K. Narayan, who died this year, had no political idea. My father, who wrote his stories in a very dark time, and for no reward, had no political idea. Perhaps it is because we have been far from authority for many centuries. It gives us a special point of view. I feel we are more inclined to see the humour and pity of things.

Nearly 30 years ago I went to Argentina. It was at the time of the guerrilla crisis. People were waiting for the old dictator Perón to come back from exile. The country was full of hate. Perónists were waiting to settle old scores. One such man said to me, 'There is good torture and bad torture.' Good torture was what you did to the enemies of the people. Bad torture was what the enemies of the people did to you. People on the other side were saying the same thing. There was no true debate about anything. There was only passion and the borrowed political jargon of Europe. I wrote, 'Where jargon turns living issues into abstractions, and where jargon ends by competing with jargon, people don't have causes. They only have enemies.'

And the passions of Argentina are still working themselves out, still defeating reason and consuming lives. No resolution is in sight.

I am near the end of my work now. I am glad to have done what I have done, glad creatively to have pushed myself as far as I could go. Because of the intuitive way in which I have written, and also because of the baffling nature of my material, every book has come as a blessing. Every book has amazed me; up to the moment of writing I never knew it was there. But the greatest miracle for me was getting started. I feel—and the anxiety is still vivid to me—that I might easily have failed before I began.

I will end as I began, with one of the marvelous little essays of Proust in *Against Sainte-Beuve*. 'The beautiful things we shall write if we have talent', Proust says, 'are inside us, indistinct, like the memory of a melody which delights us though we are unable to recapture its outline. Those who are obsessed by this blurred memory of truths they have never known are the men who are gifted ... Talent is like a sort of memory which will enable them finally to bring this indistinct music closer to them, to hear it clearly, to note it down ...'

Talent, Proust says. I would say luck, and much labour.

Gao Xingjian

The Case for Literature
2000

Born in 1940, Gao Xingjian is a writer of prose, translator, dramatist, director, critic and artist. Due to the Cultural Revolution, he could not publish his work or travel abroad until 1979. During the 1980s Gao Xingjian wrote short stories, essays, plays and four books, including Premier essai sur les techniques du roman moderne *(A Preliminary Discussion of the Art of Modern Fiction) and* In Search of a Modern Form of Dramatic Representation. *He made his theatrical debut with the experimental* Signal d'alarme *(Signal Alarm) in 1982, a pioneering play for Chinese theatre at that time.*

In 1986 Gao Xingjian's play L'autre rive *(The Other Shore) was banned and since that time none of his plays have been performed in China. He left his home country in 1987 and settled in France, surrendering membership of the Chinese Communist Party after the Tiananmen Square massacre in 1989. The regime declared Gao Xingjian* persona non grata *after the publication of his play* La fuite *(Fugitives), set in the time of this massacre. More recent works include the prodigious novel* La Montagne de l'Âme *(Soul Mountain) and the autobiographical* Le Livre d'un homme seul *(One Man's Bible).*

Gao Xingjian received the Nobel Prize 'for an œuvre of universal validity, bitter insights and linguistic ingenuity, which has opened new paths for the Chinese novel and drama'.

I have no way of knowing whether it was fate that has pushed me onto this dais but as various lucky coincidences have created this opportunity I may as well call it fate. Putting aside discussion of the existence or non-existence of God, I would like to say that despite my being an atheist I have always shown reverence for the unknowable.

A person cannot be God, certainly not replace God, and rule the world as a Superman; he will only succeed in creating more chaos and make a greater mess of the world. In the century after Nietzsche man-made disasters left the blackest records in the history of humankind. Supermen of all types called leader of the people, head of the nation and commander of the race did not baulk at resorting to various violent means in perpetrating crimes that in no way resemble the ravings of a very egotistic philosopher. However, I do not wish to waste this talk on literature by saying too much about politics and history, what I want to do is to use this opportunity to speak as one writer in the voice of an individual.

A writer is an ordinary person; perhaps he is more sensitive but people who are highly sensitive are often more frail. A writer does not speak as the spokesperson of the people or as the embodiment of righteousness. His voice is inevitably weak but it is precisely this voice of the individual that is more authentic.

What I want to say here is that literature can only be the voice of the individual and this has always been so. Once literature is contrived as the hymn of the nation, the flag of the race, the mouthpiece of a political party or the voice of a class or a group, it can be employed as a mighty and all-engulfing tool of propaganda. However, such literature loses what is inherent in literature, ceases to be literature, and becomes a substitute for power and profit.

In the century just ended literature confronted precisely this misfortune and was more deeply scarred by politics and power than in any previous period, and the writer too was subjected to unprecedented oppression.

In order that literature safeguard the reason for its own existence and not become the tool of politics it must return to the voice of the individual, for literature is primarily derived from the feelings of the individual and is the result of feelings. This is not to say that literature must therefore be divorced from politics or that it must necessarily be involved in politics. Controversies about literary trends or a writer's political inclinations were serious afflictions that tormented literature during the past century. Ideology wreaked havoc by turning related controversies over tradition and reform into controversies over what was conservative or revolutionary and thus changed literary issues into a struggle over what was progressive or reactionary. If ideology unites with power and is transformed into a real force then both literature and the individual will be destroyed.

Chinese literature in the twentieth century time and again was worn out and indeed almost suffocated because politics dictated literature: both the revolution in literature and revolutionary literature alike passed death sentences on literature and the individual. The attack on Chinese traditional culture in the name of the revolution resulted in the public prohibition and burning of books. Countless writers were shot, imprisoned, exiled or punished with hard labour in the course of the past one hundred years. This was more extreme than in any imperial dynastic period of China's history, creating enormous difficulties for writings in the Chinese language and even more for any discussion of creative freedom.

If the writer sought to win intellectual freedom the choice was either to fall silent or to flee. However, the writer relies on language and not to speak for a prolonged period is the same as suicide. The writer who sought to avoid suicide or being silenced and furthermore to express his own voice had no option but to go into exile. Surveying the history of literature in the East and the West this has always been so: from Qu Yuan to Dante, Joyce, Thomas Mann, Solzhenitsyn, and to the large numbers of Chinese intellectuals who went into exile after the Tiananmen massacre in 1989. This is the inevitable fate of the poet and the writer who continues to seek to preserve his own voice.

During the years when Mao Zedong implemented total dictatorship even fleeing was not an option. The monasteries on far away mountains that provided refuge for scholars in feudal times were totally ravaged and to write even in secret was to risk one's life. To maintain one's intellectual autonomy one could only talk to oneself, and it had to be in utmost secrecy. I should mention that it was only in this period when it was utterly impossible for literature that I came to comprehend why it was so essential: literature allows a person to preserve a human consciousness.

It can be said that talking to oneself is the starting point of literature and that using language to communicate is secondary. A person pours his feelings and thoughts into language that, written as words, becomes literature. At the time there is no thought of utility or that some day it might be published yet there is the compulsion to write because there is recompense and consolation in the pleasure of writing. I began writing my novel *Soul Mountain* to dispel my inner loneliness at the very time when works I had written with rigorous self-censorship had been banned. *Soul Mountain* was written for myself and without the hope that it would be published.

From my experience in writing, I can say that literature is inherently man's affirmation of the value of his own self and that this is validated during the writing—literature is born primarily of the writer's need for self-fulfillment. Whether it has any impact on society comes after the completion of a work and that impact certainly is not determined by the wishes of the writer.

In the history of literature there are many great enduring works which were not published in the lifetimes of the authors. If the authors had not achieved self-affirmation while writing, how could they have continued to write? As in the case of

Shakespeare, even now it is difficult to ascertain the details of the lives of the four geniuses who wrote China's greatest novels, *Journey to the West*, *Water Margin*, *Jin Ping Mei* and *Dream of Red Mansions*. All that remains is an autobiographical essay by Shi Naian and had he not as he said consoled himself by writing, how else could he have devoted the rest of his life to that huge work for which he received no recompense during life? And was this not also the case with Kafka, who pioneered modern fiction, and with Fernando Pessoa, the most profound poet of the twentieth century? Their turning to language was not in order to reform the world and while profoundly aware of the helplessness of the individual they still spoke out, for such is the magic of language.

Language is the ultimate crystallization of human civilization. It is intricate, incisive and difficult to grasp and yet it is pervasive, penetrates human perceptions and links man, the perceiving subject, to his own understanding of the world. The written word is also magical for it allows communication between separate individuals, even if they are from different races and times. It is also in this way that the shared present time in the writing and reading of literature is connected to its eternal spiritual value.

In my view, for a writer of the present to strive to emphasize a national culture is problematical. Because of where I was born and the language I use, the cultural traditions of China naturally reside within me. Culture and language are always closely related and thus characteristic and relatively stable modes of perception, thought and articulation are formed. However, a writer's creativity begins precisely with what has already been articulated in his language and addresses what has not been adequately articulated in that language. As the creator of linguistic art there is no need to stick on oneself a stock national label that can be easily recognized.

Literature transcends national boundaries—through translations it transcends languages and then specific social customs and inter-human relationships created by geographical location and history—to make profound revelations about the universality of human nature. Furthermore, the writer today receives multicultural influences outside the culture of his own race so, unless it is to promote tourism, emphasizing the cultural features of a people is inevitably suspect.

Literature transcends ideology, national boundaries and racial consciousness in the same way as the individual's existence basically transcends this or that -ism. This is because man's existential condition is superior to any theories or speculations about life. Literature is a universal observation on the dilemmas of human existence and nothing is taboo. Restrictions on literature are always externally imposed: politics, society, ethics and customs set out to tailor literature into decorations for their various frameworks.

However, literature is neither an embellishment for authority or a socially fashionable item, it has its own criterion of merit: its aesthetic quality. An aesthetic intricately related to the human emotions is the only indispensable criterion for literary works. Indeed, such judgments differ from person to person because the emotions are invariably that of different individuals. However, such subjective aesthetic judgments do have universally recognized standards. The capacity for critical appreciation nurtured by literature allows the reader to also experience the poetic feeling and the beauty, the sublime and the ridiculous, the sorrow and the absurdity, and the humor and the irony that the author has infused into his work.

Poetic feeling does not derive simply from the expression of the emotions; nevertheless, unbridled egotism, a form of infantilism, is difficult to avoid in the early stages of writing. Also, there are numerous levels of emotional expression and to reach higher levels requires cold detachment. Poetry is concealed in the distanced gaze. Furthermore, if this gaze also examines the person of the author and overarches both the characters of the book and the author to become the author's third eye, one that is as neutral as possible, the disasters and the refuse of the human world will all be worthy of scrutiny. Then as feelings of pain, hatred and abhorrence are aroused so too are feelings of concern and love for life.

An aesthetic based on human emotions does not become outdated even with the perennial changing of fashions in literature and in art. However, literary evaluations that fluctuate like fashions are premised on what is the latest: that is, whatever is new is good. This is a mechanism in general market movements and the book market is not exempted, but if the writer's aesthetic judgment follows market movements it will mean the suicide of literature. Especially in the so-called consumerist society of the present, I think one must resort to cold literature.

Ten years ago, after concluding *Soul Mountain*, which I had written over seven years, I wrote a short essay proposing this type of literature:

> Literature is not concerned with politics but is purely a matter of the individual. It is the gratification of the intellect together with an observation, a review of what has been experienced, reminiscences and feelings or the portrayal of a state of mind.
>
> The so-called writer is nothing more than someone speaking or writing and whether he is listened to or read is for others to choose. The writer is not a hero acting on orders from the people nor is he worthy of worship as an idol, and certainly he is not a criminal or enemy of the people. He is at times victimised along with his writings simply because of other's needs. When the authorities need to manufacture a few enemies to divert people's attention, writers become sacrifices and worse

still writers who have been duped actually think it is a great honour to be sacrificed.

In fact the relationship of the author and the reader is always one of spiritual communication and there is no need to meet or to socially interact, it is a communication simply through the work. Literature remains an indispensable form of human activity in which both the reader and the writer are engaged of their own volition. Hence, literature has no duty to the masses.

This sort of literature that has recovered its innate character can be called cold literature. It exists simply because humankind seeks a purely spiritual activity beyond the gratification of material desires. This sort of literature of course did not come into being today. However, whereas in the past it mainly had to fight oppressive political forces and social customs, today it has to do battle with the subversive commercial values of consumerist society. For it to exist depends on a willingness to endure the loneliness.

If a writer devotes himself to this sort of writing he will find it difficult to make a living. Hence the writing of this sort of literature must be considered a luxury, a form of pure spiritual gratification. If this sort of literature has the good fortune of being published and circulated it is due to the efforts of the writer and his friends, Cao Xueqin and Kafka are such examples. During their lifetimes, their works were unpublished so they were not able to create literary movements or to become celebrities. These writers lived at the margins and seams of society, devoting themselves to this sort of spiritual activity for which at the time they did not hope for any recompense. They did not seek social approval but simply derived pleasure from writing.

Cold literature is literature that will flee in order to survive, it is literature that refuses to be strangled by society in its quest for spiritual salvation. If a race cannot accommodate this sort of non-utilitarian literature it is not merely a misfortune for the writer but a tragedy for the race.

It is my good fortune to be receiving, during my lifetime, this great honor from the Swedish Academy, and in this I have been helped by many friends from all over the world. For years without thought of reward and not shirking difficulties they have translated, published, performed and evaluated my writings. However, I will not thank them one by one for it is a very long list of names.

I should also thank France for accepting me. In France where literature and art are revered I have won the conditions to write with freedom and I also have readers and audiences. Fortunately I am not lonely although writing, to which I have committed myself, is a solitary affair.

What I would also like to say here is that life is not a celebration and that the rest of the world is not peaceful as in Sweden where for 180 years there has been no war. This new century will not be immune to catastrophes simply because there were so many in the past century, because memories are not transmitted like genes. Humans have minds but are not intelligent enough to learn from the past and when malevolence flares up in the human mind it can endanger human survival itself.

The human species does not necessarily move in stages from progress to progress, and here I make reference to the history of human civilization. History and civilization do not advance in tandem. From the stagnation of Medieval Europe to the decline and chaos in recent times on the mainland of Asia and to the catastrophes of two world wars in the twentieth century, the methods of killing people became increasingly sophisticated. Scientific and technological progress certainly does not imply that humankind as a result becomes more civilized.

Using some scientific -ism to explain history or interpreting it with a historical perspective based on pseudo-dialectics has failed to clarify human behavior. Now that the utopian fervor and continuing revolution of the past century have crumbled to dust, there is unavoidably a feeling of bitterness among those who have survived.

The denial of a denial does not necessarily result in an affirmation. Revolution did not merely bring in new things because the new utopian world was premised on the destruction of the old. This theory of social revolution was similarly applied to literature and turned what had once been a realm of creativity into a battlefield in which earlier people were overthrown and cultural traditions were trampled upon. Everything had to start from zero, modernization was good and the history of literature too was interpreted as a continuing upheaval.

The writer cannot fill the role of the Creator so there is no need for him to inflate his ego by thinking that he is God. This will not only bring about psychological dysfunction and turn him into a madman but will also transform the world into a hallucination in which everything external to his own body is purgatory and naturally he cannot go on living. Others are clearly hell: presumably it is like this when the self loses control. Needless to say he will turn himself into a sacrifice for the future and also demand that others follow suit in sacrificing themselves.

There is no need to rush to complete the history of the twentieth century. If the world again sinks into the ruins of some ideological framework this history will have been written in vain and later people will revise it for themselves.

The writer is also not a prophet. What is important is to live in the present, to stop being hoodwinked, to cast off delusions, to look clearly at this moment of time and at the same time to scrutinize the self. This self too is total chaos and while questioning the world and others one may as well look back at one's self. Disaster and oppression do usually come from another but man's cowardice and anxiety can often intensify the suffering and furthermore create misfortune for others.

Such is the inexplicable nature of humankind's behaviour, and man's knowledge of his self is even harder to comprehend. Literature is simply man focusing his gaze on his self and while he does a thread of consciousness which sheds light on this self begins to grow.

To subvert is not the aim of literature; its value lies in discovering and revealing what is rarely known, little known, thought to be known but in fact not very well known of the truth of the human world. It would seem that truth is the unassailable and most basic quality of literature.

The new century has already arrived. I will not bother about whether or not it is in fact new but it would seem that the revolution in literature and revolutionary literature, and even ideology, may have all come to an end. The illusion of a social utopia that enshrouded more than a century has vanished and when literature throws off the fetters of this and that -ism it will still have to return to the dilemmas of human existence. However, the dilemmas of human existence have changed very little and will continue to be the eternal topic of literature.

This is an age without prophecies and promises and I think it is a good thing. The writer playing prophet and judge should also cease since the many prophecies of the past century have all turned out to be frauds. And there is no need to manufacture new superstitions about the future, it is much better to wait and see. It would be best also for the writer to revert to the role of witness and strive to present the truth.

This is not to say that literature is the same as a document. Actually, there are few facts in documented testimonies and the reasons and motives behind incidents are often concealed. However, when literature deals with the truth the whole process from a person's inner mind to the incident can be exposed without leaving anything out. This power is inherent in literature as long as the writer sets out to portray the true circumstances of human existence and is not just making up nonsense.

It is a writer's insights in grasping truth that determine the quality of a work, and word games or writing techniques cannot serve as substitutes. Indeed, there are numerous definitions of truth and how it is dealt with varies from person to person but it can be seen at a glance whether a writer is embellishing human phenomena or making a full and honest portrayal. The literary criticism of a certain ideology turned truth and untruth into semantic analysis, but such principles and tenets are of little relevance in literary creation.

However, whether or not the writer confronts truth is not just an issue of creative methodology, it is closely linked to his attitude towards writing. Truth when the pen is taken up at the same time implies that one is sincere after one puts down the pen. Here truth is not simply an evaluation of literature but at the same time has ethical connotations. It is not the writer's duty to preach morality and while striving to portray various people in the world he also unscrupulously exposes his self, even the secrets of his inner mind. For the writer truth in literature approximates ethics, it is the ultimate ethics of literature.

In the hands of a writer with a serious attitude to writing even literary fabrications are premised on the portrayal of the truth of human life, and this has been the vital life force of works that have endured from ancient times to the present. It is precisely for this reason that Greek tragedy and Shakespeare will never become outdated.

Literature does not simply make a replica of reality but penetrates the surface layers and reaches deep into the inner workings of reality; it removes false illusions, looks down from great heights at ordinary happenings, and with a broad perspective reveals happenings in their entirety.

Of course, literature also relies on the imagination but this sort of journey in the mind is not just putting together a whole lot of rubbish. Imagination that is divorced from true feelings and fabrications that are divorced from the basis of life experiences can only end up insipid and weak, and works that fail to convince the author himself will not be able to move readers. Indeed, literature does not only rely on the experiences of ordinary life nor is the writer bound by what he has personally experienced. It is possible for the things heard and seen through a language carrier and the things related in the literary works of earlier writers all to be transformed into one's own feelings. This too is the magic of the language of literature.

As with a curse or a blessing language has the power to stir body and mind. The art of language lies in the presenter being able to convey his feelings to others, it is not some sign system or semantic structure requiring nothing more than grammatical structures. If the living person behind language is forgotten, semantic expositions easily turn into games of the intellect.

Language is not merely concepts and the carrier of concepts, it simultaneously activates the feelings and the senses and this is why signs and signals cannot replace the language of living people. The will, motives, tone and emotions behind what someone says cannot be fully expressed by semantics and rhetoric alone. The connotations of the language of literature must be voiced, spoken by living people, to be fully expressed. So as well as serving as a carrier of thought literature must also appeal to the auditory senses. The human need for language is not simply for the transmission of meaning, it is at the same time listening to and affirming a person's existence.

Borrowing from Descartes, it could be said of the writer: I say and therefore I am. However, the 'I' of the writer can be the writer himself, can be equated to the narrator or become the characters of a work. As the narrator-subject can also be he and you, it is tripartite. The fixing of a key-speaker pronoun is the starting point for portraying perceptions and from this various narrative patterns take shape. It is during the process of searching for his own narrative method that the writer gives concrete form to his perceptions.

In my fiction I use pronouns instead of the usual characters and also use the pronouns I, you and he to tell about or to focus on the protagonist. The portrayal of the one character by using different pronouns creates a sense of distance. As this also provides actors on the stage with a broader psychological space I have also introduced the changing of pronouns into my drama.

The writing of fiction or drama has not and will not come to an end and there is no substance to flippant announcements of the death of certain genres of literature or art.

Born at the start of human civilization, like life, language is full of wonders and its expressive capacity is limitless. It is the work of the writer to discover and develop the latent potential inherent in language. The writer is not the Creator and he cannot eradicate the world even if it is too old. He also cannot establish some new ideal world even if the present world is absurd and beyond human comprehension. However, he can certainly make innovative statements either by adding to what earlier people have said or else starting where earlier people stopped.

To subvert literature was Cultural Revolution rhetoric. Literature did not die and writers were not destroyed. Every writer has his place on the bookshelf and he has life as long as he has readers. There is no greater consolation for a writer than to be able to leave a book in humankind's vast treasury of literature that will continue to be read in future times.

Literature is only actualized and of interest at that moment in time when the writer writes it and the reader reads it. Unless it is pretense, to write for the future only deludes oneself and others as well. Literature is for the living and moreover affirms the present of the living. It is this eternal present and this confirmation of individual life that is the absolute reason why literature is literature, if one insists on seeking a reason for this huge thing that exists of itself.

When writing is not a livelihood or when one is so engrossed in writing that one forgets why one is writing and for whom one is writing it becomes a necessity and one will write compulsively and give birth to literature. It is this non-utilitarian aspect of literature that is fundamental to literature. That the writing of literature has become a profession is an ugly outcome of the division of labour in modern society and a very bitter fruit for the writer.

This is especially the case in the present age where the market economy has become pervasive and books have also become commodities. Everywhere there are huge undiscriminating markets and not just individual writers but even the societies and movements of past literary schools have all gone. If the writer does not bend to the pressures of the market and refuses to stoop to manufacturing cultural products by writing to satisfy the tastes of fashions and trends, he must make a living by some other means. Literature is not a best-selling book or a book on a ranked list and authors promoted on television are engaged in advertising rather than in writing. Freedom in writing is not conferred and cannot be purchased but comes from an inner need in the writer himself.

Instead of saying that Buddha is in the heart, it would be better to say that freedom is in the heart and it simply depends on whether one makes use of it. If one exchanges freedom for something else then the bird that is freedom will fly off, for this is the cost of freedom.

The writer writes what he wants without concern for recompense not only to affirm his self but also to challenge society. This challenge is not pretence and the writer has no need to inflate his ego by becoming a hero or a fighter. Heroes and fighters struggle to achieve some great work or to establish some meritorious deed and these lie beyond the scope of literary works. If the writer wants to challenge society it must be through language and he must rely on the characters and incidents of his works, otherwise he can only harm literature. Literature is not angry shouting and furthermore cannot turn an individual's indignation into accusations. It is only when the feelings of the writer as an individual are dispersed in a work that his feelings will withstand the ravages of time and live on for a long time.

Therefore it is actually not the challenge of the writer to society but rather the challenge of his works. An enduring work is of course a powerful response to the times and society of the writer. The clamour of the writer and his actions may have vanished but as long as there are readers his voice in his writings continues to reverberate.

Indeed, such a challenge cannot transform society. It is merely an individual aspiring to transcend the limitations of the social ecology and taking a very inconspicuous stance. However, this is by no means an ordinary stance for it is one that takes pride in being human. It would be sad if human history is only manipulated by the unknowable laws and moves blindly with the current so that the different voices of individuals cannot be heard. It is in this sense that literature fills in the gaps of history. When the great laws of history are not used to explain humankind it will be possible for people to leave behind their own voices. History is not all that humankind possesses, there is also the legacy of literature. In literature the people are inventions but they retain an essential belief in their own self-worth.

Honorable members of the Academy, I thank you for awarding this Nobel Prize to literature, to literature that is unwavering in its independence, that avoids neither human suffering nor political oppression and that furthermore does not serve politics. I thank all of you for awarding this most prestigious prize for works that are far removed from the writings of the market, works that have aroused little attention but are actually worth reading. At the same time, I also thank the

Swedish Academy for allowing me to ascend this dais to speak before the eyes of the world. A frail individual's weak voice that is hardly worth listening to and that normally would not be heard in the public media has been allowed to address the world. However, I believe that this is precisely the meaning of the Nobel Prize and I thank everyone for this opportunity to speak.

Translated from Chinese by Mabel Lee

Günter Grass

To Be Continued ...
1999

Günter Grass was born in 1927 to Polish-German parents. Entering military service during the Second World War, he was wounded in the last year of conflict and imprisoned in an American POW camp. After the war he worked as a farm laborer and stonemason, and studied art in Düsseldorf and Berlin. He then went on to work variously as a sculptor, graphic artist and writer, first in Paris and then Berlin.

Grass is perhaps best known to English readers for The Tin Drum, *first published in 1959 and a key work in European magic realism. In 1961 came the novella* Cat and Mouse, *followed in 1963 by the novel* Dog Years. *Together these three works are now widely known as the Danzig Trilogy. The 1960s also saw Grass first become active in politics, supporting the Social Democrat party in election campaigns and in the late 1980s arguing against the reunification of Germany. His work is often categorized as part of the artistic movement known as* Vergangenheitsbewältigung, *which translates as 'coming to terms with the past'. A strong supporter of the peace and environmental movements, other novels include* The Flounder *and* The Rat, *both highly critical of modern civilization.*

The Academy praised Grass for his 'frolicsome black fables [that] portray the forgotten face of history'.

Having made this announcement, 19th-century works of fiction would go on and on. Magazines and newspapers gave them all the space they wished: the serialized novel was in its heyday. While the early chapters appeared in quick succession, the core of the work was being written out by hand, and its conclusion was yet to be conceived. Nor was it only trivial horror stories or tearjerkers that thus held the reader in thrall. Many of Dickens' novels came out in serial form, in installments. Tolstoy's *Anna Karenina* was a serialized novel. Balzac's time, a tireless provider of mass-produced serializations, gave the still anonymous writer lessons in the technique of suspense, of building to a climax at the end of a column. And nearly all Fontane's novels appeared first in newspapers and magazines as serializations. Witness the publisher of the *Vossische Zeitung*, where *Trials and Tribulations* first saw print, who exclaimed in a rage, 'Will this sluttish story never end!'

But before I go on spinning these strands of my talk or move on to others, I wish to point out that from a purely literary point of view this hall and the Swedish Academy that invited me here are far from alien to me. My novel *The Rat*, which came out almost fourteen years ago and whose catastrophic course along various oblique levels of narration one or two of my readers may recall, features a eulogy delivered before just such an audience as you, an encomium to the rat or, to be more precise, the laboratory rat.

The rat has been awarded a Nobel Prize. At last, one might say. She's been on the list for years, even the short list. Representative of millions of experimental animals—from guinea pig to rhesus monkey—the white-haired, red-eyed laboratory rat is finally getting her due. For she more than anyone—or so claims the narrator of my novel—has made possible all the Nobelified research and discoveries in the field of medicine and, as far as Nobel Laureates Watson and Crick are concerned, on the virtually boundless turf of gene manipulation. Since then maize and other vegetables—to say nothing of all sorts of animals—can be cloned more or less legally, which is why the rat-men, who increasingly take over as the novel comes to a close, that is, during the post-human era, are called Watsoncricks. They combine the best of both genera. Humans have much of the rat in them and vice versa. The world seems to use the synthesis to regain its health. After the Big Bang, when only rats, cockroaches, flies and the remains of fish and frog eggs survive and it is time to make order out of the chaos, the Watsoncricks, who miraculously escape, do more than their share.

But since this strand of the narrative could as easily have ended with 'To Be Continued ...' and the Nobel Prize speech in praise of the laboratory rat is certainly not meant to give the novel a happy end, I can now—as what might be called a matter of principle—turn to narration as a form of survival as well as a form of art.

People have always told tales. Long before humanity learned to write and gradually became literate, everybody told tales to everybody else and everybody listened to everybody else's tales. Before long it became clear that some of the still illiterate storytellers told more and better tales than others, that is, they could make more people believe their lies. And there were those among them who found artful ways of stemming the peaceful flow of their tales and diverting it into a tributary, that, far from drying up, turned suddenly and amazingly into a broad bed, though now full of flotsam and jetsam, the stuff of sub-plots. And because these primordial storytellers—who were not dependent upon day or lamp light and could carry on perfectly well in the dark, who were in fact adept at exploiting dusk or darkness to add to the suspense—because they stopped at nothing, neither dry stretches nor thundering waterfalls, except perhaps to interrupt the course of action with a 'To Be Continued ...' if they sensed their audience's attention flagging, many of their listeners felt moved to start telling tales of their own.

What tales were told when no one could yet write and therefore no one wrote them down? From the days of Cain and Abel there were tales of murder and manslaughter. Feuds—blood feuds, in particular—were always good for a story. Genocide entered the picture quite early along with floods and droughts, fat years and lean years. Lengthy lists of cattle and slaves were perfectly acceptable, and no tale could be believable without detailed genealogies of who came before whom and who came after, heroic tales especially. Love triangles, popular even now, and tales of monsters—half man, half beast—who made their way through labyrinths or lay in wait in the bulrushes attracted mass audiences from the outset, to say nothing of legends of gods and idols and accounts of sea journeys, which were then handed down, polished, enlarged upon, modified, transmogrified into their opposites, and finally written down by a storyteller whose name was supposedly Homer or, in the case of the Bible, by a collective of storytellers. In China and Persia, in India and the Peruvian highlands, wherever writing flourished, storytellers—whether as groups or individuals, anonymously or by name—turned into literati.

Writing-fixated as we are, we nonetheless retain the memory of oral storytelling, the spoken origins of literature. And a good thing too, because if we were to forget that all storytelling comes through the lips—now inarticulate, hesitant, now swift, as if driven by fear, now in whisper, to keep the secrets revealed from reaching the wrong ears, now loudly and clearly, all the way from self-serving bluster to sniffing out the very essence of life—if our faith in writing were to make us forget all that, our storytelling would be bookish, dry as dust.

Yet how good too that we have so many books available to us and that whether we read them aloud or to ourselves they are permanent. They have been my inspiration. When I was young and malleable, masters like Melville and Döblin or Luther with his Biblical German prompted me to read aloud as I wrote, to mix ink with spit. Nor have things changed much since. Well into my fifth decade of enduring, no, relishing the moil and toil called writing, I chew tough, stringy clauses into manageable mush, babble to myself in blissful isolation, and put pen to paper only when I hear the proper tone and pitch, resonance and reverberation.

Yes, I love my calling. It keeps me company, a company whose polyphonic chatter calls for literal transcription into my manuscripts. And there is nothing I like more than to meet books of mine—books that have long since flown the coop and been expropriated by readers—when I read out loud to an audience what now lies peacefully on the page. For both the young, weaned early from language, and the old, grizzled yet still rapacious, the written word becomes spoken, and the magic works again and again. It is the shaman in the author earning a bit on the side, writing against the current of time, lying his way to tenable truths. And everyone believes his tacit promise: To Be Continued ...

But how did I become a writer, poet and artist—all at once and all on frightening white paper? What homemade hubris put a child up to such craziness? After all, I was only twelve when I realized I wanted to be an artist. It coincided with the outbreak of the Second World War, when I was living on the outskirts of Danzig. But my first opportunity for professional development had to wait until the following year, when I found a tempting offer in the Hitler Youth magazine *Hilf mit!* (*Lend a Hand!*). It was a story contest. With prizes. I immediately set to writing my first novel. Influenced by my mother's background, it bore the title *The Kashubians*, but the action did not take place in the painful present of that small and dwindling people; it took place in the thirteenth century during a period of interregnum, a grim period when brigands and robber barons ruled the highways and the only recourse a peasant had to justice was a kind of kangaroo court.

All I can remember of it is that after a brief outline of the economic conditions in the Kashubian hinterland I started in on pillages and massacres with a vengeance. There was so much throttling, stabbing and skewering, so many kangaroo-court hangings and executions that by the end of the first chapter all the protagonists and a goodly number of the minor characters were dead and either buried or left to the crows. Since my sense of style did not allow me to turn corpses into spirits and the novel into a ghost story, I had to admit defeat with an abrupt end and no 'To Be Continued …' Not for good, of course, but the neophyte had learned his lesson: next time he would have to be a bit more gentle with his characters.

But first I read and read some more. I had my own way of reading: with my fingers in my ears. Let me say by way of explanation that my younger sister and I grew up in straitened circumstances, that is, in a two-room flat and hence without rooms of our own or even so much as a corner to ourselves. In the long run it turned out to be an advantage, though: I learned at an early age to concentrate in the midst of people or surrounded by noise. When I read I might have been under a bell jar; I was so involved in the world of the book that my mother, who liked a practical joke, once demonstrated her son's complete and utter absorption to a neighbor by replacing a roll I had been taking an occasional bite from with a bar of soap—Palmolive, I believe—whereupon the two women—my mother not without a certain pride—watched me reach blindly for the soap, sink my teeth into it and chew it for a good minute before it tore me away from my adventure on the page.

To this day I can concentrate as I did in my early years, but I have never read more obsessively. Our books were kept in a bookcase behind blue-curtained panes of glass. My mother belonged to a book club, and the novels of Dostoevsky and Tolstoy stood side by side and mixed in with novels by Hamsun, Raabe and Vicky Baum. Selma Lagerlöf's *Gösta Berling* was within easy reach. I later moved on to the municipal library, but my mother's collection provided the initial impulse. A punctilious businesswoman forced to sell her wares to unreliable customers on credit, she was also a great lover of beauty: she listened to opera and operetta, melodies on her primitive radio, enjoyed hearing my promising stories and frequently went to the municipal theatre, even taking me along from time to time.

The only reason I rehearse here these anecdotes of a petty bourgeois childhood after painting them with epic strokes decades ago in works peopled by fictitious characters is to help me answer the question 'What made you become a writer?' The ability to daydream at length, the job of punning and playing with language in general, the addiction to lying for its own sake rather than for mine because sticking to the truth would have been a bore—in short, what is loosely known as talent was certainly a factor, but it was the abrupt intrusion of politics into the family idyll that turned the all-too-flighty category of talent into a ballast with a certain permanence and depth.

My mother's favorite cousin, like her a Kashubian by birth, worked at the Polish post office of the Free City of Danzig. He was a regular at our house and always welcome. When the war broke out the Hevelius Square post office building held out for a time against the SS-Heimwehr, and my uncle was rounded up with those who finally surrendered. They were tried summarily and put before a firing squad. Suddenly he was no more. Suddenly and permanently his name was no longer mentioned. He became a non-person. Yet he must have lived on in me through the years when at fifteen I donned a uniform, at sixteen I learned what fear was, at seventeen I landed in an American POW camp, at eighteen I worked in the black market, studied to be a stonemason and started sculpting in stone, prepared for admission to art school and wrote and drew, drew and wrote, fleet-footed verse, quizzical one-acts, and on it went until I found the material unwieldy—I seem to have an inborn need for aesthetic pleasure. And beneath the detritus of it all lay my mother's favorite cousin, the Polish postal clerk, shot and buried, only to be found by me (who else?) and exhumed and resuscitated by literary artificial respiration under other names and guises, though this time in a novel whose major and minor characters, full of life and beans as they are, make it through a number of chapters, some even holding out till the end and thus enabling the writer to keep his recurrent promise: To Be Continued ...

And so on and so forth. The publication of my first two novels, *The Tin Drum* and *Dog Years*, and the novella I stuck between them, *Cat and Mouse*, taught me early on, as a relatively young writer, that books can cause offence, stir up fury, even hatred, that what is undertaken out of love for one's country can be taken as soiling one's nest. From then on I have been controversial.

Which means that like writers banished to Siberia or suchlike places I am in good company. So I have no grounds to complain; on the contrary, writers should consider the condition of permanent controversiality to be invigorating, part of the risk involved in choosing the profession. It is a fact of life that writers have always and with due consideration and great pleasure spat in the soup of the high and mighty. That is what makes the history of literature analogous to the development and refinement of censorship.

The ill humor of the powers-that-be forced Socrates to drain the cup of hemlock to the dregs, sent Ovid into exile, made Seneca open his veins. For centuries and to the present day the finest fruits of the western garden of literature have graced the index of the Catholic church. How much equivocation did the European Enlightenment learn from the censorship practiced by princes with absolute power? How many German, Italian, Spanish and Portuguese writers did fascism drive from their lands and languages? How many writers fell victim to the Leninist-Stalinist reign of terror? And what constraints are writers under today in countries like China, Kenya or Croatia?

I come from the land of book-burning. We know that the desire to destroy a hated book is still (or once more) part of the spirit of our times and that when necessary it finds appropriate telegenic expression and therefore a mass audience. What is much worse, however, is that the persecution of writers, including the threat of murder and murder itself, is on the rise throughout the world, so much so that the world has grown accustomed to the terror of it. True, the part of the world that calls itself free raises a hue and cry when, as in 1995 in Nigeria, a writer like Ken Saro-Wiwa and his supporters are sentenced to death and killed for taking a stand against the contamination of their country, but things immediately go back to normal, because ecological considerations might affect the profits of the world's number one oil colossus Shell.

What makes books—and with them writers—so dangerous that church and state, politburos and the mass media feel the need to oppose them? Silencing and worse are seldom the result of direct attacks on the reigning ideology. Often all it takes is a literary allusion to the idea that truth exists only in the plural—that there is no such thing as a single truth but only a multitude of truths—to make the defenders of one or another truth sense danger, mortal danger. Then there is the problem that writers are by definition unable to leave the past in peace: they are quick to open closed wounds, peer behind closed doors, find skeletons in the cupboard, consume sacred cows or, as in the case of Jonathan Swift, offer up Irish children, 'stewed, roasted, baked, or boiled', to the kitchens of the English nobility. In other words, nothing is sacred to them, not even capitalism, and that makes them offensive, even criminal. But worst of all they refuse to make common cause with the victors of history: they take pleasure milling about the fringes of the historical process with the losers, who have plenty to say but no platform to say it on. By giving them a voice, they call the victory into question, by associating with them, they join ranks with them.

Of course the powers-that-be, no matter what period costume they may be wearing, have nothing against literature as such. They enjoy it as an ornament and even promote it. At present its role is to entertain, to serve the fun culture, to de-emphasize the negative side of things and give people hope, a light in the darkness. What is basically called for, though not quite so explicitly as during the communist years, is a 'positive hero'. In the jungle of the free market economy he is likely to pave his way to success Rambo-like with corpses and a smile; he is an adventurer who is always up for a quick fuck between battles, a winner who leaves a trail of losers behind him, in short, the perfect role model for our globalized world. And the demand for the hard-boiled he-man who always lands on his feet is unfailingly met by the media: James Bond has spawned any number of Dolly-like children. Good will continue to prevail over evil as long as it assumes his cool-guy pose.

Does that make his opposite or enemy a negative hero? Not necessarily. I have my roots, as you will have noticed from your reading, in the Spanish or Moorish school of the picaresque novel. Tilting at windmills has remained a model for that school down through the ages, and the picaro's very existence derives from the comic nature of defeat. He pees on the pillars of power and saws away at the throne knowing full well he will make no dent in either: once he moves on, the exalted temple may look a bit shabby, the throne may wobble slightly, but that is all. His humor is part and parcel of his despair. While *Die Götterdämmerung* drones on before an elegant Bayreuth audience, he sits sniggering in the back row, because in his theatre comedy and tragedy go hand in hand. He scorns the fateful march of the victors and sticks his foot out to trip them, yet much as his failure makes us laugh the laughter sticks in our throat: even his wittiest cynicisms have a tragic cast to them. Besides, from the point of view of the philistine, rightist or leftist, he is a formalist—even a mannerist—of the first order: he holds the spyglass the wrong way; he sees time as a train on a siding: he puts mirrors everywhere; you can never tell whose ventriloquist he is; given his perspective, he can even accept dwarfs and giants into his entourage. The reason Rabelais was constantly on the run from the secular police and the Holy Inquisition is that his larger-than-life Gargantua and Pantagruel had turned the world according to scholasticism on its head. The laughter they unleashed was positively infernal. When Gargantua stooped bare-arsed on the towers of Notre Dame and pissed the length and breadth of Paris under water, everyone who did not drown guffawed. Or to go back to Swift: his modest culinary proposal for relieving the hunger in Ireland could be brought up to date if at the next economic summit the board set for the heads of state were groaning with lusciously prepared street children from Brazil or southern Sudan. Satire is the name of the art form I have in mind, and in satire everything is permitted, even tickling the funny bone with the grotesque.

When Heinrich Böll gave his Nobel Lecture here on 2 May, 1973, he brought the seemingly opposing positions of reason and poetry into closer and closer proximity and bemoaned the lack of time to go into another aspect of the issue: 'I have had to pass over humour, which, though no class privilege, is ignored in his poetry as a hiding place for resistance.' Now Böll knew that Jean Paul, the poet in question, had a place in the German Culture Hall of Fame, little read though he is nowadays; he knew to what extent Thomas Mann's literary oeuvre was suspected—by both the right and the left—of irony at the time (and still is, I might add). Clearly what Böll had in mind was not belly-laugh humor but rather inaudible, between-the-lines humor, the chronic susceptibility to melancholy of his clown, the desperate wit of the man who collected silence, an activity, by the way, that has become quite the thing in the media and—under the guise of 'voluntary self-control' on the part of the free West—a benign disguise for censorship.

By the early 1950s, when I had started writing consciously, Heinrich Böll was a well-known if not always well-received author. With Wolfgang Koeppen, Günter Eich and Arno Schmidt he stood apart from the culture industry. Post-war German literature, still young, was having a hard time with German, which had been corrupted by the Nazi regime. In addition, Böll's generation—but also the younger writers like myself—were stymied to a certain extent by a prohibition that came from Theodor Adorno: 'It is barbaric to write a poem after Auschwitz, and that is why it has become impossible to write poetry today …'

In other words, no more 'To Be Continued …' Though write we did. We wrote by bearing in mind, like Adorno in his *Minima Moralia: Reflections from Damaged Life* (1951), that Auschwitz marks a rift, an unbridgeable gap in the history of civilization. It was the only way we could get round the prohibition. Even so, Adorno's writing on the wall has retained its power to this day. All the writers of my generation did public battle with it. No one had the desire or ability to keep silent. It was our duty to take the goose step out of German, to lure it out of its idylls and fogged inwardness. We, the children who had had our fingers burned, we were the ones to repudiate the absolutes, the ideological black or white. Doubt and skepticism were our godparents and the multitude of gray values their present to us. In any case, such was the asceticism I imposed on myself before discovering the richness of a language I had all too sweepingly pronounced guilty: its seducible softness, its tendency to plumb the depths, its utterly supple hardness, not to mention the sheen of its dialects, its artlessness and artfulness, its eccentricities, and beauty blossoming from its subjunctives. Having won back this capital, we invested it to make more.

Despite Adorno's verdict or spurred on by it. The only way writing after Auschwitz, poetry or prose, could proceed was by becoming memory and preventing the past from coming to an end. Only then could post-war literature in German justify applying the generally valid 'To Be Continued ...' to itself and its descendants; only then could the wound be kept open and the much desired and prescribed forgetting be reversed with a steadfast 'Once upon a time'.

How many times when one or another interest group calls for considering what happened a closed chapter—we need to return to normalcy and put our shameful past behind us—how many times has literature resisted. And rightly so! Because it is a position as foolish as it is understandable; because every time the end of the post-war period is proclaimed in Germany—as it was ten years ago, with the Wall down and unity in the offing—the past catches up with us.

At that time, in February 1990, I gave a talk to students in Frankfurt entitled 'Writing After Auschwitz'. I wanted to take stock of my works book by book. In *The Diary of a Snail*, which came out in 1972 and in which past and present crisscross, but also run parallel or occasionally collide, I am asked by my sons how I define my profession, and I answer, 'A writer, children, is someone who writes against the current of time.' What I said to the students was: 'Such a view presumes that writers are not encapsulated in isolation or the sempiternal, that they see themselves as living in the here and now, and, even more, that they expose themselves to the vicissitudes of time, that they jump in and take sides. The dangers of jumping in and taking sides are well known: The distance a writer is supposed to keep is threatened; his language must live from hand to mouth; the narrowness of current events can make him narrow and curb the imagination he has trained to run free; he runs the danger of running out of breath.'

The risk I referred to then has remained with me throughout the years. But what would the profession of writer be like without risk? Granted, the writer would have the security of, say, a cultural bureaucrat, but he would be the prisoner of his fears of dirtying his hands with the present. Out of fear of losing his distance he would lose himself in realms where myths reside and lofty thoughts are all. But the present, which the past is constantly turning into, would catch up to him in the end and put him through the third degree. Because every writer is of his time, no matter how he protests being born too early or late. He does not autonomously choose what he will write about, that choice is made for him. At least I was not free to choose. Left to my own devices, I would have followed the laws of aesthetics and been perfectly happy to seek my place in texts droll and harmless.

But that was not to be. There were extenuating circumstances: mountains of rubble and cadavers, fruit of the womb of German history. The more I shovelled, the more it grew. It simply could not be ignored. Besides, I come from a family of refugees, which means that in addition to everything that drives a writer from book to book—common ambition, the fear of boredom, the mechanisms of egocentricity—I had the irreparable loss of my birthplace. If by telling tales I could not recapture a city both lost and destroyed, I could at least reconjure it. And this obsession kept me going. I wanted to make it clear to myself and my readers, not without a bit of a chip on my shoulder, that what was lost did not need to sink into oblivion, that it could be resuscitated by the art of literature in all its grandeur and pettiness: the churches and cemeteries, the sounds of the shipyards and smells of the faintly lapping Baltic, a language on its way out yet still stable-warm and grumble-rich, sins in need of confession and crimes tolerated if never exonerated.

A similar loss has provided other writers with a hotbed of obsessive topics. In a conversation dating back many years Salman Rushdie and I concurred that my lost Danzig was for me—like his lost Bombay for him—both resource and refuse pit, point of departure and navel of the world. This arrogance, this overkill lies at the very heart of literature. It is the condition for a story that can pull out all the stops. Painstaking detail, sensitive psychologizing, slice-of-life realism—no such techniques can handle our monstrous raw materials. As indebted as we are to the Enlightenment tradition of reason, the absurd course of history spurns all exclusively reasonable explanations.

Just as the Nobel Prize—once we divest it of its ceremonial garb—has its roots in the invention of dynamite, which like such other human headbirths as the splitting of the atom and the likewise Nobelified classification of the gene has wrought both weal and woe in the world, so literature has an explosive quality at its root, though the explosions literature releases have a delayed-action effect and change the world only in the magnifying glass of time, so to speak, it too wreaking cause for both joy and lamentation here below. How long did it take the European Enlightenment from Montaigne to Voltaire, Diderot, Kant, Lessing and Lichtenberg to introduce a flicker of reason into the dark corners of scholasticism? And even that flicker often died in the process, a process censorship went a long way towards inhibiting. But when the light finally did brighten things up, it turned out to be the light of cold reason, limited to the technically doable, to economic and social progress, a reason that claimed to be enlightened but that merely drummed a reason-based jargon (which amounted to instructions for making progress at all costs) into its offspring, capitalism and socialism (which were at each other's throats from the word go).

Today we can see what those brilliant failures who were the Enlightenment's offspring have wrought. We can see what a dangerous position its delayed-action, word-detonated explosion has hurled us into. And if we are trying to repair the damage with Enlightenment tools, it is only because we have no others. We look on in horror as capitalism—now that his brother, socialism, has been declared dead—rages unimpeded, megalomaniacally replaying the errors of the supposedly extinct brother. It has turned the free market into dogma, the only truth, and intoxicated by its all but limitless power, plays the wildest of games, making merger after merger with no goal than to maximize profits. No wonder capitalism is proving as impervious to reform as the communism that managed to strangle itself. Globalization is its motto, a motto it proclaims with the arrogance of infallibility: there is no alternative.

Accordingly, history has come to an end. No more 'To Be Continued …', no more suspense. Though perhaps there is hope that if not politics, which has abdicated its decision-making power to economics, then at least literature may come up with something to cause the 'new dogmatism' to falter.

How can subversive writing be both dynamite and of literary quality? Is there time enough to wait for the delayed action? Is any book capable of supplying a commodity in so short supply as the future? Is it not rather the case that literature is currently retreating from public life and that young writers are using the internet as a playground? A standstill, to which the suspicious word 'communication' lends a certain aura, is making headway. Every scrap of time is planned down to the last nervous breakdown. A cultural industry vale of tears is taking over the world. What is to be done?

My godlessness notwithstanding, all I can do is bend my knee to a saint who has never failed me and cracked some of the hardest nuts. 'O Holy and (through the grace of Camus) Nobelified Sisyphus! May thy stone not remain at the top of the hill, may we roll it down again and like thee continue to rejoice in it, and may the story told of the drudgery of our existence have no end. Amen.'

But will my prayer be heard? Or are the rumours true? Is the new breed of cloned creature destined to assure the continuation of human history?

Which brings me back to the beginning of my talk. Once more I open *The Rat* to the fifth chapter, in which the laboratory rat, representing millions of other laboratory animals in the cause of research, wins the Nobel Prize, and I am reminded how few prizes have been awarded to projects that would rid the world of the scourge of mankind: hunger. Anyone who can pay the price can get a new pair of kidneys. Hearts can be transplanted. We can phone anywhere in the world wire-free. Satellites and space stations orbit us solicitously. The latest weapon systems, conceived and developed, they too, on the basis of award-winning research, can help their masters to keep death at bay. Anything the human mind comes up with finds astonishing applications. Only hunger seems to resist. It is even increasing. Poverty deeply rooted shades into misery. Refugees are flocking all over the world accompanied by hunger. It takes political will paired with scientific know-how to root out misery of such magnitude, and no one seems resolved to undertake it.

In 1973, just when terror—with the active support of the United States—was beginning to strike in Chile, Willy Brandt spoke before the United Nations General Assembly, the first German chancellor to do so. He brought up the issue of worldwide poverty. The applause following his exclamation 'Hunger too is war!' was stunning.

I was present when he gave the speech. I was working on my novel *The Flounder* at the time. It deals with the very foundations of human existence including food, the lack and superabundance thereof, great gluttons and untold starvelings, the joys of the palate and crusts from the rich man's table.

The issue is still with us. The poor counter growing riches with growing birth rates. The affluent north and west can try to screen themselves off in security-mad fortresses, but the flocks of refugees will catch up with them: no gate can withstand the crush of the hungry.

The future will have something to say about all this. Our common novel must be continued. And even if one day people stop or are forced to stop writing and publishing, if books are no longer available, there will still be storytellers giving us mouth-to-ear artificial respiration, spinning old stories in new ways: loud and soft, heckling and halting, now close to laughter, now on the brink of tears.

Translated from German by Michael Henry Heim

José Saramago

How Characters Became the Masters and the Author Their Apprentice
1998

José Saramago was born in 1922 to a family of farmers who lived in a small village called Azinhaga, north of Lisbon. He was forced to leave high school for financial reasons and trained as a mechanic. It was then that Saramago began to explore the world of literature, visiting the public library of Lisbon during its evening opening hours.

Saramago's first book, a novel titled The Land of Sin, *was published in 1947 but his second did not appear for another nineteen years—a volume of poetry called* Possible Poems. *During that time he worked in the civil service and at a publishing company before moving for several years into newspapers. The years 1975 to 1980 saw him working mainly as a translator, but since the 1980s he has focused on his own writing.*

Saramago has produced 30 works of prose, poetry, essays and drama. His international breakthrough came in 1982 with the novel Baltazar and Blimunda, *a blasphemous and humorous love story set in eighteenth-century Portugal. Other novels include* The Year of the Death of Ricardo Reis *and* The Stone Raft. *He has lived on Lanzarote, at the northernmost end of the Canary Islands, since 1992.*

The Academy describes Saramago as a writer 'who with parables sustained by imagination, compassion and irony continually enables us once again to apprehend an elusory reality'.

The wisest man I ever knew in my whole life could not read or write. At four o'clock in the morning, when the promise of a new day still lingered over French lands, he got up from his pallet and left for the fields, taking to pasture the half-dozen pigs whose fertility nourished him and his wife. My mother's parents lived on this scarcity, on the small breeding of pigs that after weaning were sold to the neighbours in our village of Azinhaga in the province of Ribatejo. Their names were Jerónimo Meirinho and Josefa Caixinha and they were both illiterate. In winter when the cold of the night grew to the point of freezing the water in the pots inside the house, they went to the sty and fetched the weaklings among the piglets, taking them to their bed. Under the coarse blankets, the warmth from the humans saved the little animals from freezing and rescued them from certain death. Although the two were kindly people, it was not a compassionate soul that prompted them to act in that way: what concerned them, without sentimentalism or rhetoric, was to protect their daily bread, as is natural for people who, to maintain their life, have not learnt to think more than is needful. Many times I helped my grandfather Jerónimo in his swineherd's labor, many times I dug the land in the vegetable garden adjoining the house, and I chopped wood for the fire, many times, turning and turning the big iron wheel which worked the water pump. I pumped water from the community well and carried it on my shoulders. Many times, in secret, dodging from the men guarding the cornfields, I went with my grandmother, also at dawn, armed with rakes, sacking and cord, to glean the stubble, the loose straw that would then serve as litter for the livestock. And sometimes, on hot summer nights, after supper, my grandfather would tell me: 'José, tonight we're going to sleep, both of us, under the fig tree.' There were two other fig trees, but that one, certainly because it was the biggest, because it was the oldest, and timeless, was, for everybody in the house, the fig tree. More or less by antonomasia, an erudite word that I met only many years after and learned the meaning of ... Among the peace of the night, among the tree's high branches a star appeared to me and then slowly hid behind a leaf while, turning my gaze in another direction I saw rising into view like a river flowing silent through the hollow sky, the opal clarity of the Milky Way, the Road to Santiago as we still used to call it in the village. With sleep delayed, night was peopled with the stories and the cases my grandfather told and told: legends, apparitions, terrors, unique episodes, old deaths, scuffles with sticks and stones, the words of our forefathers, an untiring rumor of memories that would keep me awake while at the same time gently lulling me. I could never know if he was silent when he realized that I had fallen asleep or if he kept on talking so as not to leave half-unanswered the question I invariably asked into the most delayed pauses he placed on purpose within the account: 'And what happened next?' Maybe he repeated the stories for himself, so as not to forget them, or else to enrich them with new detail. At that age and as we all do at some time, needless to say, I imagined my grandfather Jerónimo was master of all the knowledge in the world. When at first light the singing of birds woke me up, he was not there any longer, had gone to the field with his animals, letting me sleep on. I would get up, fold the coarse blanket and barefoot—in the village I always walked barefoot till I was fourteen—and with straws still stuck in my hair, I went from the cultivated part of the yard to the other part, where the sties were, by the house. My grandmother, already afoot before my grandfather, set in front of me a big bowl of coffee with pieces of bread in and asked me if I had slept well. If I told her some bad dream, born of my grandfather's stories, she always reassured me: 'Don't make much of it, in dreams there's nothing solid.' At the time I thought, though my grandmother was also a very wise woman, she couldn't rise to the heights grandfather could, a man who, lying under a fig tree, having at his side José his grandson, could set the universe in motion just with a couple of words. It was only many years after, when my grandfather had departed from this world and I was a grown man, I finally came to realize that my grandmother, after all, also believed in dreams. There could have been no other reason why, sitting one evening at the door of her cottage where she now lived alone, staring at the biggest and smallest stars overhead, she said these words: 'The world is so beautiful and it is such a pity that I have to die.' She didn't say she was afraid of dying, but that it was a pity to die, as if her hard life of unrelenting work was, in that almost final moment, receiving the grace of a supreme and last farewell, the consolation of beauty revealed. She was sitting at the door of a house like none other I can imagine in all the world, because in it lived people who could sleep with piglets as if they were their own children, people who were sorry to leave life just because the world was beautiful; and this Jerónimo, my grandfather, swineherd and storyteller, feeling death about to arrive and take him, went and said goodbye to the trees in the yard, one by one, embracing them and crying because he knew he wouldn't see them again.

Many years later, writing for the first time about my grandfather Jerónimo and my grandmother Josefa (I haven't said so far that she was, according to many who knew her when young, a woman of uncommon beauty), I was finally aware I was transforming the ordinary people they were into literary characters: this was, probably, my way of not forgetting them, drawing and redrawing their faces with the pencil that ever changes memory, colouring and illuminating the monotony of a dull and horizonless daily routine as if creating, over the unstable map of memory, the supernatural unreality of the country where one has decided to spend one's life. The same attitude of mind that, after evoking the fascinating and enigmatic figure of a certain Berber grandfather, would lead me to describe more or less in these words an old photo (now almost 80 years old) showing my parents 'both standing, beautiful and young, facing the photographer, showing in their faces an expression of solemn seriousness, maybe fright in front of the camera at the very instant when the lens is about to capture the image they will never have again, because the following day will be, implacably, another day ... My mother is leaning her right elbow against a tall pillar and holds, in her right hand drawn in to her body, a flower. My father has his arm round my mother's back, his callused hand showing over her shoulder, like a wing. They are standing, shy, on a carpet patterned with branches. The canvas forming the fake background of the picture shows diffuse and incongruous neo-classic architecture.' And I ended, 'The day will come when I will tell these things. Nothing of this matters except to me. A Berber grandfather from North Africa, another grandfather a swineherd, a wonderfully beautiful grandmother; serious and handsome parents, a flower in a picture—what other genealogy would I care for? and what better tree would I lean against?'

I wrote these words almost 30 years ago, having no other purpose than to rebuild and register instants of the lives of those people who engendered and were closest to my being, thinking that nothing else would need explaining for people to know where I came from and what materials the person I am was made of, and what I have become little by little. But after all I was wrong, biology doesn't determine everything and as for genetics, very mysterious must have been its paths to make its voyages so long ... My genealogical tree (you will forgive the presumption of naming it this way, being so diminished in the substance of its sap) lacked not only some of those branches that time and life's successive encounters cause to burst from the main stem but also someone to help its roots penetrate the deepest subterranean layers, someone who could verify the consistency and flavor of its fruit, someone to extend and strengthen its top to make of it a shelter for birds of passage and a support for nests. When painting my parents and grandparents with the paints of literature, transforming them from common people of flesh and blood into characters, newly and in different ways builders of my life, I was, without noticing, tracing the path by which the characters I would invent later on, the others, truly literary, would construct and bring to me the materials and the tools which, at last, for better or for worse, in the sufficient and in the insufficient, in profit and loss, in all that is scarce but also in what is too much, would make of me the person whom I nowadays recognize as myself: the creator of those characters but at the same time their own creation. In one sense it could even be said that, letter by letter, word by word, page by page, book after book, I have been successively implanting in the man I was the characters I created. I believe that without them I wouldn't be the person I am today; without them maybe my life wouldn't have succeeded in becoming more than an inexact sketch, a promise that like so many others remained only a promise, the existence of someone who maybe might have been but in the end could not manage to be.

Now I can clearly see those who were my life-masters, those who most intensively taught me the hard work of living, those dozens of characters from my novels and plays that right now I see marching past before my eyes, those men and women of paper and ink, those people I believed I was guiding as I the narrator chose according to my whim, obedient to my will as an author, like articulated puppets whose actions could have no more effect on me than the burden and the tension of the strings I moved them with. Of those masters, the first was, undoubtedly, a mediocre portrait-painter, whom I called simply H, the main character of a story that I feel may reasonably be called a double initiation (his own, but also in a manner of speaking the author's) entitled *Manual of Painting and Calligraphy*, who taught me the simple honesty of acknowledging and observing, without resentment or frustration, my own limitations: as I could not and did not aspire to venture beyond my little plot of cultivated land, all I had left was the possibility of digging down, underneath, towards the roots. My own but also the world's, if I can be allowed such an immoderate ambition. It's not up to me, of course, to evaluate the merits of the results of efforts made, but today I consider it obvious that all my work from then on has obeyed that purpose and that principle.

Then came the men and women of Alentejo, that same brotherhood of the condemned of the earth where belonged my grandfather Jerónimo and my grandmother Josefa, primitive peasants obliged to hire out the strength of their arms for a wage and working conditions that deserved only to be called infamous, getting for less than nothing a life which the cultivated and civilized beings we are proud to be are pleased to call—depending on the occasion—precious, sacred or sublime. Common people I knew, deceived by a church both accomplice and beneficiary of the power of the state and of the landlords, people permanently watched by the police, people so many times innocent victims of the arbitrariness of a false justice. Three generations of a peasant family, the Badweathers, from the beginning of the century to the April Revolution of 1974 which toppled dictatorship, move through this novel, called *Risen from the Ground*, and it was with such men and women risen from the ground, real people first, figures of fiction later, that I learned how to be patient, to trust and to confide in time, that same time that simultaneously builds and destroys us in order to build and once more to destroy us. The only thing I am not sure of having assimilated satisfactorily is something that the hardship of those experiences turned into virtues in those women and men: a naturally austere attitude towards life. Having in mind, however, that the lesson learned still after more than twenty years remains intact in my memory, that every day I feel its presence in my spirit like a persistent summons: I haven't lost, not yet at least, the hope of meriting a little more the greatness of those examples of dignity proposed to me in the vast immensity of the plains of Alentejo. Time will tell.

What other lessons could I possibly receive from a Portuguese who lived in the sixteenth century, who composed the *Rimas* and the glories, the shipwrecks and the national disenchantments in the *Lusíadas*, who was an absolute poetical genius, the greatest in our literature, no matter how much sorrow this causes to Fernando Pessoa, who proclaimed himself its Super Camões? No lesson would fit me, no lesson could I learn, except the simplest, which could have been offered to me by Luís Vaz de Camões in his pure humanity, for instance the proud humility of an author who goes knocking at every door looking for someone willing to publish the book he has written, thereby suffering the scorn of the ignoramuses of blood and race, the disdainful indifference of a king and of his powerful entourage, the mockery with which the world has always received the visits of poets, visionaries and fools. At least once in life, every author has been, or will have to be, Luís de Camões, even if they haven't written the poem *Sôbolos Rios* ... Among nobles, courtiers and censors from the Holy Inquisition, among the loves of yesteryear and the disillusionments of premature old age, between the pain of writing and the joy of having written, it was this ill man, returning poor from India where so many sailed just to get rich, it was this soldier blind in one eye, slashed in his soul, it was this seducer of no fortune who will never again flutter the hearts of the ladies in the royal court, whom I put on stage in a play called *What Shall I Do with This Book?*, whose ending repeats another question, the only truly important one, the one we will never know if it will ever have a sufficient answer: 'What will you do with this book?' It was also proud humility to carry under his arm a masterpiece and to be unfairly rejected by the world. Proud humility also, and obstinate too—wanting to know what the purpose will be, tomorrow, of the books we are writing today, and immediately doubting whether they will last a long time (how long?), the reassuring reasons we are given or that are given us by ourselves. No one is better deceived than when he allows others to deceive him.

Here comes a man whose left hand was taken in war and a woman who came to this world with the mysterious power of seeing what lies beyond people's skin. His name is Baltazar Mateus and his nickname Seven-Suns; she is known as Blimunda and also, later, as Seven-Moons because it is written that where there is a sun there will have to be a moon and that only the conjoined and harmonious presence of the one and the other will, through love, make earth habitable. There also approaches a Jesuit priest called Bartolomeu who invented a machine capable of going up to the sky and flying with no other fuel than the human will, the will which, people say, can do anything, the will that could not, or did not know how to, or until today did not want to, be the sun and the moon of simple kindness or of even simpler respect. These three Portuguese fools from the eighteenth century, in a time and country where superstition and the fires of the Inquisition flourished, where vanity and the megalomania of a king raised a convent, a palace and a basilica which would amaze the outside world, if that world, in a very unlikely supposition, had eyes enough to see Portugal, eyes like Blimunda's, eyes to see what was hidden … Here also comes a crowd of thousands and thousands of men with dirty and callused hands, exhausted bodies after having lifted year after year, stone by stone, the implacable convent walls, the huge palace rooms, the columns and pilasters, the airy belfries, the basilica dome suspended over empty space. The sounds we hear are from Domenico Scarlatti's harpsichord, and he doesn't quite know if he is supposed to be laughing or crying … This is the story of *Baltazar and Blimunda*, a book where the apprentice author, thanks to what had long ago been taught to him in his grandparents' Jerónimo's and Josefa's time, managed to write some similar words not without poetry: 'Besides women's talk, dreams are what hold the world in its orbit. But it is also dreams that crown it with moons, that's why the sky is the splendour in men's heads, unless men's heads are the one and only sky.' So be it.

Of poetry the teenager already knew some lessons, learnt in his textbooks when, in a technical school in Lisbon, he was being prepared for the trade he would have at the beginning of his labour's life: mechanic. He also had good poetry masters during long evening hours in public libraries, reading at random, with finds from catalogues, with no guidance, no one to advise him, with the creative amazement of the sailor who invents every place he discovers. But it was at the Industrial School Library that *The Year of the Death of Ricardo Reis* started to be written ... There, one day the young mechanic (he was about seventeen) found a magazine entitled *Atena* containing poems signed with that name and, naturally, being very poorly acquainted with the literary cartography of his country, he thought that there really was a Portuguese poet called Ricardo Reis. Very soon, though, he found that this poet was really one Fernando Nogueira Pessoa, who signed his works with the names of non-existent poets, born of his mind. He called them heteronyms, a word that did not exist in the dictionaries of the time which is why it was so hard for the apprentice to letters to know what it meant. He learnt many of Ricardo Reis' poems by heart ('To be great, be one/Put yourself into the little things you do'); but in spite of being so young and ignorant, he could not accept that a superior mind could really have conceived, without remorse, the cruel line 'Wise is he who is satisfied with the spectacle of the world.' Later, much later, the apprentice, already with grey hairs and a little wiser in his own wisdom, dared to write a novel to show this poet of the *Odes* something about the spectacle of the world of 1936, where he had placed him to live out his last few days:

the occupation of the Rhineland by the Nazi army, Franco's war against the Spanish Republic, the creation by Salazar of the Portuguese Fascist militias. It was his way of telling him: 'Here is the spectacle of the world, my poet of serene bitterness and elegant skepticism. Enjoy, behold, since to be sitting is your wisdom ...'

The Year of the Death of Ricardo Reis ended with the melancholy words: 'Here, where the sea has ended and land awaits.' So there would be no more discoveries by Portugal, fated to one infinite wait for futures not even imaginable; only the usual fado, the same old saudade and little more ... Then the apprentice imagined that there still might be a way of sending the ships back to the water, for instance, by moving the land and setting that out to sea. An immediate fruit of collective Portuguese resentment of the historical disdain of Europe (more accurate to say fruit of my own resentment ...) the novel I then wrote—*The Stone Raft*—separated from the Continent the whole Iberian Peninsula and transformed it into a big floating island, moving of its own accord with no oars, no sails, no propellers, in a southerly direction, 'a mass of stone and land, covered with cities, villages, rivers, woods, factories and bushes, arable land, with its people and animals' on its way to a new Utopia: the cultural meeting of the Peninsular peoples with the peoples from the other side of the Atlantic, thereby defying—my strategy went that far—the suffocating rule exercised over that region by the United States of America ... A vision twice Utopian would see this political fiction as a much more generous and human metaphor: that Europe, all of it, should move South to help balance the world, as compensation for its former and its present colonial abuses. That is, Europe at last as an ethical reference. The characters in *The Stone Raft*—two women, three men and a dog—continually travel through the Peninsula as it furrows the ocean. The world is changing and they know they have to find in themselves the new persons they will become (not to mention the dog, he is not like other dogs ...). This will suffice for them.

Then the apprentice recalled that at a remote time of his life he had worked as a proofreader and that if, so to say, in *The Stone Raft* he had revised the future, now it might not be a bad thing to revise the past, inventing a novel to be called *History of the Siege of Lisbon*, where a proofreader, checking a book with the same title but a real history book and tired of watching how 'History' is less and less able to surprise, decides to substitute a 'yes' for a 'no', subverting the authority of 'historical truth'. Raimundo Silva, the proofreader, is a simple, common man, distinguished from the crowd only by believing that all things have their visible sides and their invisible ones and that we will know nothing about them until we manage to see both. He talks about this with the historian thus: 'I must remind you that proofreaders are serious people, much experienced in literature and life, My book, don't forget, deals with history. However, since I have no intention of pointing out other contradictions, in my modest opinion, Sir, everything that is not literature is life, History as well, Especially history, without wishing to give offence, And painting and music, Music has resisted since birth, it comes and goes, tries to free itself from the word, I suppose out of envy, only to submit in the end, And painting, Well now, painting is nothing more than literature achieved with paintbrushes, I trust you haven't forgotten that mankind began to paint long before it knew how to write, Are you familiar with the proverb, If you don't have a dog, go hunting with a cat, in other words, the man who cannot write, paints or draws, as if he were a child, What you are trying to say, in other words, is that literature already existed before it was born, Yes, Sir, just like man who, in a manner of speaking, existed before he came into being, It strikes me that you have missed your vocation, you should have become a philosopher, or historian, you have the flair and temperament needed for these disciplines, I lack the necessary training, Sir, and what can a simple man achieve without training, I was more than fortunate to come into the world with my genes in order, but in a raw state as it were, and then no education beyond primary school, You could have presented yourself as being self-taught, the product of your own worthy efforts, there's nothing to be ashamed of, society in the past took pride in its autodidacts, No longer, progress has come along and put an end to all of that, now the self-taught are frowned upon, only those who write entertaining verses and stories are entitled to be and go on being autodidacts, lucky for them, but as for me, I must confess that I never had any talent for literary creation, Become a philosopher, man, You have a keen sense of humour, Sir, with a distinct flair for irony, and I ask myself how you ever came to devote yourself to history, serious and profound science as it is, I'm only ironic in real life, It has always struck me that history is not real life, literature, yes, and nothing else, But history was real life at the time when it could not yet be called history, So you believe, Sir, that history is real life, Of course, I do, I meant to say that history was real life, No doubt at all, What would become of us if the deleatur did not exist, sighed the proofreader.' It is useless to add that the apprentice had learnt, with Raimundo Silva, the lesson of doubt. It was about time.

Well, probably it was this learning of doubt that made him go through the writing of *The Gospel According to Jesus Christ*. True, and he has said so, the title was the result of an optical illusion, but it is fair to ask whether it was the serene example of the proofreader who, all the time, had been preparing the ground from where the new novel would gush out. This time it was not a matter of looking behind the pages of the New Testament searching for antitheses, but of illuminating their surfaces, like that of a painting, with a low light to heighten their relief, the traces of crossings, the shadows of depressions. That's how the apprentice read, now surrounded by evangelical characters, as if for the first time, the description of the massacre of the innocents and, having read, he couldn't understand. He couldn't understand why there were already martyrs in a religion that would have to wait thirty years more to listen to its founder pronouncing the first word about it, he could not understand why the only person that could have done so dared not save the lives of the children of Bethlehem, he could not understand Joseph's lack of a minimum feeling of responsibility, of remorse, of guilt, or even of curiosity, after returning with his family from Egypt. It cannot even be argued in defense that it was necessary for the children of Bethlehem to die to save the life of Jesus: simple common sense, that should preside over all things human and divine, is there to remind us that God would not send His Son to earth, particularly with the mission of redeeming the sins of mankind, to die beheaded by a soldier of Herod at the age of two ... In that Gospel, written by the apprentice with the great respect due to great drama, Joseph will be aware of his guilt, will accept remorse as a punishment for the sin he has committed and will be taken to die almost without resistance, as if this were the last remaining thing to do to clear his accounts with the world. The apprentice's Gospel is not, consequently, one more edifying legend of blessed beings and gods, but the story of a few human beings subjected to a power they fight but cannot defeat. Jesus, who will inherit the dusty sandals with which his father had walked so many country roads, will also inherit his tragic feeling of responsibility and guilt that will never abandon him, not even when he raises his voice from the top of the cross: 'Men, forgive him because he knows not what he has done', referring certainly to the God who has sent him there, but perhaps also, if in that last agony he still remembers, his real father who has generated him humanly in flesh and blood. As you can see, the apprentice had already made a long voyage when in his heretical Gospel he wrote the last words of the temple dialogue between Jesus and the scribe: 'Guilt is a wolf that eats its cub after having devoured its father, The wolf of which you speak has already devoured my father, Then it will be soon your turn, And what about you, have you ever been devoured, Not only devoured, but also spewed up.'

Had Emperor Charlemagne not established a monastery in North Germany, had that monastery not been the origin of the city of Münster, had Münster not wished to celebrate its twelve-hundredth anniversary with an opera about the dreadful sixteenth-century war between Protestant Anabaptists and Catholics, the apprentice would not have written his play *In Nomine Dei*. Once more, with no other help than the tiny light of his reason, the apprentice had to penetrate the obscure labyrinth of religious beliefs, the beliefs that so easily make human beings kill and be killed. And what he saw was, once again, the hideous mask of intolerance, an intolerance that in Münster became an insane paroxysm, an intolerance that insulted the very cause that both parties claimed to defend. Because it was not a question of war in the name of two inimical gods, but of war in the name of a same god. Blinded by their own beliefs, the Anabaptists and the Catholics of Münster were incapable of understanding the most evident of all proofs: on Judgment Day, when both parties come forward to receive the reward or the punishment they deserve for their actions on earth, God—if His decisions are ruled by anything like human logic—will have to accept them all in Paradise, for the simple reason that they all believe in it. The terrible slaughter in Münster taught the apprentice that religions, despite all they promised, have never been used to bring men together and that the most absurd of all wars is a holy war, considering that God cannot, even if he wanted to, declare war on himself ...

Blind. The apprentice thought, 'we are blind', and he sat down and wrote *Blindness* to remind those who might read it that we pervert reason when we humiliate life, that human dignity is insulted every day by the powerful of our world, that the universal lie has replaced the plural truths, that man stopped respecting himself when he lost the respect due to his fellow creatures. Then the apprentice, as if trying to exorcise the monsters generated by the blindness of reason, started writing the simplest of all stories: one person is looking for another, because he has realized that life has nothing more important to demand from a human being. The book is called *All the Names*. Unwritten, all our names are there. The names of the living and the names of the dead.

I conclude. The voice that read these pages wished to be the echo of the conjoined voices of my characters. I don't have, as it were, more voice than the voices they had. Forgive me if what has seemed little to you, to me is all.

Translated from Portuguese by Tim Crosfield and Fernando Rodrigues

Dario Fo

Contra Jogulatores Obloquentes (Against Jesters Who Defame and Insult)
1997

Dario Fo, born in 1926, was surrounded by rich narrative traditions as a child; his grandfather was a well-known fabulatore *in the village of Sangiano in Lombardy, Italy. Fo studied art and architecture in Milan, and in 1952 began to write satirical cabaret, making his debut as an actor in the same year. He married the actress Franca Rame in 1954 and five years later they set up their own theatre company. Fo first won international acclaim in 1960 with his play* Gli arcangeli non giocano a flipper *(Archangels Don't Play Pinball).*

Now one of the foremost figures in modern farce and political drama, Fo's collected plays include some seventy works, such as Morte accidentale di un anarchico *(Accidental Death of an Anarchist) and* Il papa e la strega *(The Pope and the Witch). Fo is opposed to conformism and possesses a strong commitment to social and political causes. This has seen him embroiled in various court cases and controversies with the Italian state, the police, the censors, the television industry and the Vatican. He has written a series of monologues with Rame, including* Tutta casa, letto e chiesa *(All Home, Bed and Church), inspired by the fight of Italy's women to win the right to divorce and legal abortion.*

According to the Academy, Fo 'emulates the jesters of the Middle Ages in scourging authority and upholding the dignity of the downtrodden'.

> 'Against jesters who defame and insult'.
>
> > Law issued by Emperor Frederick II (Messina 1221), declaring that anyone may commit violence against jesters without incurring punishment or sanction.

The drawings I'm showing you are mine. Copies of these, slightly reduced in size, have been distributed among you.

For some time it's been my habit to use images when preparing a speech: rather than write it down, I illustrate it. This allows me to improvise, to exercise my imagination—and to oblige you to use yours.

As I proceed, I will from time to time indicate to you where we are in the manuscript. That way you won't lose the thread. This will be of help especially to those of you who don't understand either Italian or Swedish. English speakers will have a tremendous advantage over the rest because they will imagine things I've neither said nor thought. There is of course the problem of the two laughters: those who understand Italian will laugh immediately, those who don't will have to wait for Anna [Barsotti]'s Swedish translation. And then there are those of you who won't know whether to laugh the first time or the second. Anyway, let's get started.

Ladies and gentlemen, the title I've selected for this little chat is 'contra jogulatores obloquentes', which you all recognize as Latin, medieval Latin to be precise. It's the title of a law issued in Sicily in 1221 by Emperor Frederick II of Swabia, an emperor 'anointed by God', who we were taught in school to regard a sovereign of extraordinary enlightenment, a liberal. 'Jogulatores obloquentes' means 'jesters who defame and insult'. The law in question allowed any and all citizens to insult jesters, to beat them and even—if they were in that mood—to kill them, without running any risk of being brought to trial and condemned. I hasten to assure you that this law no longer is in vigour, so I can safely continue.

Ladies and gentlemen,
Friends of mine, noted men of letters, have in various radio and television interviews declared: 'The highest prize should

no doubt be awarded to the members of the Swedish Academy, for having had the courage this year to award the Nobel Prize to a jester.' I agree. Yours is an act of courage that borders on provocation.

It's enough to take stock of the uproar it has caused: sublime poets and writers who normally occupy the loftiest of spheres, and who rarely take interest in those who live and toil on humbler planes, are suddenly bowled over by some kind of whirlwind.

Like I said, I applaud and concur with my friends.

These poets had already ascended to the Parnassian heights when you, through your insolence, sent them toppling to earth, where they fell face and belly down in the mire of normality.

Insults and abuse are hurled at the Swedish Academy, at its members and their relatives back to the seventh generation. The wildest of them clamour: 'Down with the King ... of Norway!' It appears they got the dynasty wrong in the confusion.

(At this point you may turn the page. As you see there is an image of a naked poet bowled over by a whirlwind.)

Some landed pretty hard on their nether parts. There were reports of poets and writers whose nerves and livers suffered terribly. For a few days thereafter there was not a pharmacy in Italy that could muster up a single tranquilliser.

But, dear members of the Academy, let's admit it, this time you've overdone it. I mean come on, first you give the prize to a black man, then to a Jewish writer. Now you give it to a clown. What gives? As they say in Naples: *pazziàmme*? Have we lost our senses?

Also the higher clergy have suffered their moments of madness. Sundry potentates—great electors of the Pope, bishops, cardinals and prelates of Opus Dei—have all gone through the ceiling, to the point that they have even petitioned for the reinstatement of the law that allowed jesters to be burned at the stake. Over a slow fire.

On the other hand I can tell you there is an extraordinary number of people who rejoice with me over your choice. And

Dario Fo 145

so I bring you the most festive thanks, in the name of a multitude of mummers, jesters, clowns, tumblers and storytellers.

(This is where we are now [indicates a page].)

GUITTI
GIULLARI
CLOWN
SALTIMBANCHI
FABULATORI DEL LAGO

FAVOLE ASSURDE CHE NOI RAGAZZI
COMMENTAVAMO CON SCHIGNAZZI

And speaking of storytellers, I mustn't forget those of the small town on Lago Maggiore where I was born and raised, a town with a rich oral tradition.

They were the old storytellers, the master glass-blowers who taught me and other children the craftsmanship, the art, of spinning fantastic yarns. We would listen to them, bursting with laughter—laughter that would stick in our throats as the tragic allusion that surmounted each sarcasm would dawn on us. To this day I keep fresh in my mind the story of the Rock of Caldé.

'MANY YEARS AGO,' began the old glass-blower, 'way up on the crest of that steep cliff that rises from the lake there was a town called Caldé. As it happened, this town was sitting on a loose splinter of rock that slowly, day by day, was sliding down towards the precipice. It was a splendid little town, with a campanile, a fortified tower at the very peak and a cluster of houses, one after the other. It's a town that once was and that now is gone. It disappeared in the fifteenth century.

"Hey," shouted the peasants and fishermen down in the valley below. "You're sliding, you'll fall down from there."

'But the cliff dwellers wouldn't listen to them, they even laughed and made fun of them: "You think you're pretty smart, trying to scare us into running away from our houses and our land so you can grab them instead. But we're not that stupid."

'So they continued to prune their vines, sow their fields, marry and make love. They went to mass. They felt the rock slide under their houses but they didn't think much about it. "Just the rock settling. Quite normal," they said, reassuring each other.

'The great splinter of rock was about to sink into the lake. "Watch out, you've got water up to your ankles," shouted the people along the shore. "Nonsense, that's just drainage water from the fountains, it's just a bit humid," said the people of the town, and so, slowly but surely, the whole town was swallowed by the lake.

'Gurgle ... gurgle ... splash ... they sink ... houses, men, women, two horses, three donkeys ... heehaw ... gurgle. Undaunted, the priest continued to receive the confession of a nun: "Te absolvi ... animus ... santi ... guurgle ... Aame ... gurgle ..." The tower disappeared, the campanile sank with bells and all: Dong ... ding ... dop ... plock ...

'Even today,' continued the old glass-blower, 'if you look down into the water from that outcrop that still juts out from the lake, and if in that same moment a thunderstorm breaks out, and the lightning illuminates the bottom of the lake, you can still see—incredible as it may seem!—the submerged town, with its streets still intact and even the inhabitants themselves, walking around and glibly repeating to themselves: "Nothing has happened." The fish swim back and forth before their eyes, even into their ears. But they just brush them off: "Nothing to worry about. It's just some kind of fish that's learned to swim in the air."

'"Atchoo!" "God bless you!" "Thank you ... it's a bit humid today ... more than yesterday ... but everything's fine." They've reached rock bottom, but as far as they're concerned, nothing has happened at all.'

DISTURBING THOUGH IT MAY BE, there's no denying that a tale like this still has something to tell us.

I repeat, I owe much to these master glass-blowers of mine, and they—I assure you—are immensely grateful to you, members of this Academy, for rewarding one of their disciples.

And they express their gratitude with explosive exuberance. In my home town, people swear that on the night the news arrived that one of their own storytellers was to be awarded the Nobel Prize, a kiln that had been standing cold for some fifty years suddenly erupted in a broadside of flames, spraying high into the air—like a fireworks *finale*—a myriad splinters of coloured glass, which then showered down on the surface of the lake, releasing an impressive cloud of steam.

(While you applaud, I'll have a drink of water. [Turning to the interpreter:] Would you like some?

It's important that you talk among yourselves while we drink, because if you try to hear the gurgle gurgle gurgle the water makes as we swallow we'll choke on it and start coughing. So instead you can exchange niceties like 'Oh, what a lovely evening it is, isn't it?'

End of intermission: we turn to a new page, but don't worry, it'll go faster from here.)

ABOVE ALL OTHERS, this evening you're due the loud and solemn thanks of an extraordinary master of the stage, little-known not only to you and to people in France, Norway, Finland ... but also to the people of Italy. Yet he was, until Shakespeare, doubtless the greatest playwright of Renaissance Europe. I'm referring to Ruzzante Beolco, my greatest master along with Molière: both actor-playwrights, both mocked by the leading men of letters of their times. Above all, they were despised for bringing onto the stage the everyday life, joys and desperation of the common people; the hypocrisy and the arrogance of the high and mighty; and the incessant injustice. And their major, unforgivable fault was this: in telling these things, they made people laugh. Laughter does not please the mighty.

Ruzzante, the true father of the *Commedia dell'Arte*, also constructed a language of his own, a language of and for the theater, based on a variety of tongues: the dialects of the Po Valley, expressions in Latin, Spanish, even German, all mixed with onomatopoeic sounds of his own invention. It is from him, from Beolco Ruzzante, that I've learned to free myself from conventional literary writing and to express myself with words that you can chew, with unusual sounds, with various techniques of rhythm and breathing, even with the rambling nonsense-speech of the *grammelot*.

Allow me to dedicate a part of this prestigious prize to Ruzzante.

A FEW DAYS AGO, a young actor of great talent said to me: 'Maestro, you should try to project your energy, your enthusiasm, to young people. You have to give them this charge of yours. You have to share your professional knowledge and experience with them.' Franca—that's my wife—and I looked at each other and said: 'He's right.' But when we teach others our art, and share this charge of fantasy, what end will it serve? Where will it lead?

In the past couple of months, Franca and I have visited a number of university campuses to hold workshops and seminars before young audiences. It has been surprising—not to say disturbing—to discover their ignorance about the times we live in. We told them about the proceedings now in course in Turkey against the accused culprits of the massacre in Sivas. Thirty-seven of the country's foremost democratic intellectuals, meeting in the Anatolian town to celebrate the memory of a famous medieval jester of the Ottoman period, were burned alive in the dark of the night, trapped inside their hotel. The fire was the handiwork of a group of fanatical fundamentalists that enjoyed protection from elements within the government itself. In one night, 37 of the country's most celebrated artists, writers, directors, actors and Kurdish dancers were erased from this earth.

In one blow these fanatics destroyed some of the most important exponents of Turkish culture.

Thousands of students listened to us. The looks in their faces spoke of their astonishment and incredulity. They had never heard of the massacre. But what impressed me the most is that not even the teachers and professors present had heard of it. There Turkey is, on the Mediterranean, practically in front of us, insisting on joining the European Community, yet no one had heard of the massacre. Salvini, a noted Italian democrat, was right on the mark when he observed: 'The widespread ignorance of events is the main buttress of injustice.' But this absentmindedness on the part of the young has been conferred upon them by those who are charged to educate and inform them: among the absentminded and uninformed, school teachers and other educators deserve first mention.

Young people easily succumb to the bombardment of gratuitous banalities and obscenities that each day is served to them by the mass media: heartless TV action films where in the space of ten minutes they are treated to three rapes, two assassinations, one beating and a serial crash involving ten cars on a bridge that then collapses, whereupon everything—cars, drivers and passengers—precipitates into the sea ... only one person survives the fall, but he doesn't know how to swim and so drowns, to the cheers of the crowd of curious onlookers that suddenly has appeared on the scene.

AT ANOTHER UNIVERSITY we spoofed the project—alas well under way—to manipulate genetic material, or more specifically, the proposal by the European Parliament to allow patent rights on living organisms. We could feel how the subject sent a chill through the audience. Franca and I explained how our

Eurocrats, kindled by powerful and ubiquitous multinationals, are preparing a scheme worthy the plot of a sci-fi/horror movie entitled 'Frankenstein's pig brother'. They're trying to get the approval of a directive which (and get this!) would authorize industries to take patents on living beings, or on parts of them, created with techniques of genetic manipulation that seem taken straight out of 'The Sorcerer's Apprentice'.

This is how it would work: by manipulating the genetic make-up of a pig, a scientist succeeds in making the pig more human-like. By this arrangement it becomes much easier to remove from the pig the organ of your choice—a liver, a kidney—and to transplant it into a human. But to assure that the transplanted pig-organs aren't rejected, it's also necessary to transfer certain pieces of genetic information from the pig to the human. The result: a human pig (even though you will say that there are already plenty of those).

And every part of this new creature, this humanised pig, will be subject to patent laws; and whosoever wishes a part of it will have to pay copyright fees to the company that 'invented' it. Secondary illnesses, monstrous deformations, infectious diseases—all are optionals, included in the price ...

The Pope has forcefully condemned this monstrous genetic witchcraft. He has called it an offence against humanity, against the dignity of man, and has gone to pains to underscore the project's total and irrefutable lack of moral value.

The astonishing thing is that while this is happening, an American scientist, a remarkable magician—you've probably read about him in the papers—has succeeded in transplanting the head of a baboon. He cut the heads off two baboons and switched them. The baboons didn't feel all that great after the operation. In fact, it left them paralyzed, and they both died shortly thereafter, but the experiment worked, and that's the great thing.

But here's the rub: this modern-day Frankenstein, a certain Professor White, is all the while a distinguished member of the Vatican Academy of Sciences. Somebody should warn the Pope.

So, WE ENACTED these criminal farces to the kids at the universities, and they laughed their heads off. They would say of Franca and me: 'They're a riot, they come up with the most fantastic stories.' Not for a moment, not even with an inkling in their spines, did they grasp that the stories we told were true.

These encounters have strengthened us in our conviction that our job is—in keeping with the exhortation of the great Italian poet Savinio—'to tell our own story'. Our task as intellectuals, as persons who mount the pulpit or the stage, and who, most importantly, address to young people, our task is not just to teach them method, like how to use the arms, how to control breathing, how to use the stomach, the voice, the falsetto, the *contracampo*. It's not enough to teach a technique or a style: we have to show them what is happening around us. They have to be able to tell their own story. A theatre, a literature, an artistic expression that does not speak for its own time has no relevance.

RECENTLY, I TOOK PART in a large conference with lots of people where I tried to explain, especially to the younger participants, the ins and outs of a particular Italian court case. The original case resulted in seven separate proceedings, at the end of which three Italian left-wing politicians were sentenced to 21 years of imprisonment each, accused of having murdered a police commissioner. I've studied the documents of the case—as I did when I prepared *Accidental Death of an Anarchist*—and at the conference I recounted the facts pertaining to it, which are really quite absurd, even farcical. But at a certain point I realized I was speaking to deaf ears, for the simple reason that my audience was ignorant not only of the case itself, but of what had happened five years earlier, ten years earlier: the violence, the terrorism. They knew nothing about the massacres that occurred in Italy, the trains that blew up, the bombs in the *piazze* or the farcical court cases that have dragged on since then.

The terribly difficult thing is that in order to talk about what is happening today, I have to start with what happened 30 years ago and then work my way forward. It's not enough to speak about the present. And pay attention, this isn't just about Italy: the same thing happens everywhere, all over Europe. I've tried in Spain and encountered the same difficulty; I've tried in France, in Germany, I've yet to try in Sweden, but I will.

TO CONCLUDE, let me share this medal with Franca.

Franca Rame, my companion in life and in art who you, members of the Academy, acknowledge in your motivation of the prize as actress and author; who has had a hand in many of the texts of our theatre.

(At this very moment, Franca is on stage in a theatre in Italy but will join me the day after tomorrow. Her flight arrives midday, if you like we can all head out together to pick her up at the airport.)

Franca has a very sharp wit, I assure you. A journalist put the following question to her: 'So how does it feel to be the wife of a Nobel Prize winner? To have a monument in your home?' To which she answered: 'I'm not worried. Nor do I feel at all at a disadvantage; I've been in training for a long time. I do my exercises each morning: I go down on my hand and knees, and that way I've accustomed myself to becoming a pedestal to a monument. I'm pretty good at it.'

Like I said, she has a sharp wit. At times she even turns her irony against herself.

Without her at my side, where she has been for a lifetime, I would never have accomplished the work you have seen fit to honour. Together we've staged and recited thousands of performances, in theaters, occupied factories, at university sit-ins, even in deconsecrated churches, in prisons and city parks, in sunshine and pouring rain, always together. We've had to endure abuse, assaults by the police, insults from the right-thinking and violence. And it is Franca who has had to suffer the most atrocious aggression. She has had to pay more dearly than any one of us, with her neck and limb in the balance, for the solidarity with the humble and the beaten that has been our premise.

The day it was announced that I was to be awarded the Nobel Prize I found myself in front of the theatre on Via di Porta Romana in Milan where Franca, together with Giorgio Albertazzi, was performing *The Devil with Tits*. Suddenly I was surrounded by a throng of reporters, photographers and camera-wielding TV crews. A passing tram stopped, unexpectedly, the driver stepped out to greet me, then all the passengers stepped out too, they applauded me, and everyone wanted to shake my hand and congratulate me ... when at a certain point they all stopped in their tracks and, as with a single voice, shouted 'Where's Franca?' They began to holler 'Francaaa' until, after a little while, she appeared. Discombobulated and moved to tears, she came down to embrace me.

At that moment, as if out of nowhere, a band appeared, playing nothing but wind instruments and drums. It was made up of kids from all parts of the city and, as it happened, they were playing together for the first time. They struck up 'Porta Romana bella, Porta Romana' in samba beat. I've never heard anything played so out of tune, but it was the most beautiful music Franca and I had ever heard.

Believe me, this prize belongs to both of us.

Thank you.

Translated from Italian by Paul Claesson

Wislawa Szymborska

The Poet and the World
1996

Born in 1923 in Kornik in western Poland, Wislawa Szymborska has lived in Krakow since 1931. She studied Polish literature and sociology at Jagiellonian University, and her first published poem, 'Szukam slowa' ('I Am Looking for a Word') appeared in March 1945 in the daily newspaper Dziennik Polski. *She continued to publish poetry in various newspapers and periodicals in the years following the war. From 1953 to 1981 she was the poetry editor and a columnist for the literary weekly* Zycie Literackie.

The majority of Szymborska's poems run to less than a page each, outlining their underlying philosophical themes in miniature and exploring realms such as ethics and the human condition in modern society. She has published sixteen collections of poetry, among them Dlatego zyjemy *(That's Why We Are Alive),* Sól *(Salt),* Sto pociech *(No End of Fun),* Ludzie na moscie *(People on the Bridge) and* Widok z ziarnkiem piasku *(View with a Grain of Sand). She has also translated French poetry, and her own work has been translated into numerous languages, including English, German, Swedish, Italian, Danish, Hebrew, Arabic and Japanese.*

In the words of the Academy, Szymborska writes 'poetry that with ironic precision allows the historical and biological context to come to light in fragments of human reality'.

They say the first sentence in any speech is always the hardest. Well, that one's behind me, anyway. But I have a feeling that the sentences to come—the third, the sixth, the tenth and so on, up to the final line—will be just as hard, since I'm supposed to talk about poetry. I've said very little on the subject, next to nothing, in fact. And whenever I have said anything, I've always had the sneaking suspicion that I'm not very good at it. This is why my lecture will be rather short. All imperfection is easier to tolerate if served up in small doses.

Contemporary poets are skeptical and suspicious even, or perhaps especially, about themselves. They publicly confess to being poets only reluctantly, as if they were a little ashamed of it. But in our clamorous times it's much easier to acknowledge your faults, at least if they're attractively packaged, than to recognize your own merits, since these are hidden deeper and you never quite believe in them yourself ... When filling in questionnaires or chatting with strangers, that is, when they can't avoid revealing their profession, poets prefer to use the general term 'writer' or replace 'poet' with the name of whatever job they do in addition to writing. Bureaucrats and bus passengers respond with a touch of incredulity and alarm when they find out that they're dealing with a poet. I suppose philosophers may meet with a similar reaction. Still, they're in a better position, since as often as not they can embellish their calling with some kind of scholarly title. Professor of philosophy—now that sounds much more respectable.

But there are no professors of poetry. This would mean, after all, that poetry is an occupation requiring specialized study, regular examinations, theoretical articles with bibliographies and footnotes attached, and finally, ceremoniously conferred diplomas. And this would mean, in turn, that it's not enough to cover pages with even the most exquisite poems in order to become a poet. The crucial element is some slip of paper bearing an official stamp. Let us recall that the pride of Russian poetry, the future Nobel Laureate Joseph Brodsky, was once sentenced to internal exile precisely on such grounds. They called him 'a parasite', because he lacked official certification granting him the right to be a poet ...

Several years ago, I had the honour and pleasure of meeting

Brodsky in person. And I noticed that, of all the poets I've known, he was the only one who enjoyed calling himself a poet. He pronounced the word without inhibitions.

Just the opposite—he spoke it with defiant freedom. It seems to me that this must have been because he recalled the brutal humiliations he had experienced in his youth.

In more fortunate countries, where human dignity isn't assaulted so readily, poets yearn, of course, to be published, read and understood, but they do little, if anything, to set themselves above the common herd and the daily grind. And yet it wasn't so long ago, in this century's first decades, that poets strove to shock us with their extravagant dress and eccentric behavior. But all this was merely for the sake of public display. The moment always came when poets had to close the doors behind them, strip off their mantles, fripperies and other poetic paraphernalia, and confront—silently, patiently awaiting their own selves—the still white sheet of paper. For this is finally what really counts.

It's not accidental that film biographies of great scientists and artists are produced in droves. The more ambitious directors seek to reproduce convincingly the creative process that led to important scientific discoveries or the emergence of a masterpiece. And one can depict certain kinds of scientific labour with some success. Laboratories, sundry instruments, elaborate machinery brought to life: such scenes may hold the audience's interest for a while. And those moments of uncertainty—will the experiment, conducted for the thousandth time with some tiny modification, finally yield the desired result?—can be quite dramatic. Films about painters can be spectacular, as they go about recreating every stage of a famous painting's evolution, from the first penciled line to the final brush-stroke. Music swells in films about composers: the first bars of the melody that rings in the musician's ears finally emerge as a mature work in symphonic form. Of course this is all quite naive and doesn't explain the strange mental state popularly known as inspiration, but at least there's something to look at and listen to.

But poets are the worst. Their work is hopelessly unphotogenic. Someone sits at a table or lies on a sofa while staring motionless at a wall or ceiling. Once in a while this person writes down seven lines only to cross out one of them fifteen minutes later, and then another hour passes, during which nothing happens ... Who could stand to watch this kind of thing?

I've mentioned inspiration. Contemporary poets answer evasively when asked what it is, and if it actually exists. It's not that they've never known the blessing of this inner impulse. It's just not easy to explain something to someone else that you don't understand yourself.

When I'm asked about this on occasion, I hedge the question too. But my answer is this: inspiration is not the exclusive privilege of poets or artists generally. There is, has been and will always be a certain group of people whom inspiration visits. It's made up of all those who've consciously chosen their calling and do their job with love and imagination. It may include doctors, teachers, gardeners—and I could list a hundred more professions. Their work becomes one continuous adventure as long as they manage to keep discovering new challenges in it. Difficulties and setbacks never quell their curiosity. A swarm of new questions emerges from every problem they solve. Whatever inspiration is, it's born from a continuous 'I don't know.'

There aren't many such people. Most of the earth's inhabitants work to get by. They work because they have to. They didn't pick this or that kind of job out of passion; the circumstances of their lives did the choosing for them. Loveless work, boring work, work valued only because others haven't got even that much, however loveless and boring—this is one of the harshest human miseries. And there's no sign that coming centuries will produce any changes for the better as far as this goes.

And so, though I may deny poets their monopoly on inspiration, I still place them in a select group of Fortune's darlings.

At this point, though, certain doubts may arise in my audience. All sorts of torturers, dictators, fanatics and demagogues struggling for power by way of a few loudly shouted slogans also enjoy their jobs, and they too perform their duties with inventive fervour. Well, yes, but they 'know'. They know, and whatever they know is enough for them once and for all. They don't want to find out about anything else, since that might diminish their arguments' force. And any knowledge that doesn't lead to new questions quickly dies out: it fails to maintain the temperature required for sustaining life. In the most extreme cases, cases well known from ancient and modern history, it even poses a lethal threat to society.

This is why I value that little phrase 'I don't know' so highly. It's small, but it flies on mighty wings. It expands our lives to include the spaces within us as well as those outer expanses in which our tiny earth hangs suspended. If Isaac Newton had never said to himself 'I don't know', the apples in his little orchard might have dropped to the ground like hailstones and at best he would have stooped to pick them up and gobble them with gusto. Had my compatriot Marie Skłodowska-Curie never said to herself 'I don't know', she probably would have wound up teaching chemistry at some private high school for young ladies from good families, and would have ended her days performing this otherwise perfectly respectable job. But she kept on saying 'I don't know', and these words led her, not just once but twice, to Stockholm, where restless, questing spirits are occasionally rewarded with the Nobel Prize.

Poets, if they're genuine, must also keep repeating 'I don't know.' Each poem marks an effort to answer this statement, but as soon as the final period hits the page, the poet begins to hesitate, starts to realize that this particular answer was pure makeshift that's absolutely inadequate to boot. So the poets keep on trying, and sooner or later the consecutive results of their self-dissatisfaction are clipped together with a giant paperclip by literary historians and called their 'oeuvre' ...

I sometimes dream of situations that can't possibly come true. I audaciously imagine, for example, that I get a chance to chat with the Ecclesiastes, the author of that moving lament on the vanity of all human endeavours. I would bow very deeply before him, because he is, after all, one of the greatest poets, for me at least. That done, I would grab his hand. '"There's nothing new under the sun": that's what you wrote, Ecclesiastes. But you yourself were born new under the sun. And the poem you created is also new under the sun, since no one wrote it down before you. And all your readers are also new under the sun, since those who lived before you couldn't read your poem. And that cypress that you're sitting under hasn't been growing since the dawn of time. It came into being by way of another cypress similar to yours, but not exactly the same. And Ecclesiastes, I'd also like to ask you what new thing under the sun you're planning to work on now? A further supplement to the thoughts you've already expressed? Or maybe you're tempted to contradict some of them now? In your earlier work you mentioned joy—so what if it's fleeting? So maybe your new-under-the-sun poem will be about joy? Have you taken notes yet, do you have drafts? I doubt you'll say, "I've written everything down, I've got nothing left to add." There's no poet in the world who can say this, least of all a great poet like yourself.'

The world—whatever we might think when terrified by its vastness and our own impotence, or embittered by its indifference to individual suffering, of people, animals and perhaps even plants, for why are we so sure that plants feel no pain;

whatever we might think of its expanses pierced by the rays of stars surrounded by planets we've just begun to discover, planets already dead? still dead? we just don't know; whatever we might think of this measureless theatre to which we've got reserved tickets, but tickets whose lifespan is laughably short, bounded as it is by two arbitrary dates; whatever else we might think of this world—it is astonishing.

But 'astonishing' is an epithet concealing a logical trap. We're astonished, after all, by things that deviate from some well-known and universally acknowledged norm, from an obviousness we've grown accustomed to. Now the point is, there is no such obvious world. Our astonishment exists per se and isn't based on comparison with something else.

Granted, in daily speech, where we don't stop to consider every word, we all use phrases like 'the ordinary world', 'ordinary life', 'the ordinary course of events' ... But in the language of poetry, where every word is weighed, nothing is usual or normal. Not a single stone and not a single cloud above it. Not a single day and not a single night after it. And above all, not a single existence, not anyone's existence in this world.

It looks like poets will always have their work cut out for them.

Translated from Polish by Stanislaw Baranczak and Clare Cavanagh

Seamus Heaney

Crediting Poetry
1995

Seamus Heaney spent his childhood on a farm in County Derry, Northern Ireland. His father was a farmer and cattle herder, while his mother's relations were employed at the local linen mill. The tension between the cattle-herding Gaelic past and the Ulster of the Industrial Revolution has been significant in Heaney's background, as well as the tension within the family home between the talkativeness of the poet's mother and the silence of his father. Heaney believes this duality has been fundamental to the 'quarrel with himself' from which his poetry comes.

Heaney's poems first came to notice in the mid 1960s, when he was part of a group of poets subsequently recognized as constituting a 'Northern School' within Irish writing. Born into a society deeply divided along political and religious lines, Heaney has sought to create a productive relationship between his work and the issues in Irish political life. His poetry has been published in many volumes, including Death of a Naturalist, North, Station Island *and* Electric Light, *and his plays include* The Cure at Troy *and* The Burial at Thebes, *versions of Sophocles'* Philoctetes *and* Antigone *respectively.*

The Academy awarded the prize to Heaney 'for works of lyrical beauty and ethical depth, which exalt everyday miracles and the living past'.

When I first encountered the name of the city of Stockholm, I little thought that I would ever visit it, never mind end up being welcomed to it as a guest of the Swedish Academy and the Nobel Foundation. At the time I am thinking of, such an outcome was not just beyond expectation: it was simply beyond conception. In the 1940s, when I was the eldest child of an ever-growing family in rural County Derry, we crowded together in the three rooms of a traditional thatched farmstead and lived a kind of den-life which was more or less emotionally and intellectually proofed against the outside world. It was an intimate, physical, creaturely existence in which the night sounds of the horse in the stable beyond one bedroom wall mingled with the sounds of adult conversation from the kitchen beyond the other. We took in everything that was going on, of course—rain in the trees, mice on the ceiling, a steam train rumbling along the railway line one field back from the house—but we took it in as if we were in the doze of hibernation. Ahistorical, pre-sexual, in suspension between the archaic and the modern, we were as susceptible and impressionable as the drinking water that stood in a bucket in our scullery: every time a passing train made the earth shake, the surface of that water used to ripple delicately, concentrically and in utter silence.

But it was not only the earth that shook for us: the air around and above us was alive and signalling too. When a wind stirred in the beeches, it also stirred an aerial wire attached to the topmost branch of the chestnut tree. Down it swept, in through a hole bored in the corner of the kitchen window, right on into the innards of our wireless set where a little pandemonium of burbles and squeaks would suddenly give way to the voice of a BBC newsreader speaking out of the unexpected like a *deus ex machina*. And that voice too we could hear in our bedroom, transmitting from beyond and behind the voices of the adults in the kitchen; just as we could often hear, behind and beyond every voice, the frantic, piercing signaling of morse code.

We could pick up the names of neighbours being spoken in the local accents of our parents, and in the resonant English tones of the newsreader the names of bombers and of cities bombed, of war fronts and army divisions, the numbers of planes lost and of prisoners taken, of casualties suffered and advances made; and always, of course, we would pick up too those other, solemn and oddly bracing words, 'the enemy' and 'the allies'. But even so, none of the news of these world-spasms entered me as terror. If there was something ominous in the newscaster's tones, there was something torpid about our understanding of what was at stake; and if there was something culpable about such political ignorance in that time and place, there was something positive about the security I inhabited as a result of it.

The wartime, in other words, was pre-reflective time for me. Pre-literate too. Pre-historical in its way. Then as the years went on and my listening became more deliberate, I would climb up on an arm of our big sofa to get my ear closer to the wireless speaker. But it was still not the news that interested me; what I was after was the thrill of story, such as a detective serial about a British special agent called Dick Barton or perhaps a radio adaptation of one of Capt. W. E. Johns' adventure tales about an RAF flying ace called Biggles. Now that the other children were older and there was so much going on in the kitchen, I had to get close to the actual radio set in order to concentrate my hearing, and in that intent proximity to the dial I grew familiar with the names of foreign stations, with Leipzig and Oslo and Stuttgart and Warsaw and, of course, with Stockholm.

I also got used to hearing short bursts of foreign languages as the dial hand swept round from BBC to Radio Eireann, from the intonations of London to those of Dublin, and even though I did not understand what was being said in those first encounters with the gutturals and sibilants of European speech, I had already begun a journey into the wideness of the world beyond. This in turn became a journey into the wideness of language, a journey where each point of arrival—whether in one's poetry or one's life—turned out to be a stepping stone rather than a destination, and it is that journey which has brought me now to this honoured spot. And yet the platform here feels more like a space station than a stepping stone, so that is why, for once in my life, I am permitting myself the luxury of walking on air.

I CREDIT POETRY for making this spacewalk possible. I credit it immediately because of a line I wrote fairly recently instructing myself (and whoever else might be listening) to 'walk on air against your better judgment'. But I credit it ultimately because poetry can make an order as true to the impact of external reality and as sensitive to the inner laws of the poet's being as the ripples that rippled in and rippled out across the water in that scullery bucket fifty years ago. An order where we can at last grow up to that which we stored up as we grew. An order which satisfies all that is appetitive in the intelligence and prehensile in the affections. I credit poetry, in other words, both for being itself and for being a help, for making possible a fluid and restorative relationship between the mind's centre and its circumference, between the child gazing at the word 'Stockholm' on the face of the radio dial and the man facing the faces that he meets in Stockholm at this most privileged moment. I credit it because credit is due to it, in our time and in all time, for its truth to life, in every sense of that phrase.

TO BEGIN WITH, I wanted that truth to life to possess a concrete reliability, and rejoiced most when the poem seemed most direct, an upfront representation of the world it stood in for or stood up for or stood its ground against. Even as a schoolboy, I loved John Keats' ode 'To Autumn' for being an ark of the covenant between language and sensation; as an adolescent, I loved Gerard Manley Hopkins for the intensity of his exclamations which were also equations for a rapture and an ache I didn't fully know I knew until I read him; I loved Robert Frost for his farmer's accuracy and his wily down-to-earthness; and Chaucer too for much the same reasons. Later on I would find a different kind of accuracy, a moral down-to-earthness to which I responded deeply and always will, in the war poetry of Wilfred Owen, a poetry where a New Testament sensibility suffers and absorbs the shock of the new century's barbarism. Then later again, in the pure consequence of Elizabeth Bishop's style, in the sheer obduracy of Robert Lowell's and in the barefaced confrontation of Patrick Kavanagh's, I encountered further reasons for believing in poetry's ability—and responsibility—to say what happens, to 'pity the planet', to be 'not concerned with Poetry'.

This temperamental disposition towards an art that was earnest and devoted to things as they are was corroborated by the experience of having been born and brought up in Northern Ireland and of having lived with that place even though I have lived out of it for the past quarter of a century. No place in the world prides itself more on its vigilance and realism, no place considers itself more qualified to censure any flourish of rhetoric or extravagance of aspiration. So, partly as a result of having internalized these attitudes through growing up with them, and partly as a result of growing a skin to protect myself against them, I went for years half-avoiding and half-resisting the opulence and extensiveness of poets as different as Wallace Stevens and Rainer Maria Rilke; crediting insufficiently the crystalline inwardness of Emily Dickinson, all those forked lightnings and fissures of association; and missing the visionary strangeness of Eliot. And these more or less costive attitudes were fortified by a refusal to grant the poet any more license than any other citizen; and they were further induced by having to conduct oneself as a poet in a situation of ongoing political violence and public expectation. A public expectation, it has to be said, not of poetry as such but of political positions variously approvable by mutually disapproving groups.

In such circumstances, the mind still longs to repose in what Samuel Johnson once called with superb confidence 'the stability of truth', even as it recognizes the destabilizing nature of its own operations and inquiries. Without needing to be theoretically instructed, consciousness quickly realizes that it is the site of variously contending discourses. The child in the bedroom, listening simultaneously to the domestic idiom of his Irish home and the official idioms of the British broadcaster while picking up from behind both the signals of some other distress, that child was already being schooled for the complexities of his adult predicament, a future where he would have to adjudicate among promptings variously ethical, aesthetical, moral, political, metrical, sceptical, cultural, topical, typical, post-colonial and, taken all together, simply impossible. So it was that I found myself in the mid 1970s in another small house, this time in County Wicklow south of Dublin, with a young family of my own and a slightly less imposing radio set, listening to the rain in the trees and to the news of bombings closer to home—not only those by the Provisional IRA in Belfast but equally atrocious assaults in Dublin by loyalist paramilitaries from the north. Feeling puny in my predicaments as I read about the tragic logic of Osip Mandelstam's fate in the 1930s, feeling challenged yet steadfast in my noncombatant status when I heard, for example, that one particularly sweet-natured school friend had been interned without trial because he was suspected of having been involved in a political killing. What I was longing for was not quite stability but an active escape from the quicksand of relativism, a way of crediting poetry without anxiety or apology. In a poem called 'Exposure' I wrote then:

> If I could come on meteorite!
> Instead, I walk through damp leaves,
> Husks, the spent flukes of autumn,
>
> Imagining a hero
> On some muddy compound,
> His gift like a slingstone
> Whirled for the desperate.
>
> How did I end up like this?
> I often think of my friends'
> Beautiful prismatic counselling
> And the anvil brains of some who hate me
>
> As I sit weighing and weighing
> My responsible *tristia*.
> For what? For the ear? For the people?
> For what is said behind-backs?
>
> Rain comes down through the alders,
> Its low conducive voices
> Mutter about let-downs and erosions
> And yet each drop recalls
>
> The diamond absolutes.
> I am neither internee nor informer;
> An inner émigré, a grown long-haired
> And thoughtful; a wood-kerne
>
> Escaped from the massacre,
> Taking protective colouring
> From bole and bark, feeling
> Every wind that blows;

Who, blowing up these sparks
For their meagre heat, have missed
The once in a lifetime portent,
The comet's pulsing rose.

> (from *North*)

In one of the poems best known to students in my generation, a poem which could be said to have taken the nutrients of the symbolist movement and made them available in capsule form, the American poet Archibald MacLeish affirmed that 'A poem should be equal to/not true.' As a defiant statement of poetry's gift for telling truth but telling it slant, this is both cogent and corrective. Yet there are times when a deeper need enters, when we want the poem to be not only pleasurably right but compellingly wise, not only a surprising variation played upon the world, but a re-tuning of the world itself. We want the surprise to be transitive like the impatient thump which unexpectedly restores the picture to the television set, or the electric shock which sets the fibrillating heart back to its proper rhythm. We want what the woman wanted in the prison queue in Leningrad, standing there blue with cold and whispering for fear, enduring the terror of Stalin's regime and asking the poet Anna Akhmatova if she could describe it all, if her art could be equal to it. And this is the want I too was experiencing in those far more protected circumstances in County Wicklow when I wrote the lines I have just quoted, a need for poetry that would merit the definition of it I gave a few moments ago, as an order 'true to the impact of external reality and ... sensitive to the inner laws of the poet's being'.

THE EXTERNAL REALITY and inner dynamic of happenings in Northern Ireland between 1968 and 1974 were symptomatic of change, violent change admittedly, but change nevertheless, and for the minority living there, change had been long overdue. It should have come early, as the result of the ferment of protest on the streets in the late 1960s, but that was not to be and the eggs of danger which were always incubating got hatched out very quickly. While the Christian moralist in oneself was impelled to deplore the atrocious nature of the IRA's campaign of bombings and killings, and the 'mere Irish' in oneself was appalled by the ruthlessness of the British Army on occasions like Bloody Sunday in Derry in 1972, the minority citizen in oneself, the one who had grown up conscious that his group was distrusted and discriminated against in all kinds of official and unofficial ways, this citizen's perception was at one with the poetic truth of the situation in recognizing that if life in Northern Ireland were ever really to flourish, change had to take place. But that citizen's perception was also at one with the truth in recognizing that the very brutality of the means by which the IRA were pursuing change was destructive of the trust upon which new possibilities would have to be based.

Nevertheless, until the British government caved in to the strong-arm tactics of the Ulster loyalist workers after the Sunningdale Conference in 1974, a well-disposed mind could still hope to make sense of the circumstances, to balance what was promising with what was destructive and do what W. B. Yeats had tried to do half a century before, namely, 'to hold in a single thought reality and justice'. After 1974, however, for the twenty long years between then and the ceasefires of August 1994, such a hope proved impossible. The violence from below was then productive of nothing but a retaliatory violence from above, the dream of justice became subsumed into the callousness of reality, and people settled in to a quarter century of life-waste and spirit-waste, of hardening attitudes and narrowing possibilities that were the natural result of political solidarity, traumatic suffering and sheer emotional self-protectiveness.

ONE OF THE MOST harrowing moments in the whole history of the harrowing of the heart in Northern Ireland came when a minibus full of workers being driven home one January evening in 1976 was held up by armed and masked men and the occupants of the van ordered at gunpoint to line up at the side of the road. Then one of the masked executioners said to them, 'Any Catholics among you, step out here.' As it happened, this particular group, with one exception, were all Protestants, so the presumption must have been that the masked men were Protestant paramilitaries about to carry out a tit-for-tat sectarian killing of the Catholic as the odd man out, the one who would have been presumed to be in sympathy with the IRA and all its actions. It was a terrible moment for him, caught between dread and witness, but he did make a motion to step forward. Then, the story goes, in that split second of decision, and in the relative cover of the winter evening darkness, he felt the hand of the Protestant worker next to him take his hand and squeeze it in a signal that said no, don't move, we'll not betray you, nobody need know what faith or party you belong to. All in vain, however, for the man stepped out of the line; but instead of finding a gun at his temple, he was thrown backward and away as the gunmen opened fire on those remaining in the line, for these were not Protestant terrorists, but members, presumably, of the Provisional IRA.

IT IS DIFFICULT at times to repress the thought that history is about as instructive as an abattoir; that Tacitus was right and that peace is merely the desolation left behind after the decisive operations of merciless power. I remember, for example, shocking myself with a thought I had about that friend who was imprisoned in the 1970s upon suspicion of having been involved with a political murder: I shocked myself by thinking that even if he were guilty, he might still perhaps be helping the future to be born, breaking the repressive forms and liberating new potential in the only way that worked, that is to say the violent way—which therefore became, by extension, the right way. It was like a moment of exposure to interstellar cold, a reminder of the scary element, both inner and outer, in which human beings must envisage and conduct their lives. But it was only a moment. The birth of the future we desire is surely in the contraction which that terrified Catholic felt on the roadside when another hand gripped his hand, not in the gunfire that followed, so absolute and so desolate, if also so much a part of the music of what happens.

As writers and readers, as sinners and citizens, our realism and our aesthetic sense make us wary of crediting the positive note. The very gunfire braces us and the atrocious confers a worth upon the effort which it calls forth to confront it. We are rightly in awe of the torsions in the poetry of Paul Celan and rightly enamoured of the suspiring voice in Samuel Beckett because these are evidence that art can rise to the occasion and somehow be the corollary of Celan's stricken destiny as Holocaust survivor and Beckett's demure heroism as a member of the French Resistance. Likewise, we are rightly suspicious of that which gives too much consolation in these circumstances; the very extremity of our late twentieth-century knowledge puts much of our cultural heritage to an extreme test. Only the very stupid or the very deprived can any longer help knowing that the documents of civilization have been written in blood and tears, blood and tears no less real for being very remote. And when this intellectual predisposition coexists with the actualities of Ulster and Israel and Bosnia and Rwanda and a host of other wounded spots on the face of the earth, the inclination is not only not to credit human nature with much constructive potential but not to credit anything too positive in the work of art.

Which is why for years I was bowed to the desk like some monk bowed over his *prie-dieu*, some dutiful contemplative pivoting his understanding in an attempt to bear his portion of the weight of the world, knowing himself incapable of heroic virtue or redemptive effect, but constrained by his obedience to his rule to repeat the effort and the posture. Blowing up sparks for meagre heat. Forgetting faith, straining towards good works. Attending insufficiently to the diamond absolutes, among which must be counted the sufficiency of that which is absolutely imagined. Then finally and happily, and not in obedience to the dolorous circumstances of my native place but in despite of them, I straightened up. I began a few years ago to try to make space in my reckoning and imagining for the marvellous as well as for the murderous. And once again I shall try to represent the import of that changed orientation with a story out of Ireland.

This is a story about another monk holding himself up valiantly in the posture of endurance. It is said that once upon a time St Kevin was kneeling with his arms stretched out in the form of a cross in Glendalough, a monastic site not too far from where we lived in County Wicklow, a place which to this day is one of the most wooded and watery retreats in the whole of the country. Anyhow, as Kevin knelt and prayed, a blackbird mistook his outstretched hand for some kind of roost and swooped down upon it, laid a clutch of eggs in it and proceeded to nest in it as if it were the branch of a tree. Then, overcome with pity and constrained by his faith to love the life in all creatures great and small, Kevin stayed immobile for hours and days and nights and weeks, holding out his hand until the eggs hatched and the fledglings grew wings, true to life if subversive of common sense, at the intersection of natural process and the glimpsed ideal, at one and the same time a signpost and a reminder. Manifesting that order of poetry where we can at last grow up to that which we stored up as we grew.

St Kevin's story is, as I say, a story out of Ireland. But it strikes me that it could equally well come out of India or Africa or the Arctic or the Americas. By which I do not mean merely to consign it to a typology of folktales, or to dispute its value by questioning its culture-bound status within a multicultural context. On the contrary, its trustworthiness and its travel-worthiness have to do with its local setting. I can, of course, imagine it being deconstructed nowadays as a paradigm of colonialism, with Kevin figuring as the benign imperialist (or the missionary in the wake of the imperialist), the one who intervenes and appropriates the indigenous life and interferes with its pristine ecology. And I have to admit that there is indeed an irony that it was such a one who recorded and preserved this instance of the true beauty of the Irish heritage: Kevin's story, after all, appears in the writings of Giraldus Cambrensis, one of the Normans who invaded Ireland in the twelfth century, one whom the Irish-language annalist Geoffrey Keating would call, five hundred years later, 'the bull of the herd of those who wrote the false history of Ireland'. But even so, I still cannot persuade myself that this manifestation of early Christian civilization should be construed all that simply as a way into whatever is exploitative or barbaric in our history, past and present. The whole conception strikes me rather as being another example of the kind of work I saw a few weeks ago in the small museum in Sparta, on the morning before the news of this year's Nobel Prize in literature was announced.

This was art which sprang from a cult very different from the faith espoused by St Kevin. Yet in it there was a representation of a roosted bird and an entranced beast and a self-enrapturing man, except that this time the man was Orpheus and the rapture came from music rather than prayer. The work itself was a small carved relief and I could not help making a sketch of it; but neither could I help copying out the information typed on the card which accompanied and identified the exhibit. The image moved me because of its antiquity and durability, but the description on the card moved me also because it gave a name and credence to that which I see myself as having been engaged upon for the past three decades: 'Votive panel', the identification card said, 'possibly set up to Orpheus by local poet. Local work of the Hellenistic period.'

ONCE AGAIN, I hope I am not being sentimental or simply fetishizing—as we have learnt to say—the local. I wish instead to suggest that images and stories of the kind I am invoking here do function as bearers of value. The century has witnessed the defeat of Nazism by force of arms; but the erosion of the Soviet regimes was caused, among other things, by the sheer persistence, beneath the imposed ideological conformity, of cultural values and psychic resistances of a kind that these stories and images enshrine. Even if we have learned to be rightly and deeply fearful of elevating the cultural forms and conservatisms of any nation into normative and exclusivist systems, even if we have terrible proof that pride in an ethnic and religious heritage can quickly degrade into the fascistic, our vigilance on that score should not displace our love and trust in the good of the indigenous per se. On the contrary, a trust in the staying power and travel-worthiness of such good should encourage us to credit the possibility of a world where respect for the validity of every tradition will issue in the creation and maintenance of a salubrious political space. In spite of devastating and repeated acts of massacre, assassination and extirpation, the huge acts of faith which have marked the new relations between Palestinians and Israelis, Africans and Afrikaners, and the way in which walls have come down in Europe and iron curtains have opened, all this inspires a hope that new possibility can still open up in Ireland as well. The crux of that problem involves an ongoing partition of the island between British and Irish jurisdictions, and an equally persistent partition of the affections in Northern Ireland between the British and Irish heritages; but surely every dweller in the country must hope that the governments involved in its governance can devise institutions which will allow that partition to become a bit more like the net on a tennis court, a demarcation allowing for agile give and take, for encounter and contending, prefiguring a future where the vitality that flowed in the beginning from those bracing words 'enemy' and 'allies' might finally derive from a less binary and altogether less binding vocabulary.

WHEN THE POET W. B. Yeats stood on this platform more than seventy years ago, Ireland was emerging from the throes of a traumatic civil war that had followed fast on the heels of a war of independence fought against the British. The struggle that ensued had been brief enough; it was over by May 1923, some seven months before Yeats sailed to Stockholm, but it was bloody, savage and intimate, and for generations to come it would dictate the terms of politics within the 26 independent counties of Ireland, that part of the island known first of all as the Irish Free State and then subsequently as the Republic of Ireland.

Yeats barely alluded to the civil war or the war of independence in his Nobel speech. Nobody understood better than he the connection between the construction or destruction of state institutions and the founding or foundering of cultural life, but on this occasion he chose to talk instead about the Irish Dramatic Movement. His story was about the creative purpose of that movement and its historic good fortune in having not only his own genius to sponsor it, but also the genius of his friends John Millington Synge and Lady Augusta Gregory. He came to Sweden to tell the world that the local work of poets and dramatists had been as important to the transformation of his native place and times as the ambushes of guerrilla armies; and his boast in that elevated prose was essentially the same as the one he would make in verse more than a decade later in his poem 'The Municipal Gallery Revisited'. There Yeats presents himself amongst the portraits and heroic narrative paintings which celebrate the events and personalities of recent history and all of a sudden realises that something truly epoch-making has occurred: '"This is not", I say,/"The dead Ireland of my youth, but an Ireland/The poets have imagined, terrible and gay."' And the poem concludes with two of the most quoted lines of his entire oeuvre:

> Think where man's glory most begins and ends,
> And say my glory was I had such friends.

And yet, expansive and thrilling as these lines are, they are an instance of poetry flourishing itself rather than proving itself, they are the poet's lap of honour, and in this respect if in no other they resemble what I am doing in this lecture. In fact, I should quote here on my own behalf some other words from the poem: 'You that would judge me, do not judge alone/This book or that.' Instead, I ask you to do what Yeats asked his audience to do and think of the achievement of Irish poets and dramatists and novelists over the past forty years, among whom I am proud to count great friends. In literary matters, Ezra Pound advised against accepting the opinion of those 'who haven't themselves produced notable work', and it is advice I have been privileged to follow, since it is the good opinion of notable workers—and not just those in my own country—that has fortified my endeavour since I began to write in Belfast more than thirty years ago. The Ireland I now inhabit is one that these Irish contemporaries have helped to imagine.

Yeats, however, was by no means all flourish. To the credit of poetry in our century there must surely be entered in any reckoning his two great sequences of poems entitled 'Nineteen Hundred and Nineteen' and 'Meditations in Time of Civil War', the latter of which contains the famous lyric about the bird's nest at his window, where a starling or stare had built in a crevice of the old wall. The poet was living then in a Norman tower which had been very much a part of the military history of the country in earlier and equally troubled times, and as his thoughts turned upon the irony of civilizations being consolidated by violent and powerful conquerors who end up commissioning the artists and the architects, he began to associate the sight of a mother bird feeding its young with the image of the honey bee, an image deeply lodged in poetic tradition and always suggestive of the ideal of an industrious, harmonious, nurturing commonwealth:

> The bees build in the crevices
> Of loosening masonry, and there
> The mother birds bring grubs and flies.
> My wall is loosening; honey-bees,
> Come build in the empty house of the stare.
>
> We are closed in, and the key is turned
> On our uncertainty; somewhere
> A man is killed, or a house burned,
> Yet no clear fact to be discerned:
> Come build in the empty house of the stare.

> A barricade of stone or of wood;
> Some fourteen days of civil war;
> Last night they trundled down the road
> That dead young soldier in his blood:
> Come build in the empty house of the stare.
>
> We had fed the heart on fantasies,
> The heart's grown brutal from the fare;
> More substance in our enmities
> Than in our love; O honey-bees,
> Come build in the empty house of the stare.

I have heard this poem repeated often, in whole and in part, by people in Ireland over the past 25 years, and no wonder, for it is as tender-minded towards life itself as St Kevin was and as tough-minded about what happens in and to life as Homer. It knows that the massacre will happen again on the roadside, that the workers in the minibus are going to be lined up and shot down just after quitting time; but it also credits as a reality the squeeze of the hand, the actuality of sympathy and protectiveness between living creatures. It satisfies the contradictory needs which consciousness experiences at times of extreme crisis, the need on the one hand for a truth-telling that will be hard and retributive, and on the other hand, the need not to harden the mind to a point where it denies its own yearnings for sweetness and trust.

It is a proof that poetry can be equal to and true at the same time, an example of that completely adequate poetry which the Russian woman sought from Anna Akhmatova and which William Wordsworth produced at a corresponding moment of historical crisis and personal dismay almost exactly two hundred years ago.

WHEN THE BARD Demodocus sings of the fall of Troy and of the slaughter that accompanied it, Odysseus weeps and Homer says that his tears were like the tears of a wife on a battle-field weeping for the death of a fallen husband. His epic simile continues:

> At the sight of the man panting and dying there,
> she slips down to enfold him, crying out;
> then feels the spears, prodding her back and shoulders,
> and goes bound into slavery and grief.
> Piteous weeping wears away her cheeks:
> but no more piteous than Odysseus' tears,
> cloaked as they were, now, from the company.

Even today, three thousand years later, as we channel-surf over so much live coverage of contemporary savagery, highly informed but nevertheless in danger of growing immune, familiar to the point of over-familiarity with old newsreels of the concentration camp and the gulag, Homer's image can still bring us to our senses. The callousness of those spear shafts on the woman's back and shoulders survives time and translation. The image has that documentary adequacy which answers all that we know about the intolerable.

But there is another kind of adequacy which is specific to lyric poetry. This has to do with the 'temple inside our hearing' which the passage of the poem calls into being. It is an adequacy deriving from what Mandelstam called 'the steadfastness of speech articulation', from the resolution and independence which the entirely realized poem sponsors. It has as much to do with the energy released by linguistic fission and fusion, with the buoyancy generated by cadence and tone and rhyme and stanza, as it has to do with the poem's concerns or the poet's truthfulness. In fact, in lyric poetry, truthfulness becomes recognizable as a ring of truth within the medium itself. And it is the unappeasable pursuit of this note, a note tuned to its most extreme in Emily Dickinson and Paul Celan and orchestrated to its most opulent in John Keats, it is this which keeps the poet's ear straining to hear the totally persuasive voice behind all the other informing voices.

Which is a way of saying that I have never quite climbed down from the arm of that sofa. I may have grown more attentive to the news and more alive to the world history and world sorrow behind it. But the thing uttered by the speaker I strain towards is still not quite the story of what is going on; it is more reflexive than that, because as a poet I am in fact straining towards a strain, seeking repose in the stability conferred by a musically satisfying order of sounds. As if the ripple at its widest desired to be verified by a reformation of itself, to be drawn in and drawn out through its point of origin.

I also strain towards this in the poetry I read. And I find it, for example, in the repetition of that refrain of Yeats', 'Come build in the empty house of the stare', with its tone of supplication, its pivots of strength in the words 'build' and 'house' and its acknowledgement of dissolution in the word 'empty'. I find it also in the triangle of forces held in equilibrium by the triple rhyme of 'fantasies' and 'enmities' and 'honey-bees', and in the sheer in-placeness of the whole poem as a given form within the language. Poetic form is both the ship and the anchor. It is at once a buoyancy and a steadying, allowing for the simultaneous gratification of whatever is centrifugal and whatever is centripetal in mind and body. And it is by such means that Yeats' work does what the necessary poetry always does, which is to touch the base of our sympathetic nature while taking in at the same time the unsympathetic nature of the world to which that nature is constantly exposed. The form of the poem, in other words, is crucial to poetry's power to do the thing which always is and always will be to poetry's credit:

the power to persuade that vulnerable part of our consciousness of its rightness in spite of the evidence of wrongness all around it, the power to remind us that we are hunters and gatherers of values, that our very solitudes and distresses are creditable, in so far as they, too, are an earnest of our veritable human being.

Kenzaburo Oe

Japan, the Ambiguous, and Myself
1994

Kenzaburo Oe was born in 1935 in the village of Ose-mura, on the island of Shikoku. Japan's defeat in the Second World War brought democratic principles to the remote village, replacing the militaristic education that had been taught there during the war. This glimpse of a different world spurred Oe to travel to Tokyo. His clan had lived in the village for several hundred years, and he was the first member of his family to leave. At Tokyo University he studied French Literature under Professor Kazuo Watanabe, and became an avid reader of contemporary French and American literature.

There are several phases in Oe's work. His early fiction was deeply influenced by the history and myths of his home village, such as his first novel, Memushiri kōchi *(Bud-Nipping, Lamb Shooting), published in 1958. Subsequent phases saw him tackling issues such as the occupation of Japan and violence in society, with the latter works embracing existentialism and picaresque literature. This fiction includes* Man'en gan'nen no futtobōru *(The Silent Cry) and* Pinchi ran'naa chōsho *(The Pinch Runner Memorandum). He has also written several volumes about his handicapped son, Hikari, among them* Kojinteki na taiken *(A Personal Matter) and* Atarashii hito yo mezameyo! *(Rouse Up, O Young Men of the New Age!).*

The Academy honoured Oe for the 'poetic force [that] creates an imagined world, where life and myth condense to form a disconcerting picture of the human predicament today'.

During the last catastrophic world war I was a little boy and lived in a remote, wooded valley on Shikoku Island in the Japanese Archipelago, thousands of miles away from here. At that time there were two books by which I was really fascinated: *The Adven-*

tures of Huckleberry Finn and *The Wonderful Adventures of Nils*. The whole world was then engulfed by waves of horror. By reading *Huckleberry Finn* I felt I was able to justify my act of going into the mountain forest at night and sleeping among the trees with a sense of security which I could never find indoors. The protagonist of *The Adventures of Nils* is transformed into a little creature, understands birds' language and makes an adventurous journey. I derived from the story sensuous pleasures of various kinds. Firstly, living as I was in a deep wood on the island of Shikoku just as my ancestors had done long ago, I had a revelation that this world and this way of life there were truly liberating. Secondly, I felt sympathetic and identified myself with Nils, a naughty little boy, who while traversing Sweden, collaborating with and fighting for the wild geese, transforms himself into a boy, still innocent, yet full of confidence as well as modesty. On coming home at last, Nils speaks to his parents. I think that the pleasure I derived from the story at its highest level lies in the language, because I felt purified and uplifted by speaking along with Nils. His words run as follows (in French and English translation):

> 'Maman, Papa! Je suis grand, je suis de nouveau un homme!' cria-t-il.
> 'Mother and father!' he cried. 'I'm a big boy. I'm a human being again!'

I was fascinated by the phrase 'je suis de nouveau un homme!' in particular. As I grew up, I was continually to suffer hardships in different realms of life—in my family, in my relationship to Japanese society and in my way of living at large in the latter half of the twentieth century. I have survived by representing these sufferings of mine in the form of the novel. In that process I have found myself repeating, almost sighing, 'je suis de nouveau un homme!' Speaking like this as regards myself is perhaps inappropriate to this place and to this occasion. However, please allow me to say that the fundamental style of my writing has been to start from my personal matters and then to link it up with society, the state and the world. I hope you will forgive me for talking about my personal matters a little further.

Half a century ago, while living in the depth of that forest, I read *The Adventures of Nils* and felt within it two prophecies. One was that I might one day become able to understand the language of birds. The other was that I might one day fly off with my beloved wild geese—preferably to Scandinavia.

After I got married, the first child born to us was mentally handicapped. We named him Hikari, meaning 'Light' in Japanese. As a baby he responded only to the chirps of wild birds and never to human voices. One summer when he was six years old we were staying at our country cottage. He heard a pair of water rails (*Rallus aquaticus*) warbling from the lake beyond a grove, and he said with the voice of a commentator on a recording of wild birds: 'They are water rails.' This was the first moment my son ever uttered human words. It was from then on that my wife and I began having verbal communication with our son.

Hikari now works at a vocational training center for the handicapped, an institution based on ideas we learnt from Sweden. In the meantime he has been composing works of music. Birds were the originators that occasioned and mediated his composition of human music. On my behalf Hikari has thus accomplished the prophecy that I might one day understand the language of birds. I must say also that my life would have been impossible but for my wife with her abundant female force and wisdom. She has been the very incarnation of Akka, the leader of Nils' wild geese. Together with her I have flown to Stockholm and the second of the prophecies has also, to my utmost delight, now been realized.

Kawabata Yasunari, the first Japanese writer who stood on this platform as a winner of the Nobel Prize for Literature, delivered a lecture entitled 'Japan, the Beautiful, and Myself'. It was at once very beautiful and *vague*. I have used the English word 'vague' as an equivalent of that word in Japanese, *aimaina*. This Japanese adjective could have several alternatives for its English translation. The kind of vagueness that Kawabata adopted deliberately is implied in the title itself of his lecture. It can be transliterated as 'myself *of* beautiful Japan'. The vagueness of the whole title derives from the Japanese particle 'no' (literally 'of') linking 'Myself' and 'Beautiful Japan'.

The vagueness of the title leaves room for various interpretations of its implications. It can imply 'myself as a part of beautiful Japan', the particle 'no' indicating the relationship of the noun following it to the noun preceding it as one of possession, belonging or attachment. It can also imply 'beautiful Japan and myself', the particle in this case linking the two nouns in apposition, as indeed they are in the English title of Kawabata's lecture translated by one of the most eminent American specialists of Japanese literature. He translates 'Japan, the beautiful *and* myself'. In this expert translation the *traduttore* (translator) is not in the least a *traditore* (betrayer).

Under that title Kawabata talked about a unique kind of mysticism which is found not only in Japanese thought but also more widely Oriental thought. By 'unique' I mean here a tendency towards Zen Buddhism. Even as a twentieth-century writer Kawabata depicts his state of mind in terms of the poems written by medieval Zen monks. Most of these poems are concerned with the linguistic impossibility of telling truth. According to such poems words are confined within their closed shells. The readers cannot expect that words will ever come out of these poems and get through to us. One can never understand or feel sympathetic towards these Zen poems except by giving oneself up and willingly penetrating into the closed shells of those words.

Why did Kawabata boldly decide to read those extremely esoteric poems in Japanese before the audience in Stockholm? I look back almost with nostalgia upon the straightforward bravery which he attained towards the end of his distinguished career and with which he made such a confession of his faith. Kawabata had been an artistic pilgrim for decades during which he produced a host of masterpieces. After those years of his pilgrimage, only by making a confession as to how he was fascinated by such inaccessible Japanese poems that baffle any attempt fully to understand them, was he able to talk about 'Japan, the Beautiful, and Myself', that is, about the world in which he lived and the literature which he created.

It is noteworthy, furthermore, that Kawabata concluded his lecture as follows:

> My works have been described as works of emptiness, but it is not to be taken for the nihilism of the West. The spiritual foundation would seem to be quite different. Dogen entitled his poem about the seasons 'Innate Reality', and even as he sang of the beauty of the seasons he was deeply immersed in Zen.
>
> (Translation by Edward Seidensticker)

Here also I detect a brave and straightforward self-assertion. On the one hand Kawabata identifies himself as belonging essentially to the tradition of Zen philosophy and aesthetic sensibilities pervading the classical literature of the Orient. Yet on the other he goes out of his way to differentiate emptiness as an attribute of his works from the nihilism of the West. By doing so he was wholeheartedly addressing the coming generations of mankind with whom Alfred Nobel entrusted his hope and faith.

To tell you the truth, rather than with Kawabata my compatriot who stood here 26 years ago, I feel more spiritual affinity with the Irish poet William Butler Yeats, who was awarded a Nobel Prize for Literature 71 years ago when he was at about the same age as me. Of course I would not presume to rank myself with the poetic genius Yeats. I am merely a humble follower living in a country far removed from his. As William Blake, whose work Yeats revalued and restored to the high place it holds in this century, once wrote: 'Across Europe & Asia to China & Japan like lightnings'.

During the last few years I have been engaged in writing a trilogy which I wish to be the culmination of my literary activities. So far the first two parts have been published and I have recently finished writing the third and final part. It is entitled in Japanese *A Flaming Green Tree*. I am indebted for this title to a stanza from Yeats' poem 'Vacillation':

> A tree there is that from its topmost bough
> Is half all glittering flame and half all green
> Abounding foliage moistened with the dew ...
>
> ('Vacillation', 11–13)

In fact my trilogy is so soaked in the overflowing influence of Yeats' poems as a whole. On the occasion of Yeats' winning the Nobel Prize the Irish Senate proposed a motion to congratulate him, which contained the following sentences:

> ... the recognition which the nation has gained, as a prominent contributor to the world's culture, through his success.
> ... a race that hitherto had not been accepted into the comity of nations.
> ... Our civilization will be assessed on the name of Senator Yeats.

> ... there will always be the danger that there may be a stampeding of people who are sufficiently removed from insanity in enthusiasm for destruction.
>
> (The Nobel Prize: Congratulations to Senator Yeats)

Yeats is the writer in whose wake I would like to follow. I would like to do so for the sake of another nation that has now been 'accepted into the comity of nations' but rather on account of the technology in electrical engineering and its manufacture of automobiles. Also I would like to do so as a citizen of such a nation which was stamped into 'insanity in enthusiasm of destruction' both on its own soil and on that of the neighbouring nations.

As someone living in the present world such as this one and sharing bitter memories of the past imprinted on my mind, I cannot utter in unison with Kawabata the phrase 'Japan, the Beautiful, and Myself'. A moment ago I touched upon the 'vagueness' of the title and content of Kawabata's lecture. In the rest of my lecture I would like to use the word 'ambiguous' in accordance with the distinction made by the eminent British poet Kathleen Raine; she once said of William Blake that he was not so much vague as ambiguous. I cannot talk about myself otherwise than by saying 'Japan, the Ambiguous, and Myself'.

My observation is that after one hundred and twenty years of modernization since the opening of the country, present-day Japan is split between two opposite poles of ambiguity. I too am living as a writer with this polarization imprinted on me like a deep scar.

This ambiguity which is so powerful and penetrating that it splits both the state and its people is evident in various ways. The modernization of Japan has been orientated toward learning from and imitating the West. Yet Japan is situated in Asia and has firmly maintained its traditional culture. The ambiguous orientation of Japan drove the country into the position of an invader in Asia. On the other hand, the culture of modern Japan, which implied being thoroughly open to the West or at least that impeded understanding by the West. What was more, Japan was driven into isolation from other Asian countries, not only politically but also socially and culturally.

In the history of modern Japanese literature the writers most sincere and aware of their mission were those 'post-war writers' who came onto the literary scene immediately after the last war, deeply wounded by the catastrophe yet full of hope for a rebirth. They tried with great pains to make up for the inhuman atrocities committed by Japanese military forces in Asian countries, as well as to bridge the profound gaps that existed not only between the developed countries of the West and Japan but also between African and Latin American countries and Japan. Only by doing so did they think that they could seek with some humility reconciliation with the rest of the world. It has always been my aspiration to cling to the very end of the line of that literary tradition inherited from those writers.

The contemporary state of Japan and its people in their postmodern phase cannot but be ambivalent. Right in the middle of the history of Japan's modernization came the Second World War, a war which was brought about by the very aberration of the modernization itself. The defeat in this war 50 years ago occasioned an opportunity for Japan and the Japanese as the very agent of the war to attempt a rebirth out of the great misery and sufferings that were depicted by the 'Postwar School' of Japanese writers. The moral props for Japanese aspiring to such a rebirth were the idea of democracy and their determination never to wage a war again. Paradoxically, the people and state of Japan living on such moral props were not innocent but had been stained by their own past history of invading other Asian countries. Those moral props mattered also to the deceased victims of the nuclear weapons that were used for the first time in Hiroshima and Nagasaki, and for the survivors and their offspring affected by radioactivity (including tens of thousands of those whose mother tongue is Korean).

In the recent years there have been criticisms levelled against Japan suggesting that she should offer more military forces to United Nations forces and thereby play a more active role in the keeping and restoration of peace in various parts of the world. Our heart sinks whenever we hear these criticisms. After the end of the Second World War it was a categorical imperative for us to declare that we renounced war forever in a central article of the new Constitution. The Japanese chose the principle of eternal peace as the basis of morality for our rebirth after the war.

I trust that the principle can best be understood in the West with its long tradition of tolerance for conscientious rejection of military service. In Japan itself there have all along been attempts by some to obliterate the article about renunciation of war from the Constitution and for this purpose they have taken every opportunity to make use of pressures from abroad. But to obliterate from the Constitution the principle of eternal peace will be nothing but an act of betrayal against the peoples of Asia and the victims of the atom bombs in Hiroshima and Nagasaki. It is not difficult for me as a writer to imagine what would be the outcome of that betrayal.

The pre-war Japanese Constitution that posited an absolute power transcending the principle of democracy had sustained some support from the populace. Even though we now have the half-century-old new Constitution, there is a popular sentiment of support for the old one that lives on in reality in some quarters. If Japan were to institutionalize a principle other than the one to which we have adhered for the last 50 years, the determination we made in the post-war ruins of our collapsed effort at modernization—that determination of ours to establish the concept of universal humanity would come to nothing. This is the spectre that rises before me, speaking as an ordinary individual.

What I call Japan's 'ambiguity' in my lecture is a kind of chronic disease that has been prevalent throughout the modern age. Japan's economic prosperity is not free from it either, accompanied as it is by all kinds of potential dangers in the light of the structure of world economy and environmental conservation. The 'ambiguity' in this respect seems to be accelerating. It may be more obvious to the critical eyes of the world at large than to us within the country. At the nadir of the postwar economic poverty we found a resilience to endure it, never losing our hope for recovery. It may sound curious to say so, but we seem to have no less resilience to endure our anxiety about the ominous consequence emerging out of the present prosperity. From another point of view, a new situation now seems to be arising in which Japan's prosperity is going to be incorporated into the expanding potential power of both production and consumption in Asia at large.

I am one of the writers who wish to create serious works of literature which dissociate themselves from those novels which are mere reflections of the vast consumer cultures of Tokyo and the subcultures of the world at large. What kind of identity as a Japanese should I seek? W. H. Auden once defined the novelist as follows:

> ... among the dust
> Be just, among the Filthy filthy too,
> And in his own weak person, if he can,
> Must suffer dully all the wrongs of Man.
>
> ('The Novelist', 11–14)

This is what has become my 'habit of life' (in Flannery O'Connor's words) through being a writer as my profession.

To define a desirable Japanese identity I would like to pick out the word 'decent' which is among the adjectives that George Orwell often used, along with words like 'humane', 'sane' and 'comely', for the character types that he favoured. This deceptively simple epithet may starkly set off and contrast with the word 'ambiguous', used for my identification in 'Japan, the Ambiguous, and Myself'. There is a wide and ironical discrepancy between what the Japanese seem like when viewed from outside and what they wish to look like.

I hope Orwell would not raise an objection if I used the word 'decent' as a synonym of 'humanist' or 'humaniste' in French, because both words share in common qualities such as tolerance and humanity. Among our ancestors were some pioneers who made painstaking efforts to build up the Japanese identity as 'decent' or 'humanist'.

One such person was the late Professor Kazuo Watanabe, a scholar of French Renaissance literature and thought. Surrounded by the insane ardour of patriotism on the eve and in the middle of the Second World War, Watanabe had a lonely dream of grafting the humanist view of man onto the traditional Japanese sense of beauty and sensitivity to Nature, which fortunately had not been entirely eradicated. I must hasten to add that Professor Watanabe had a conception of beauty and Nature different from that conceived of by Kawabata in his 'Japan, the Beautiful, and Myself'.

The way Japan had tried to build up a modern state modeled on the West was cataclysmic. In ways different from, yet partly corresponding to, that process Japanese intellectuals had tried to bridge the gap between the West and their own country at its deepest level. It must have been a laborious task or *travail* but it was also one that brimmed with joy. Professor Watanabe's study of François Rabelais was thus one of the most distinguished and rewarding scholarly achievements of the Japanese intellectual world.

Watanabe studied in Paris before the Second World War. When he told his academic supervisor about his ambition to translate Rabelais into Japanese, the eminent elderly French scholar answered the aspiring young Japanese student with the phrase: 'L'entreprise inouie de la traduction de l'intraduisible Rabelais' ('The unprecedented enterprise of translating into Japanese untranslatable Rabelais'). Another French scholar answered with blunt astonishment: 'Belle entreprise Pantagruélique' ('An admirably Pantagruel-like enterprise'). In spite of all this not only did Watanabe accomplish his great enterprise in a poverty-stricken environment during the war and the American occupation, but he also did his best to transplant into the confused and disorientated Japan of that time the life and thought of those French humanists who were the forerunners, contemporaries and followers of François Rabelais.

In both my life and writing I have been a pupil of Professor Watanabe's. I was influenced by him in two crucial ways. One was in my method of writing novels. I learnt concretely from his translation of Rabelais what Mikhail Bakhtin formulated as 'the image system of grotesque realism or the culture of popular laughter'; the importance of material and physical principles; the correspondence between the cosmic, social and physical elements; the overlapping of death and passions for rebirth; and the laughter that subverts hierarchical relationships.

The image system made it possible to seek literary methods of attaining the universal for someone like me, born and brought up in a peripheral, marginal, off-centre region of the peripheral, marginal, off-center country, Japan. Starting from such a background I do not represent Asia as a new economic power but an Asia impregnated with ever-lasting poverty and a mixed-up fertility. By sharing old, familiar yet living metaphors I align myself with writers like Kim Ji-ha of Korea, Chon I and Mu Jen, both of China. For me the brotherhood of world literature consists in such relationships in concrete terms. I once took part in a hunger strike for the political freedom of a gifted Korean poet. I am now deeply worried about the destiny of those gifted Chinese novelists who have been deprived of their freedom since the Tiananmen Square incident.

Another way in which Professor Watanabe has influenced me is in his idea of humanism. I take it to be the quintessence of Europe as a living totality. It is an idea which is also perceptible in Milan Kundera's definition of the spirit of the novel. Based on his accurate reading of historical sources Watanabe wrote critical biographies, with Rabelais at their center, of people from Erasmus to Sébastien Castellion, and of women connected with Henri IV from Queen Marguerite to Gabrielle Destré. By doing so Watanabe intended to teach the Japanese about humanism, about the importance of tolerance, about man's vulnerability to his preconceptions or machines of his own making. His sincerity led him to quote the remark by the Danish philologist Kristoffer Nyrop: 'Those who do not protest against war are accomplices of war.' In his attempt to transplant into Japan humanism as the very basis of Western thought Watanabe was bravely venturing on both 'l'entreprise inouïe' and the 'belle entreprise Pantagruélique'.

As someone influenced by Watanabe's humanism I wish my task as a novelist to enable both those who express themselves with words and their readers to recover from their own sufferings and the sufferings of their time, and to cure their souls of the wounds. I have said I am split between the opposite poles of ambiguity characteristic of the Japanese. I have been making efforts to be cured of and restored from those pains and wounds by means of literature. I have made my efforts also to pray for the cure and recovery off my fellow Japanese.

If you will allow me to mention him again, my mentally handicapped son Hikari was awakened by the voices of birds to the music of Bach and Mozart, eventually composing his own works. The little pieces that he first composed were full of fresh splendour and delight. They seemed like dew glittering on grass leaves. The word *innocence* is composed of *in*—'not'—and *nocere*—'hurt'—that is, 'not to hurt'. Hikari's music was in this sense a natural effusion of the composer's own innocence.

As Hikari went on to compose more works, I could not but hear in his music also 'the voice of a crying and dark soul'. Mentally handicapped as he was, his strenuous effort furnished his act of composing or his 'habit of life' with the growth of compositional techniques and a deepening of his conception. That in turn enabled him to discover in the depth of his heart a mass of dark sorrow which he had hitherto been unable to identify with words.

'The voice of a crying and dark soul' is beautiful, and his act of expressing it in music cures him of his dark sorrow in an act of recovery. Furthermore, his music has been accepted as one that cures and restores his contemporary listeners as well. Herein I find the grounds for believing in the exquisite healing power of art.

This belief of mine has not been fully proved. 'Weak person' though I am, with the aid of this unverifiable belief, I would like to 'suffer dully all the wrongs' accumulated throughout the twentieth century as a result of the monstrous development of technology and transport. As one with a peripheral, marginal and off-centre existence in the world I would like to seek how—with what I hope is a modest, decent and humanist contribution—I can be of some use in a cure and reconciliation of mankind.

Toni Morrison

The Bird Is In Your Hands
1993

Toni Morrison was born Chloe Anthony Wofford in Lorain, Ohio. Her family was working class, her father a welder. Morrison was a voracious reader as a child, and throughout her childhood the family home was filled with storytelling and the songs and folktales of black culture. These influences subsequently found their way into Morrison's work.

The strength of Morrison's writing lies in its treatment of epic themes and expressive depictions of African American life, examining in particular the struggle of black women to find themselves and build a coherent cultural identity within a racist culture. Morrison is also credited with possessing a finely tuned ear for dialogue. Her novels include The Bluest Eye, Song of Solomon, Jazz *and* Paradise. *She won the Pulitzer Prize for Fiction in 1988 for her novel* Beloved, *which was based on the true story of an escaped slave woman who on recapture killed her infant daughter to spare the child a life of slavery. She has provided encouragement to other black writers through her membership of the National Council of the Arts and the Institute of Arts and Letters.*

The Academy stated that Morrison, 'in novels characterized by visionary force and poetic import, gives life to an essential aspect of American reality'.

'Once upon a time there was an old woman. Blind but wise.' Or was it an old man? A guru, perhaps. Or a griot soothing restless children. I have heard this story, or one exactly like it, in the lore of several cultures.

'Once upon a time there was an old woman. Blind. Wise.'

In the version I know the woman is the daughter of slaves, black, American, and lives alone in a small house outside of town. Her reputation for wisdom is without peer and without question. Among her people she is both the law and its transgression. The honour she is paid and the awe in which she is held reach beyond her neighbourhood to places far away; to the city where the intelligence of rural prophets is the source of much amusement.

One day the woman is visited by some young people who seem to be bent on disproving her clairvoyance and showing her up for the fraud they believe she is. Their plan is simple: they enter her house and ask the one question the answer to which rides solely on her difference from them, a difference they regard as a profound disability: her blindness. They stand before her, and one of them says, 'Old woman, I hold in my hand a bird. Tell me whether it is living or dead.'

She does not answer, and the question is repeated. 'Is the bird I am holding living or dead?'

Still she doesn't answer. She is blind and cannot see her visitors, let alone what is in their hands. She does not know their colour, gender or homeland. She only knows their motive.

The old woman's silence is so long, the young people have trouble holding their laughter.

Finally she speaks and her voice is soft but stern. 'I don't know,' she says. 'I don't know whether the bird you are holding is dead or alive, but what I do know is that it is in your hands. It is in your hands.'

Her answer can be taken to mean: if it is dead, you have either found it that way or you have killed it. If it is alive, you can still kill it. Whether it is to stay alive, it is your decision. Whatever the case, it is your responsibility.

For parading their power and her helplessness, the young visitors are reprimanded, told they are responsible not only for the act of mockery but also for the small bundle of life sacrificed to achieve its aims. The blind woman shifts attention away from assertions of power to the instrument through which that power is exercised.

Speculation on what (other than its own frail body) that bird-in-the-hand might signify has always been attractive to me, but especially so now thinking, as I have been, about the work I do that has brought me to this company. So I choose to read the bird as language and the woman as a practiced writer. She is worried about how the language she dreams in, given to her at birth, is handled, put into service, even withheld from her for certain nefarious purposes. Being a writer she thinks of language partly as a system, partly as a living thing over which one has control, but mostly as agency—as an act with consequences. So the question the children put to her: 'Is it living or dead?' is not unreal because she thinks of language as susceptible to death, erasure; certainly imperilled and salvageable only by an effort of the will. She believes that if the bird in the hands of her visitors is dead the custodians are responsible for the corpse. For her a dead language is not only one no longer spoken or written, it is unyielding language content to admire its own paralysis. Like statist language, censored and censoring. Ruthless in its policing duties, it has no desire or purpose other than maintaining the free range of its own narcotic narcissism, its own exclusivity and dominance. However moribund, it is not without effect for it actively thwarts the intellect, stalls conscience, suppresses human potential. Unreceptive to interrogation, it cannot form or tolerate new ideas, shape other thoughts, tell another story, fill baffling silences. Official language smitheryed to sanction ignorance and preserve privilege is a suit of armour polished to shocking glitter, a husk from which the knight departed long ago. Yet there it is: dumb, predatory, sentimental. Exciting reverence in schoolchildren, providing shelter for despots, summoning false memories of stability, harmony among the public.

She is convinced that when language dies, out of carelessness, disuse, indifference and absence of esteem, or killed by fiat, not only she herself, but all users and makers are accountable for its demise. In her country children have bitten their tongues off and use bullets instead to iterate the voice of speechlessness, of disabled and disabling language, of language adults have abandoned altogether as a device for grappling with meaning, providing guidance, or expressing love. But she knows tongue-suicide is not only the choice of children. It is common among the infantile heads of state and power merchants whose evacuated language leaves them with no access to what is left of their human instincts for they speak only to those who obey, or in order to force obedience.

The systematic looting of language can be recognized by the tendency of its users to forgo its nuanced, complex, mid-wifery properties for menace and subjugation. Oppressive language does more than represent violence; it is violence; does more than represent the limits of knowledge; it limits knowledge. Whether it is obscuring state language or the faux-language of mindless media; whether it is the proud but calcified language of the academy or the commodity-driven language of science; whether it is the malign language of law-without-ethics, or language designed for the estrangement of minorities, hiding its racist plunder in its literary cheek—it must be rejected, altered and exposed. It is the language that drinks blood, laps vulnerabilities, tucks its fascist boots under crinolines of respectability and patriotism as it moves relentlessly toward the bottom line and the bottomed-out mind. Sexist language, racist language, theistic language—all are typical of the policing languages of mastery, and cannot, do not permit new knowledge or encourage the mutual exchange of ideas.

The old woman is keenly aware that no intellectual mercenary, nor insatiable dictator, no paid-for politician or demagogue; no counterfeit journalist would be persuaded by her thoughts. There is and will be rousing language to keep citizens armed and arming; slaughtered and slaughtering in the malls, courthouses, post offices, playgrounds, bedrooms and boulevards; stirring, memorialising language to mask the pity and waste of needless death. There will be more diplomatic language to countenance rape, torture, assassination. There is and will be more seductive, mutant language designed to throttle women, to pack their throats like paté-producing geese with their own unsayable, transgressive words; there will be more of the language of surveillance disguised as research; of politics and history calculated to render the suffering of millions mute; language glamorised to thrill the dissatisfied and bereft into assaulting their neighbours; arrogant pseudo-empirical language crafted to lock creative people into cages of inferiority and hopelessness.

Underneath the eloquence, the glamour, the scholarly associations, however stirring or seductive, the heart of such language is languishing, or perhaps not beating at all—if the bird is already dead.

She has thought about what could have been the intellectual history of any discipline if it had not insisted upon, or been forced into, the waste of time and life that rationalisations for and representations of dominance required—lethal discourses of exclusion blocking access to cognition for both the excluder and the excluded.

The conventional wisdom of the Tower of Babel story is that the collapse was a misfortune. That it was the distraction, or the weight of many languages that precipitated the tower's failed architecture. That one monolithic language would have expedited the building and heaven would have been reached. Whose heaven, she wonders? And what kind? Perhaps the achievement of Paradise was premature, a little hasty if no one could take the time to understand other languages, other views, other narratives period. Had they, the heaven they imagined might have been found at their feet. Complicated, demanding, yes, but a view of heaven as life; not heaven as post-life.

She would not want to leave her young visitors with the impression that language should be forced to stay alive merely to be. The vitality of language lies in its ability to limn the actual, imagined and possible lives of its speakers, readers, writers. Although its poise is sometimes in displacing experience it is not a substitute for it. It arcs toward the place where meaning may lie. When a president of the United States thought about the graveyard his country had become, and said, 'The world will little note nor long remember what we say here. But it will never forget what they did here,' his simple words are exhilarating in their life-sustaining properties because they refused to encapsulate the reality of 600,000 dead men in a cataclysmic race war. Refusing to monumentalize, disdaining the 'final word', the precise 'summing up', acknowledging their 'poor power to add or detract', his words signal deference to the uncapturability of the life it mourns. It is the deference that moves her, that recognition that language can never live up to life once and for all. Nor should it. Language can never 'pin down' slavery, genocide, war. Nor should it yearn for the arrogance to be able to do so. Its force, its felicity is in its reach toward the ineffable.

Be it grand or slender, burrowing, blasting or refusing to sanctify; whether it laughs out loud or is a cry without an alphabet, the choice word, the chosen silence, unmolested language surges toward knowledge, not its destruction. But who does not know of literature banned because it is interrogative; discredited because it is critical; erased because alternate? And how many are outraged by the thought of a self-ravaged tongue?

Word-work is sublime, she thinks, because it is generative; it makes meaning that secures our difference, our human difference—the way in which we are like no other life.

We die. That may be the meaning of life. But we do language. That may be the measure of our lives.

'Once upon a time ...' visitors ask an old woman a question. Who are they, these children? What did they make of that encounter? What did they hear in those final words: 'The bird is in your hands'? A sentence that gestures towards possibility or one that drops a latch? Perhaps what the children heard was 'It's not my problem. I am old, female, black, blind. What wisdom I have now is in knowing I cannot help you. The future of language is yours.'

They stand there. Suppose nothing was in their hands? Suppose the visit was only a ruse, a trick to get to be spoken to, taken seriously as they have not been before? A chance to interrupt, to violate the adult world, its miasma of discourse about them, for them, but never to them? Urgent questions are at stake, including the one they have asked: 'Is the bird we hold living or dead?' Perhaps the question meant: 'Could someone tell us what is life? What is death?' No trick at all; no silliness. A straightforward question worthy of the attention of a wise one. An old one. And if the old and wise who have lived life and faced death cannot describe either, who can?

But she does not; she keeps her secret; her good opinion of herself; her gnomic pronouncements; her art without commitment. She keeps her distance, enforces it and retreats into the singularity of isolation, in sophisticated, privileged space.

Nothing, no word follows her declaration of transfer. That silence is deep, deeper than the meaning available in the words she has spoken. It shivers, this silence, and the children, annoyed, fill it with language invented on the spot.

'Is there no speech,' they ask her, 'no words you can give us that helps us break through your dossier of failures? Through the education you have just given us that is no education at all because we are paying close attention to what you have done as well as to what you have said? To the barrier you have erected between generosity and wisdom?

'We have no bird in our hands, living or dead. We have only you and our important question. Is the nothing in our hands something you could not bear to contemplate, to even guess? Don't you remember being young when language was magic without meaning? When what you could say, could not mean? When the invisible was what imagination strove to see? When questions and demands for answers burned so brightly you trembled with fury at not knowing?

'Do we have to begin consciousness with a battle heroines and heroes like you have already fought and lost leaving us with nothing in our hands except what you have imagined is there? Your answer is artful, but its artfulness embarrasses us and ought to embarrass you. Your answer is indecent in its self-congratulation. A made-for-television script that makes no sense if there is nothing in our hands.

'Why didn't you reach out, touch us with your soft fingers, delay the sound bite, the lesson, until you knew who we were? Did you so despise our trick, our modus operandi you could not see that we were baffled about how to get your attention? We are young. Unripe. We have heard all our short lives that we have to be responsible. What could that possibly mean in the catastrophe this world has become; where, as a poet said, 'nothing needs to be exposed since it is already barefaced'. Our inheritance is an affront. You want us to have your old, blank eyes and see only cruelty and mediocrity. Do you think we are stupid enough to perjure ourselves again and again with the fiction of nationhood? How dare you talk to us of duty when we stand waist deep in the toxin of your past?

'You trivialise us and trivialise the bird that is not in our hands. Is there no context for our lives? No song, no literature, no poem full of vitamins, no history connected to experience that you can pass along to help us start strong? You are an adult. The old one, the wise one. Stop thinking about saving your face. Think of our lives and tell us your particularised world. Make up a story. Narrative is radical, creating us at the very moment it is being created. We will not blame you if your reach exceeds your grasp; if love so ignites your words they go down in flames and nothing is left but their scald. Or if, with the reticence of a surgeon's hands, your words suture only the places where blood might flow. We know you can never do it properly—once and for all. Passion is never enough; neither is skill. But try. For our sake and yours forget your name in the street; tell us what the world has been to you in the dark places and in the light. Don't tell us what to believe, what to fear. Show us belief's wide skirt and the stitch that unravels fear's caul. You, old woman, blessed with blindness, can speak the language that tells us what only language can: how to see without pictures. Language alone protects us from the scariness of things with no names. Language alone is meditation.

'Tell us what it is to be a woman so that we may know what it is to be a man. What moves at the margin. What it is to have no home in this place. To be set adrift from the one you knew. What it is to live at the edge of towns that cannot bear your company.

'Tell us about ships turned away from shorelines at Easter, placenta in a field. Tell us about a wagonload of slaves, how they sang so softly their breath was indistinguishable from the falling snow. How they knew from the hunch of the nearest shoulder that the next stop would be their last. How, with hands prayered in their sex, they thought of heat, then sun. Lifting their faces as though it was there for the taking. Turning as though there for the taking. They stop at an inn. The driver and his mate go in with the lamp leaving them humming in the dark. The horse's void steams into the snow beneath its hooves and its hiss and melt are the envy of the freezing slaves.

'The inn door opens: a girl and a boy step away from its light. They climb into the wagon bed. The boy will have a gun in three years, but now he carries a lamp and a jug of warm cider. They pass it from mouth to mouth. The girl offers bread, pieces of meat and something more: a glance into the eyes of the one she serves. One helping for each man, two for each woman. And a look. They look back. The next stop will be their last. But not this one. This one is warmed.'

It's quiet again when the children finish speaking, until the woman breaks into the silence.

'Finally', she says, 'I trust you now. I trust you with the bird that is not in your hands because you have truly caught it. Look. How lovely it is, this thing we have done—together.'

Derek Walcott

The Antilles: Fragments of Epic Memory
1992

Derek Walcott, poet and playwright, was born in 1930 on one of the Windward Islands in the Lesser Antilles, in the town of Castries in Saint Lucia. His birthplace, an isolated, volcanic island and an ex-British colony, resonates throughout his work. Walcott's mother ran the local Methodist school and his father, a Bohemian watercolourist, died when Walcott was only a few years old.

In 1953 Walcott moved to Trinidad, and worked in the theatre and as an art critic. His first poetry collection, 25 Poems, *was published when he was eighteen, but his breakthrough came with the collection* In a Green Night, *published in 1962. He has published more than twenty plays, the majority of which have been produced by the Trinidad Theatre Workshop, which he founded in 1959.*

Walcott has travelled widely, but has always strongly identified with Caribbean society and its fusion of African, Asiatic and European cultures. The effects of colonisation are often explored in his plays, and he has focused on creating an indigenous drama for the region. His plays include Ti-Jean and His Brothers, Dream on Monkey Mountain *and* The Isle Is Full of Noises.

Walcott received the Nobel Prize 'for a poetic oeuvre of great luminosity, sustained by a historical vision, the outcome of a multicultural commitment'.

Felicity is a village in Trinidad on the edge of the Caroni plain, the wide central plain that still grows sugar and to which indentured cane cutters were brought after emancipation, so the small population of Felicity is East Indian, and on the afternoon that I visited it with friends from America, all the faces along its road were Indian, which, as I hope to show, was a moving, beautiful thing, because this Saturday afternoon *Ramleela*, the epic dramatization of the Hindu epic the *Ramayana*, was going to be performed, and the costumed actors from the village were assembling on a field strung with different-coloured flags, like a new gas station, and beautiful Indian boys in red and black were aiming arrows haphazardly into the afternoon light. Low blue mountains on the horizon, bright grass, clouds that would gather colour before the light went. Felicity! What a gentle Anglo-Saxon name for an epical memory.

Under an open shed on the edge of the field, there were two huge armatures of bamboo that looked like immense cages. They were parts of the body of a god, his calves or thighs, which, fitted and reared, would make a gigantic effigy. This effigy would be burnt as a conclusion to the epic. The cane structures flashed a predictable parallel: Shelley's sonnet on the fallen statue of Ozymandias and his empire, that 'colossal wreck' in its empty desert.

Drummers had lit a fire in the shed and they eased the skins of their tablas nearer the flames to tighten them. The saffron flames, the bright grass and the hand-woven armatures of the fragmented god who would be burnt were not in any desert where imperial power had finally toppled but were part of a ritual, evergreen season that, like the cane-burning harvest, is annually repeated, the point of such sacrifice being its repetition, the point of the destruction being renewal through fire.

Deities were entering the field. What we generally call 'Indian music' was blaring from the open platformed shed from which the epic would be narrated. Costumed actors were arriving. Princes and gods, I supposed. What an unfortunate confession! 'Gods, I suppose' is the shrug that embodies our African and Asian diasporas. I had often thought of but never seen *Ramleela*, and had never seen this theatre, an open field, with village children as warriors, princes and gods. I had no idea what the epic story was, who its hero was, what enemies he fought, yet I had recently adapted the *Odyssey* for a theatre in England, presuming that the audience knew the trials of Odysseus, hero of another Asia Minor epic, while nobody in Trinidad knew any more than I did about Rama, Kali, Shiva, Vishnu, apart from the Indians, a phrase I use pervertedly because that is the kind of remark you can still hear in Trinidad: 'apart from the Indians'.

It was as if, on the edge of the Central Plain, there was another plateau, a raft on which the *Ramayana* would be poorly performed in this ocean of cane, but that was my writer's view of things, and it is wrong. I was seeing the *Ramleela* at Felicity as theatre when it was faith.

Multiply that moment of self-conviction when an actor, made-up and costumed, nods to his mirror before stepping on stage in the belief that he is a reality entering an illusion and you would have what I presumed was happening to the actors of this epic. But they were not actors. They had been chosen; or they themselves had chosen their roles in this sacred story that would go on for nine afternoons over a two-hour period till the sun set. They were not amateurs but believers. There was no theatrical term to define them. They did not have to psych themselves up to play their roles. Their acting would probably be as buoyant and as natural as those bamboo arrows crisscrossing the afternoon pasture. They believed in what they were playing, in the sacredness of the text, the validity of India, while I, out of the writer's habit, searched for some sense of elegy, of loss, even of degenerative mimicry in the happy faces of the boy-warriors or the heraldic profiles of the village princes. I was polluting the afternoon with doubt and with the patronage of admiration. I misread the event through a visual echo of History—the cane fields, indenture, the evocation of vanished armies, temples and trumpeting elephants—when all around me there was quite the opposite: elation, delight in the boys' screams, in the sweets-stalls, in more and more costumed characters appearing; a delight of conviction, not loss. The name Felicity made sense.

Consider the scale of Asia reduced to these fragments: the small white exclamations of minarets or the stone balls of temples in the cane fields, and one can understand the self-mockery and embarrassment of those who see these rites as parodic, even degenerate. These purists look on such ceremonies as grammarians look at a dialect, as cities look on provinces and empires on their colonies. Memory that yearns to join the centre, a limb remembering the body from which it has been severed, like those bamboo thighs of the god. In other words, the way that the Caribbean is still looked at, illegitimate, rootless, mongrelised. 'No people there', to quote Froude, 'in the true sense of the word.' No people. Fragments and echoes of real people, unoriginal and broken.

The performance was like a dialect, a branch of its original language, an abridgement of it, but not a distortion or even a reduction of its epic scale. Here in Trinidad I had discovered that one of the greatest epics of the world was seasonally performed, not with that desperate resignation of preserving a culture, but with an openness of belief that was as steady as the wind bending the cane lances of the Caroni plain. We had to leave before the play began to go through the creeks of the Caroni Swamp, to catch the scarlet ibises coming home at dusk. In a performance as natural as those of the actors of the *Ramleela*, we watched the flocks come in as bright as the scarlet of the boy archers, as the red flags, and cover an islet until it turned into a flowering tree, an anchored immortelle. The sigh of History meant nothing here. These two visions, the *Ramleela* and the arrowing flocks of scarlet ibises, blent into a single gasp of gratitude. Visual surprise is natural in the Caribbean; it comes with the landscape, and faced with its beauty, the sigh of History dissolves.

We make too much of that long groan which underlines the past. I felt privileged to discover the ibises as well as the scarlet archers of Felicity.

The sigh of History rises over ruins, not over landscapes, and in the Antilles there are few ruins to sigh over, apart from the ruins of sugar estates and abandoned forts. Looking around slowly, as a camera would, taking in the low blue hills over Port of Spain, the village road and houses, the warrior-archers, the god-actors and their handlers, and music already on the soundtrack, I wanted to make a film that would be a long-drawn sigh over Felicity. I was filtering the afternoon with evocations of a lost India, but why 'evocations'? Why not 'celebrations of a real presence'? Why should India be 'lost' when none of these villagers ever really knew it, and why not 'continuing', why not the perpetuation of joy in Felicity and in all the other nouns of the Central Plain: Couva, Chaguanas, Charley Village? Why was I not letting my pleasure open its windows wide? I was enticed like any Trinidadian to the ecstasies of their claim, because ecstasy was the pitch of the sinuous drumming in the loudspeakers. I was entitled to the feast of Husein, to the mirrors and crepe-paper temples of the Muslim epic, to the Chinese Dragon Dance, to the rites of that Sephardic Jewish synagogue that was once on Something Street. I am only one-eighth the writer I might have been had I contained all the fragmented languages of Trinidad.

Break a vase, and the love that reassembles the fragments is stronger than that love which took its symmetry for granted when it was whole. The glue that fits the pieces is the sealing of its original shape. It is such a love that reassembles our African and Asiatic fragments, the cracked heirlooms whose restoration shows its white scars. This gathering of broken pieces is the care and pain of the Antilles, and if the pieces are disparate, ill-fitting, they contain more pain than their original sculpture, those icons and sacred vessels taken for granted in their ancestral places. Antillean art is this restoration of our shattered histories, our shards of vocabulary, our archipelago becoming a synonym for pieces broken off from the original continent.

And this is the exact process of the making of poetry, or what should be called not its 'making' but its remaking, the fragmented memory, the armature that frames the god, even the rite that surrenders it to a final pyre; the god assembled cane by cane, reed by weaving reed, line by plaited line, as the artisans of Felicity would erect his holy echo.

Poetry, which is perfection's sweat but which must seem as fresh as the raindrops on a statue's brow, combines the natural and the marmoreal; it conjugates both tenses simultaneously: the past and the present, if the past is the sculpture and the present the beads of dew or rain on the forehead of the past. There is the buried language and there is the individual vocabulary, and the process of poetry is one of excavation and of self-discovery. Tonally the individual voice is a dialect; it shapes its own accent, its own vocabulary and melody in defiance of an imperial concept of language, the language of Ozymandias, libraries and dictionaries, law courts and critics, and churches, universities, political dogma, the diction of institutions. Poetry is an island that breaks away from the main. The dialects of my archipelago seem as fresh to me as those raindrops on the statue's forehead, not the sweat made from the classic exertion of frowning marble, but the condensations of a refreshing element, rain and salt.

Deprived of their original language, the captured and indentured tribes create their own, accreting and secreting fragments of an old, an epic vocabulary, from Asia and from Africa, but to an ancestral, an ecstatic rhythm in the blood that cannot be subdued by slavery or indenture, while nouns are renamed and the given names of places accepted like Felicity village or Choiseul. The original language dissolves from the exhaustion of distance like fog trying to cross an ocean, but this process of renaming, of finding new metaphors, is the same process that the poet faces every morning of his working day, making his own tools like Crusoe, assembling nouns from necessity, from Felicity, even renaming himself. The stripped man is driven back to that self-astonishing, elemental force, his mind. That is the basis of the Antillean experience, this shipwreck of fragments, these echoes, these shards of a huge tribal vocabulary, these partially remembered customs, and they are not decayed but strong. They survived the Middle Passage and the *Fatel Rozack*, the ship that carried the first indentured Indians from the port of Madras to the cane fields of Felicity, that carried the chained Cromwellian convict and the Sephardic Jew, the Chinese grocer and the Lebanese merchant selling cloth samples on his bicycle.

And here they are, all in a single Caribbean city, Port of Spain, the sum of history, Trollope's 'non-people'. A downtown babel of shop signs and streets, mongrelised, polyglot, a ferment without a history, like heaven. Because that is what such a city is, in the New World, a writer's heaven.

A culture, we all know, is made by its cities.

Another first morning home, impatient for the sunrise—a broken sleep. Darkness at five, and the drapes not worth opening; then, in the sudden light, a cream-walled, brown-roofed police station bordered with short royal palms, in the colonial style, back of it frothing trees and taller palms, a pigeon fluttering into the cover of an alcove, a rain-stained block of once-modern apartments, the morning side road into the station without traffic. All part of a surprising peace. This quiet happens with every visit to a city that has deepened itself in me. The flowers and the hills are easy, affection for them predictable; it is the architecture that, for the first morning, disorients. A return from American seductions used to make the traveller feel that something was missing, something was trying to complete itself, like the stained concrete apartments.

Pan left along the window and the excrescences rear—a city trying to soar, trying to be brutal, like an American city in silhouette, stamped from the same mould as Columbus or Des Moines. An assertion of power, its decor bland, its air-conditioning pitched to the point where its secretarial and executive staff sport competing cardigans; the colder the offices the more important, an imitation of another climate. A longing, even an envy of feeling cold.

In serious cities, in grey, militant winter with its short afternoons, the days seem to pass by in buttoned overcoats, every building appears as a barracks with lights on in its windows, and when snow comes, one has the illusion of living in a Russian novel, in the nineteenth century, because of the literature of winter. So visitors to the Caribbean must feel that they are inhabiting a succession of postcards. Both climates are shaped by what we have read of them. For tourists, the sunshine cannot be serious. Winter adds depth and darkness to life as well as to literature, and in the unending summer of the tropics not even poverty or poetry (in the Antilles poverty is poetry with a V, *une vie*, a condition of life as well as of imagination) seems capable of being profound because the nature around it is so exultant, so resolutely ecstatic, like its music. A culture based on joy is bound to be shallow. Sadly, to sell itself, the Caribbean encourages the delights of mindlessness, of brilliant vacuity, as a place to flee not only winter but that seriousness that comes only out of culture with four seasons. So how can there be a people there, in the true sense of the word?

They know nothing about seasons in which leaves let go of the year, in which spires fade in blizzards and streets whiten, of the erasures of whole cities by fog, of reflection in fireplaces; instead, they inhabit a geography whose rhythm, like their music, is limited to two stresses: hot and wet, sun and rain, light and shadow, day and night, the limitations of an incomplete meter, and are therefore a people incapable of the subtleties of contradiction, of imaginative complexity. So be it. We cannot change contempt.

Ours are not cities in the accepted sense, but no one wants them to be. They dictate their own proportions, their own definitions in particular places and in a prose equal to that of their detractors, so that now it is not just St James but the streets and yards that Naipaul commemorates, its lanes as short and brilliant as his sentences; not just the noise and jostle of Tunapuna but the origins of C. L. R. James' *Beyond a Boundary*, not just Felicity village on the Caroni plain, but Selvon Country, and that is the way it goes up the islands now: the old Dominica of Jean Rhys still very much the way she wrote of it; and the Martinique of the early Cesaire; Perse's Guadeloupe, even without the pith helmets and the mules; and what delight and privilege there was in watching a literature—one literature in several imperial languages, French, English, Spanish—bud and open island after island in the early morning of a culture, not timid, not derivative, any more than the hard white petals of the frangipani are derivative and timid. This is not a belligerent boast but a simple celebration of inevitability: that this flowering had to come.

On a heat-stoned afternoon in Port of Spain, some alley white with glare, with love vine spilling over a fence, palms and a hazed mountain appear around a corner to the evocation of Vaughn or Herbert's 'that shady city of palm-trees', or to the memory of a Hammond organ from a wooden chapel in Castries, where the congregation sang 'Jerusalem, the Golden'. It is hard for me to see such emptiness as desolation. It is that patience that is the width of Antillean life, and the secret is not to ask the wrong thing of it, not to demand of it an ambition it has no interest in. The traveller reads this as lethargy, as torpor.

Here there are not enough books, one says, no theatres, no museums, simply not enough to do. Yet, deprived of books, a man must fall back on thought, and out of thought, if he can learn to order it, will come the urge to record, and in extremity, if he has no means of recording, recitation, the ordering of memory which leads to meter, to commemoration. There can be virtues in deprivation, and certainly one virtue is salvation from a cascade of high mediocrity, since books are now not so much created as remade. Cities create a culture, and all we have are these magnified market towns, so what are the proportions of the ideal Caribbean city? A surrounding, accessible countryside with leafy suburbs, and if the city is lucky, behind it, spacious plains. Behind it, fine mountains; before it, an indigo sea. Spires would pin its center and around them would be leafy, shadowy parks. Pigeons would cross its sky in alphabetic patterns, carrying with them memories of a belief in augury, and at the heart of the city there would be horses, yes, horses, those animals last seen at the end of the 19th century drawing broughams and carriages with top-hatted citizens, horses that live in the present tense without elegiac echoes from their hooves, emerging from paddocks at the Queen's Park Savannah at sunrise, when mist is unthreading from the cool mountains above the roofs, and at the center of the city seasonally there would be races, so that citizens could roar at the speed and grace of these 19th-century animals. Its docks, not obscured by smoke or deafened by too much machinery, and above all, it would be so racially various that the cultures of the world—the Asiatic, the Mediterranean, the European, the African—would be represented in it, its humane variety more exciting than Joyce's Dublin. Its citizens would intermarry as they chose, from instinct, not tradition, until their children find it increasingly futile to trace their genealogy. It would not have too many avenues difficult or dangerous for pedestrians, its mercantile area would be a cacophony of accents, fragments of the old language that would be silenced immediately at five o'clock, its docks resolutely vacant on Sundays.

This is Port of Spain to me, a city ideal in its commercial and human proportions, where a citizen is a walker and not a pedestrian, and this is how Athens may have been before it became a cultural echo.

The finest silhouettes of Port of Spain are idealisations of the craftsman's handiwork, not of concrete and glass, but of baroque woodwork, each fantasy looking more like an involved drawing of itself than the actual building. Behind the city is the Caroni plain, with its villages, Indian prayer flags and fruit vendors' stalls along the highway over which ibises come like floating flags. Photogenic poverty! Postcard sadnesses! I am not re-creating Eden; I mean, by 'the Antilles', the reality of light, of work, of survival. I mean a house on the side of a country road, I mean the Caribbean Sea, whose smell is the smell of refreshing possibility as well as survival. Survival is the triumph of stubbornness, and spiritual stubbornness, a sublime stupidity, is what makes the occupation of poetry endure, when there are so many things that should make it futile. Those things added together can go under one collective noun: 'the world'.

This is the visible poetry of the Antilles, then. Survival.

If you wish to understand that consoling pity with which the islands were regarded, look at the tinted engravings of Antillean forests, with their proper palm trees, ferns and waterfalls. They have a civilizing decency, like botanical gardens, as if the sky were a glass ceiling under which a colonized vegetation is arranged for quiet walks and carriage rides. Those views are incised with a pathos that guides the engraver's tool and the topographer's pencil, and it is this pathos which, tenderly ironic, gave villages names like Felicity. A century looked at a landscape furious with vegetation in the wrong light and with the wrong eye. It is such pictures that are saddening rather than the tropics itself. These delicate engravings of sugar mills and harbours, of native women in costume, are seen as a part of History, that History which looked over the shoulder of the engraver and, later, the photographer. History can alter the eye and the moving hand to conform a view of itself; it can rename places for the nostalgia in an echo; it can temper the glare of tropical light to elegiac monotony in prose, the tone of judgment in Conrad, in the travel journals of Trollope.

These travellers carried with them the infection of their own malaise, and their prose reduced even the landscape to melancholia and self-contempt. Every endeavour is belittled as imitation, from architecture to music. There was this conviction in Froude that since History is based on achievement, and since the history of the Antilles was so genetically corrupt, so depressing in its cycles of massacres, slavery and indenture, a culture was inconceivable and nothing could ever be created in those ramshackle ports, those monotonously feudal sugar estates. Not only the light and salt of Antillean mountains defied this, but the demotic vigour and variety of their inhabitants. Stand close to a waterfall and you will stop hearing its roar. To be still in the 19th century, like horses, as Brodsky has written, may not be such a bad deal, and much of our life in the Antilles still seems to be in the rhythm of the last century, like the West Indian novel.

By writers even as refreshing as Graham Greene, the Caribbean is looked at with elegiac pathos, a prolonged sadness to which Levi-Strauss has supplied an epigraph: *Tristes Tropiques*. Their *tristesse* derives from an attitude to the Caribbean dusk, to rain, to uncontrollable vegetation, to the provincial ambition of Caribbean cities where brutal replicas of modern architecture dwarf the small houses and streets. The mood is understandable, the melancholy as contagious as the fever of a sunset, like the gold fronds of diseased coconut palms, but there is something alien and ultimately wrong in the way such a sadness, even a morbidity, is described by English, French, or some of our exiled writers. It relates to a misunderstanding of the light and the people on whom the light falls.

These writers describe the ambitions of our unfinished cities, their unrealized, homiletic conclusion, but the Caribbean city may conclude just at that point where it is satisfied with its own scale, just as Caribbean culture is not evolving but already shaped. Its proportions are not to be measured by the traveller or the exile, but by its own citizenry and architecture. To be told you are not yet a city or a culture requires this response. I am not your city or your culture. There might be less of *Tristes Tropiques* after that.

Here, on the raft of this dais, there is the sound of the applauding surf: our landscape, our history recognized, 'at last'. *At Last* is one of the first Caribbean books. It was written by the Victorian traveler Charles Kingsley. It is one of the early books to admit the Antillean landscape and its figures into English literature. I have never read it but gather that its tone is benign. The Antillean archipelago was there to be written about, not to write itself, by Trollope, by Patrick Leigh-Fermor, in the very tone in which I almost wrote about the village spectacle at Felicity, as a compassionate and beguiled outsider, distancing myself from Felicity village even while I was enjoying it. What is hidden cannot be loved. The traveller cannot love, since love is stasis and travel is motion. If he returns to what he loved in a landscape and stays there, he is no longer a traveller but in stasis and concentration, the lover of that particular part of earth, a native. So many people say they 'love the Caribbean', meaning that someday they plan to return for a visit but could never live there, the usual benign insult of the traveller, the tourist. These travellers, at their kindest, were devoted to the same patronage, the islands passing in profile, their vegetal luxury, their backwardness and poverty. Victorian prose dignified them. They passed by in beautiful profiles and were forgotten, like a vacation.

Alexis Saint-Legér Léger, whose writer's name is Saint-John Perse, was the first Antillean to win this prize for poetry. He was born in Guadeloupe and wrote in French, but before him, there was nothing as fresh and clear in feeling as those poems of his childhood, that of a privileged white child on an Antillean plantation, *Pour Feter une Enfance*, *Éloges* and later *Images a Crusoe*. At last, the first breeze on the page, salt-edged and self-renewing as the trade winds, the sound of pages and palm trees turning as 'the odour of coffee ascents the stairs'.

Caribbean genius is condemned to contradict itself. To celebrate Perse, we might be told, is to celebrate the old plantation system, to celebrate the beque or plantation rider, verandahs and mulatto servants, a white French language in a white pith helmet, to celebrate a rhetoric of patronage and hauteur; and even if Perse denied his origins, great writers often have this folly of trying to smother their source, we cannot deny him any more than we can the African Aime Cesaire. This is not accommodation, this is the ironic republic that is poetry, since, when I see cabbage palms moving their fronds at sunrise, I think they are reciting Perse.

The fragrant and privileged poetry that Perse composed to celebrate his white childhood and the recorded Indian music behind the brown young archers of Felicity, with the same cabbage palms against the same Antillean sky, pierce me equally. I feel the same poignancy of pride in the poems as in the faces. Why, given the history of the Antilles, should this be remarkable? The history of the world, by which of course we mean Europe, is a record of intertribal lacerations, of ethnic cleansings. At last, islands not written about but writing themselves! The palms and the Muslim minarets are Antillean exclamations. At last! the royal palms of Guadeloupe recite *Éloges* by heart.

Later, in *Anabase*, Perse assembled fragments of an imaginary epic, with the clicking teeth of frontier gates, barren wadis with the froth of poisonous lakes, horsemen burnoused in sandstorms, the opposite of cool Caribbean mornings, yet not necessarily a contrast any more than some young brown archer at Felicity, hearing the sacred text blared across the flagged field, with its battles and elephants and monkey-gods, in a contrast to the white child in Guadeloupe assembling fragments of his own epic from the lances of the cane fields, the estate carts and oxens, and the calligraphy of bamboo leaves from the ancient languages, Hindi, Chinese and Arabic, on the Antillean sky. From the *Ramayana* to Anabasis, from Guadeloupe to Trinidad, all that archaeology of fragments lying around, from the broken African kingdoms, from the crevasses of Canton, from Syria and Lebanon, vibrating not under the earth but in our raucous, demotic streets.

A boy with weak eyes skims a flat stone across the flat water of an Aegean inlet, and that ordinary action with the scything elbow contains the skipping lines of the *Iliad* and the *Odyssey*, and another child aims a bamboo arrow at a village festival, another hears the rustling march of cabbage palms in a Caribbean sunrise, and from that sound, with its fragments of tribal myth, the compact expedition of Perse's epic is launched, centuries and archipelagoes apart. For every poet it is always morning in the world. History a forgotten, insomniac night; History and elemental awe are always our early beginning, because the fate of poetry is to fall in love with the world, in spite of History.

There is a force of exultation, a celebration of luck, when a writer finds himself a witness to the early morning of a culture that is defining itself, branch by branch, leaf by leaf, in that self-defining dawn, which is why, especially at the edge of the sea, it is good to make a ritual of the sunrise. Then the noun, the 'Antilles' ripples like brightening water, and the sounds of leaves, palm fronds and birds are the sounds of a fresh dialect, the native tongue. The personal vocabulary, the individual melody whose meter is one's biography, joins in that sound, with any luck, and the body moves like a walking, a waking island.

This is the benediction that is celebrated, a fresh language and a fresh people, and this is the frightening duty owed.

I stand here in their name, if not their image—but also in the name of the dialect they exchange like the leaves of the trees whose names are suppler, greener, more morning-stirred than English—*laurier canelles, bois-flot, bois-canot*—or the valleys the trees mention—*Fond St Jacques, Matoonya, Forestier, Roseau, Mahaut*—or the empty beaches—*L'Anse Ivrogne, Case en Bas, Paradis*—all songs and histories in themselves, pronounced not in French—but in patois.

One rose hearing two languages, one of the trees, one of school children reciting in English:

> I am monarch of all I survey,
> My right there is none to dispute;
> From the centre all round to the sea
> I am lord of the fowl and the brute.
> Oh, solitude! where are the charms
> That sages have seen in thy face?
> Better dwell in the midst of alarms,
> Than reign in this horrible place ...

While in the country to the same meter, but to organic instruments, handmade violin, chac-chac and goatskin drum, a girl named Sensenne singing:

> Si mwen di 'ous ça fait mwen la peine
> 'Ous kai dire ça vrai.
> (If I told you that caused me pain
> You'll say, 'It's true.')
> Si mwen di 'ous ça pentetrait mwen
> 'Ous peut dire ça vrai
> (If I told you that you pierced my heart
> You'd say, 'It's true.')
> Ces mamailles actuellement
> Pas ka faire l'amour z'autres pour un rien.
> (Children nowadays
> Don't make love for nothing.)

It is not that History is obliterated by this sunrise. It is there in Antillean geography, in the vegetation itself. The sea sighs with the drowned from the Middle Passage, the butchery of its aborigines, Carib and Aruac and Taino, bleeds in the scarlet of the immortelle, and even the actions of surf on sand cannot erase the African memory, or the lances of cane as a green prison where indentured Asians, the ancestors of Felicity, are still serving time.

That is what I have read around me from boyhood, from the beginnings of poetry, the grace of effort. In the hard mahogany of woodcutters: faces, resinous men, charcoal burners; in a man with a cutlass cradled across his forearm, who stands on the verge with the usual anonymous khaki dog; in the extra clothes he put on this morning, when it was cold when he rose in the thinning dark to go and make his garden in the heights—the heights, the garden, being miles away from his house, but that is where he has his land—not to mention the fishermen, the footmen on trucks, groaning up mornes, all fragments of Africa originally but shaped and hardened and rooted now in the island's life, illiterate in the way leaves are illiterate; they do not read, they are there to be read, and if they are properly read, they create their own literature.

But in our tourist brochures the Caribbean is a blue pool into which the republic dangles the extended foot of Florida as inflated rubber islands bob and drinks with umbrellas float towards her on a raft. This is how the islands from the shame of necessity sell themselves; this is the seasonal erosion of their identity, that high-pitched repetition of the same images of service that cannot distinguish one island from the other, with a future of polluted marinas, land deals negotiated by ministers, and all of this conducted to the music of Happy Hour and the rictus of a smile. What is the earthly paradise for our visitors? Two weeks without rain and a mahogany tan, and, at sunset, local troubadours in straw hats and floral shirts beating 'Yellow Bird' and 'Banana Boat Song' to death. There is a territory wider than this—wider than the limits made by the map of an island—which is the illimitable sea and what it remembers.

All of the Antilles, every island, is an effort of memory; every mind, every racial biography culminating in amnesia and fog. Pieces of sunlight through the fog and sudden rainbows, *arcs-en-ciel*. That is the effort, the labour of the Antillean imagination, rebuilding its gods from bamboo frames, phrase by phrase.

Decimation from the Aruac downwards is the blasted root of Antillean history, and the benign blight that is tourism can infect all of those island nations, not gradually, but with imperceptible speed, until each rock is whitened by the guano of white-winged hotels, the arc and descent of progress.

Before it is all gone, before only a few valleys are left, pockets of an older life, before development turns every artist into an anthropologist or folklorist, there are still cherishable places, little valleys that do not echo with ideas, a simplicity of re-beginnings, not yet corrupted by the dangers of change. Not nostalgic sites but occluded sanctities as common and simple as their sunlight. Places as threatened by this prose as a headland is by the bulldozer or a sea almond grove by the surveyor's string, or from blight, the mountain laurel.

One last epiphany: A basic stone church in a thick valley outside Soufrière, the hills almost shoving the houses around into a brown river, a sunlight that looks oily on the leaves, a backward place, unimportant, and one now being corrupted into significance by this prose. The idea is not to hallow or invest the place with anything, not even memory. African children in Sunday frocks come down the ordinary concrete steps into the church, banana leaves hang and glisten, a truck is parked in a yard and old women totter towards the entrance. Here is where a real fresco should be painted, one without importance, but one with real faith, mapless, Historyless.

How quickly it could all disappear! And how it is beginning to drive us further into where we hope are impenetrable places, green secrets at the end of bad roads, headlands where the next view is not of a hotel but of some long beach without a figure and the hanging question of some fisherman's smoke at its far end. The Caribbean is not an idyll, not to its natives. They draw their working strength from it organically, like trees, like the sea almond or the spice laurel of the heights. Its peasantry and its fishermen are not there to be loved or even photographed; they are trees who sweat, and whose bark is filmed with salt, but every day on some island, rootless trees in suits are signing favourable tax breaks with entrepreneurs, poisoning the sea almond and the spice laurel of the mountains to their roots. A morning could come in which governments might ask what happened not merely to the forests and the bays but to a whole people.

They are here again, they recur, the faces, corruptible angels, smooth black skins and white eyes huge with an alarming joy, like those of the Asian children of Felicity at *Ramleela*; two different religions, two different continents, both filling the heart with the pain that is joy.

But what is joy without fear? The fear of selfishness that, here on this podium with the world paying attention not to them but to me, I should like to keep these simple joys inviolate, not because they are innocent, but because they are true. They are as true as when, in the grace of this gift, Perse heard the fragments of his own epic of Asia Minor in the rustling of cabbage palms, that inner Asia of the soul through which imagination wanders, if there is such a thing as imagination as opposed to the collective memory of our entire race, as true as the delight of that warrior-child who flew a bamboo arrow over the flags in the field at Felicity; and now as grateful a joy and a blessed fear as when a boy opened an exercise book and, within the discipline of its margins, framed stanzas that might contain the light of the hills on an island blest by obscurity, cherishing our insignificance.

Nadine Gordimer

Writing and Being
1991

Nadine Gordimer was a founding member of the Congress of South African Writers, and has lived for most of her life in her home country. She was born in 1923 in Springs, an East Rand mining town near Johannesburg, to Isidore and Nan Gordimer.

In its time a strong critic of the apartheid policy, Gordimer explores in much of her work the moral and psychological tensions caused by the racial division of her country. She won the Man Booker Prize in 1974 for her novel The Conservationist, *and her body of work is prodigious. It includes fourteen novels, among them* A Guest of Honour, Burger's Daughter, July's People, A Sport of Nature, My Son's Story *and her most recent,* None to Accompany Me; *thirteen short story collections, with* Loot and Other Stories *published in 2003; and five volumes of non-fiction, including* The Essential Gesture, On the Mines *and* The Black Interpreters. *She has received numerous honorary degrees, from institutions such as Yale, Harvard, Cambridge and the universities of Cape Town and Witwatersrand, as well as France's* Commandeur de l'Ordre des Arts et des Lettres.

Gordimer, 'through her magnificent epic writing has—in the words of Alfred Nobel—been of very great benefit to humanity'.

In the beginning was the Word. The Word was with God, signified God's Word, the word that was Creation. But over the centuries of human culture the word has taken on other meanings, secular as well as religious. To have the word has come to be synonymous with ultimate authority, with prestige, with awesome, sometimes dangerous persuasion, to have Prime Time, a TV talk show, to have the gift of the gab as well as that of speaking in tongues. The word flies through space, it is bounced from satellites, now nearer than it has ever been to the heaven from which it was believed to have come. But its most significant transformation occurred for me and my kind long ago, when it was first scratched on a stone tablet or traced on papyrus, when it materialized from sound to spectacle, from being heard to being read as a series of signs, and then a script; and traveled through time from parchment to Gutenberg. For this is the genesis story of the writer. It is the story that wrote her or him into being.

It was, strangely, a double process, creating at the same time both the writer and the very purpose of the writer as a mutation in the agency of human culture. It was both ontogenesis as the origin and development of an individual being, and the adaptation, in the nature of that individual, specifically to the exploration of ontogenesis, the origin and development of the individual being. For we writers are evolved for that task. Like the prisoners incarcerated with the jaguar in Borges' story[1], 'The God's Script', who was trying to read, in a ray of light which fell only once a day, the meaning of being from the marking on the creature's pelt, we spend our lives attempting to interpret through the word the readings we take in the societies, the world of which we are part. It is in this sense, this inextricable, ineffable participation, that writing is always and at once an exploration of self and of the world; of individual and collective being.

Being here.

Humans, the only self-regarding animals, blessed or cursed with this torturing higher faculty, have always wanted to know why. And this is not just the great ontological question of why we are here at all, for which religions and philosophies have tried to answer conclusively for various peoples at various times, and science tentatively attempts dazzling bits of explanation such as that we are perhaps going to die out in our millennia, like dinosaurs, without having developed the necessary comprehension to understand as a whole. Since humans became self-regarding they have sought, as well, explanations for the common phenomena of procreation, death, the cycle of seasons, the earth, sea, wind and stars, sun and moon, plenty and disaster. With myth, the writer's ancestors, the oral storytellers, began to feel out and formulate these mysteries, using the elements of daily life—observable reality—and the faculty of the imagination—the power of projection into the hidden—to make stories.

Roland Barthes[2] asks, 'What is characteristic of myth?' And answers: 'To transform a meaning into form.' Myths are stories that mediate in this way between the known and unknown. Claude Levi-Strauss[3] wittily de-mythologizes myth as a genre between a fairytale and a detective story. Being here; we don't know who-dun-it. But something satisfying, if not the answer, can be invented. Myth was the mystery plus the fantasy—gods, anthropomorphized animals and birds, chimera, phantasmagorical creatures—that posits out of the imagination some sort of explanation for the mystery. Humans and their fellow creatures were the materiality of the story, but as Nikos Kazantzakis[4] once wrote, 'Art is the representation not of the body but of the forces which created the body.'

There are many proven explanations for natural phenomena now; and there are new questions of being arising out of some of the answers. For this reason, the genre of myth has never been entirely abandoned, although we are inclined to think of it as archaic. If it dwindled to the children's bedtime tale in some societies, in parts of the world protected by forests or deserts from international megaculture it has continued, alive, to offer art as a system of mediation between the individual and being. And it has made a whirling comeback out of Space, an Icarus in the avatar of Batman and his kind, who never fall into the ocean of failure to deal with the gravity forces of life. These new myths, however, do not seek so much to enlighten and provide some sort of answers as to distract, to provide a fantasy escape route for people who no longer want to face even the hazard of answers to the terrors of their existence. (Perhaps it is the positive knowledge that humans now possess the means to destroy their whole planet, the fear that they have in this way themselves become the gods, dreadfully charged with their own continued existence, that has made comic-book and movie myth escapist.) The forces of being remain. They are what the writer, as distinct from the contemporary popular mythmaker, still engage today, as myth in its ancient form attempted to do.

How writers have approached this engagement and continue to experiment with it has been and is, perhaps more than ever, the study of literary scholars. The writer in relation to the nature of perceivable reality and what is beyond—imperceivable reality—is the basis for all these studies, no matter what resulting concepts are labeled, and no matter in what categorized microfiles writers are stowed away for the annals of literary historiography. Reality is constructed out of many elements and entities, seen and unseen, expressed, and left unexpressed for breathing-space in the mind. Yet from what is regarded as old-hat psychological analysis to modernism and postmodernism, structuralism and post-structuralism, all literary studies are aimed at the same end: to pin down to a consistency (and what is consistency if not the principle hidden within the riddle?); to make definitive through methodology the writer's grasp at the forces of being. But life is aleatory in itself; being is constantly pulled and shaped this way and that by circumstances and different levels of consciousness. There is no pure state of being, and it follows that there is no pure text, 'real' text, totally incorporating the aleatory. It surely cannot be reached by any critical methodology, however interesting the attempt. To deconstruct a text is in a way a contradiction, since to deconstruct it is to make another construction out of the pieces, as Roland Barthes[5] does so fascinatingly, and admits to, in his linguistic and semantical dissection of Balzac's story, 'Sarrasine'. So the literary scholars end up being some kind of storyteller, too.

Perhaps there is no other way of reaching some understanding of being than through art? Writers themselves don't analyse what they do; to analyse would be to look down while crossing a canyon on a tightrope. To say this is not to mystify the process of writing but to make an image out of the intense inner concentration the writer must have to cross the chasms of the aleatory and make them the word's own, as an explorer plants a flag. Yeats' inner 'lonely impulse of delight' in the pilot's solitary flight, and his 'terrible beauty' born of mass uprising, both opposed and conjoined; E. M. Forster's modest 'only connect'; Joyce's chosen, wily 'silence, cunning and exile'; more contemporary, Gabriel García Márquez's labyrinth in which power over others, in the person of Simon Bolivar, is led to the thrall of the only unassailable power, death—these are some examples of the writer's endlessly varied ways of approaching the state of being through the word. Any writer of any worth at all hopes to play only a pocket-torch of light— and rarely, through genius, a sudden flambeau—into the bloody yet beautiful labyrinth of human experience, of being.

Anthony Burgess[6] once gave a summary definition of literature as 'the aesthetic exploration of the world'. I would say that writing only begins there, for the exploration of much beyond, which nevertheless only aesthetic means can express.

How does the writer become one, having been given the word? I do not know if my own beginnings have any particular interest. No doubt they have much in common with those of others, have been described too often before as a result of this yearly assembly before which a writer stands. For myself, I have said that nothing factual that I write or say will be as truthful as my fiction. The life, the opinions, are not the work, for it is in the tension between standing apart and being involved that the imagination transforms both. Let me give some minimal account of myself. I am what I suppose would be called a natural writer. I did not make any decision to become one. I did not, at the beginning, expect to earn a living by being read. I wrote as a child out of the joy of apprehending life through my senses—the look and scent and feel of things; and soon out of the emotions that puzzled me or raged within me and which took form, found some enlightenment, solace and delight, shaped in the written word. There is a little Kafka[7] parable that goes like this:

> I have three dogs: Hold-him, Seize-him and Nevermore. Hold-him and Seize-him are ordinary little Schipperkes and nobody would notice them if they were alone. But there is Nevermore, too. Nevermore is a mongrel Great Dane and has an appearance that centuries of the most careful breeding could never have produced. Nevermore is a gypsy.

In the small South African gold-mining town where I was growing up I was Nevermore the mongrel (although I could scarcely have been described as a Great Dane ...) in whom the accepted characteristics of the townspeople could not be traced. I was the Gypsy, tinkering with words second-hand, mending my own efforts at writing by learning from what I read. For my school was the local library. Proust, Chekhov and Dostoevsky, to name only a few to whom I owe my existence as a writer, were my professors. In that period of my life, yes, I was evidence of the theory that books are made out of other books ... But I did not remain so for long, nor do I believe any potential writer could.

With adolescence comes the first reaching out to otherness through the drive of sexuality. For most children, from then on the faculty of the imagination, manifest in play, is lost in the focus on daydreams of desire and love, but for those who are going to be artists of one kind or another the first life-crisis after that of birth does something else in addition: the imagination gains range and extends by the subjective flex of new and turbulent emotions. There are new perceptions. The writer begins to be able to enter into other lives. The process of standing apart and being involved has come.

Unknowingly, I had been addressing myself on the subject of being, whether, as in my first stories, there was a child's contemplation of death and murder in the necessity to finish off, with a death blow, a dove mauled by a cat, or whether there was wondering dismay and early consciousness of racism that came of my walk to school, when on the way I passed storekeepers, themselves East European immigrants kept lowest in the ranks of the Anglo-Colonial social scale for whites in the mining town, roughly those whom colonial society ranked lowest of all, discounted as less than human—the black miners who were the stores' customers. Only many years later was I to realize that if I had been a child in that category—black—I might not have become a writer at all, since the library that made this possible for me was not open to any black child. For my formal schooling was sketchy, at best.

To address oneself to others begins a writer's next stage of development. To publish to anyone who would read what I wrote. That was my natural, innocent assumption of what publication meant, and it has not changed, that is what it means to me today, in spite of my awareness that most people refuse to believe that a writer does not have a particular audience in mind; and my other awareness: of the temptations, conscious and unconscious, which lure the writer into keeping a corner of the eye on who will take offense, who will approve what is on the page—a temptation that, like Eurydice's straying glance, will lead the writer back into the Shades of a destroyed talent.

The alternative is not the malediction of the ivory tower, another destroyer of creativity. Borges once said he wrote for his friends and to pass the time. I think this was an irritated, flippant response to the crass question—often an accusation—'For whom do you write?', just as Sartre's admonition that there are times when a writer should cease to write, and act upon being only in another way, was given in the frustration of an unresolved conflict between distress at injustice in the world and the knowledge that what he knew how to do best was write. Both Borges and Sartre, from their totally different extremes of denying literature a social purpose, were certainly perfectly aware that it has its implicit and unalterable social role in exploring the state of being, from which all other roles, personal among friends, public at the protest demonstration, derive. Borges was not writing for his friends, for he published and we all have received the bounty of his work. Sartre did not stop writing, although he stood at the barricades in 1968.

The question of for whom do we write nevertheless plagues the writer, a tin can attached to the tail of every work published. Principally it jangles the inference of tendentiousness as praise or denigration. In this context, Camus[8] dealt with the question best. He said that he liked individuals who take sides more than literatures that do. 'One either serves the whole of man or does not serve him at all. And if man needs bread and justice, and if what has to be done must be done to serve this need, he also needs pure beauty which is the bread of his heart.' So Camus called for 'Courage in and talent in one's work.' And Márquez[9] redefined tender fiction thus: The best way a writer can serve a revolution is to write as well as he can.

I believe that these two statements might be the credo for all of us who write. They do not resolve the conflicts that have come, and will continue to come, to contemporary writers. But they state plainly an honest possibility of doing so, they turn the face of the writer squarely to her and his existence, the reason to be, as a writer, and the reason to be, as a responsible human, acting, like any other, within a social context.

Being here: in a particular time and place. That is the existential position with particular implications for literature. Czeslaw Milosz[10] once wrote the cry: 'What is poetry which does not serve nations or people?' and Brecht[11] wrote of a time when 'to speak of trees is almost a crime'. Many of us have had such despairing thoughts while living and writing through such times, in such places, and Sartre's solution makes no sense in a world where writers were—and still are—censored and forbidden to write, where, far from abandoning the word, lives were and are at risk in smuggling it, on scraps of paper, out of prisons. The state of being whose ontogenesis we explore has overwhelmingly included such experiences. Our approaches, in Nikos Kazantzakis'[12] words, have to 'make the decision which harmonizes with the fearsome rhythm of our time'.

Some of us have seen our books lie for years unread in our own countries, banned, and we have gone on writing. Many writers have been imprisoned. Looking at Africa alone— Soyinka, Ngugi wa Thiong'o, Jack Mapanje, in their countries, and in my own country, South Africa, Jeremy Cronin, Mongane Wally Serote, Breyten Breytenbach, Dennis Brutus, Jaki Seroke: all these went to prison for the courage shown in their lives, and have continued to take the right, as poets, to speak of trees. Many of the greats, from Thomas Mann to Chinua Achebe, cast out by political conflict and oppression in different countries, have endured the trauma of exile, from which some never recover as writers, and some do not survive at all. I think of the South Africans, Can Themba, Alex la Guma, Nat Nakasa, Todd Matshikiza. And some writers, over half a century from Joseph Roth to Milan Kundera, have had to publish new works first in the word that is not their own, a foreign language.

Then in 1988 the fearsome rhythm of our time quickened in an unprecedented frenzy to which the writer was summoned to submit the word. In the broad span of modern times since the Enlightenment writers have suffered opprobrium, bannings and even exile for other than political reasons. Flaubert dragged into court for indecency, over *Madame Bovary*, Strindberg arraigned for blasphemy, over *Marrying*, Lawrence's *Lady Chatterley's Lover* banned—there have been many examples of so-called offence against hypocritical bourgeois mores, just as there have been of treason against political dictatorships. But in a period when it would be unheard of for countries such as France, Sweden and Britain to bring such charges against freedom of expression, there has risen a force that takes its appalling authority from something far more widespread than social mores, and far more powerful than the power of any single political regime. The edict of a world religion has sentenced a writer to death.

For more than three years, now, wherever he is hidden, wherever he might go, Salman Rushdie has existed under the Muslim pronouncement upon him of the fatwa. There is no asylum for him anywhere. Every morning when this writer sits down to write, he does not know if he will live through the day; he does not know whether the page will ever be filled. Salman Rushdie happens to be a brilliant writer, and the novel for which he is being pilloried, *The Satanic Verses*, is an innovative exploration of one of the most intense experiences of being in our era, the individual personality in transition between two cultures brought together in a postcolonial world. All is re-examined through the refraction of the imagination; the meaning of sexual and filial love, the rituals of social acceptance, the meaning of a formative religious faith for individuals removed from its subjectivity by circumstance opposing different systems of belief, religious and secular, in a different context of living. His novel is a true mythology. But although he has done for the postcolonial consciousness in Europe what Günter Grass did for the post-Nazi one with *The Tin Drum* and *Dog Years*, perhaps even has tried to approach what Beckett did for our existential anguish in *Waiting For Godot*, the level of his achievement should not matter. Even if he were a mediocre writer, his situation is the terrible concern of every fellow writer for, apart from his personal plight, what implications, what new threat against the carrier of the word does it bring? It should be the concern of individuals and above all, of governments and human rights organisations all over the world. With dictatorships apparently vanquished, this murderous new dictate invoking the power of international terrorism in the name of a great and respected religion should and can be dealt with only by democratic governments and the United Nations as an offence against humanity.

I return from the horrific singular threat to those that have been general for writers of this century now in its final, summing-up decade. In repressive regimes anywhere—whether in what was the Soviet bloc, Latin America, Africa, China—most imprisoned writers have been shut away for their activities as citizens striving for liberation against the oppression of the general society to which they belong. Others have been condemned by repressive regimes for serving society by writing as well as they can; for this aesthetic venture of ours becomes subversive when the shameful secrets of our times are explored deeply, with the artist's rebellious integrity to the state of being manifest in life around her or him; then the writer's themes and characters inevitably are formed by the pressures and distortions of that society as the life of the fisherman is determined by the power of the sea.

There is a paradox. In retaining this integrity, the writer sometimes must risk both the state's indictment of treason, and the liberation forces' complaint of lack of blind commitment. As a human being, no writer can stoop to the lie of Manichean 'balance'. The devil always has lead in his shoes, when placed on his side of the scale. Yet, to paraphrase coarsely Márquez's dictum given by him both as a writer and a fighter for justice, the writer must take the right to explore, warts and all, both the enemy and the beloved comrade in arms, since only a try for the truth makes sense of being, only a try for the truth edges towards justice just ahead of Yeats' beast slouching to be born. In literature, from life,

> we page through each other's faces
> we read each looking eye
> ... It has taken lives to be able to do so.

These are the words of the South African poet and fighter for justice and peace in our country, Mongane Serote.[13]

The writer is of service to humankind only insofar as the writer uses the word even against his or her own loyalties, trusts the state of being, as it is revealed, to hold somewhere in its complexity filaments of the cord of truth, able to be bound together, here and there, in art: trusts the state of being to yield somewhere fragmentary phrases of truth, which is the final word of words, never changed by our stumbling efforts to spell it out and write it down, never changed by lies, by semantic sophistry, by the dirtying of the word for the purposes of racism, sexism, prejudice, domination, the glorification of destruction, the curses and the praise-songs.

---

1 'The God's Script' from *Labyrinths & Other Writings* by Jorge Luis Borges, translator unknown, edited by Donald H. Yates & James E. Kirby, Penguin Modern Classics, page 71.

2 *Mythologies* by Roland Barthes, translated by Annette Lavers, Hill & Wang, page 131.

3 *Historie de Lynx* by Claude Lévi-Strauss, '... je les situais à mi-chemin entre le conte de fées et le roman policier.' Plon, page 13.

4 *Report to Greco* by Nikos Kazantzakis, Faber & Faber, page 150.

5 *S/Z* by Roland Barthes, translated by Richard Miller, Jonathan Cape.
6 London *Observer* review, 19/4/81, Anthony Burgess.
7 The Third Octavo Notebook from *Wedding Preparations in the Country* by Franz Kafka, Definitive Edition, Secker & Warburg.
8 *Carnets* 1942–5 by Albert Camus.
9 Gabriel García Márquez, in an interview; my notes do not give the journal or date.
10 'Dedication' from *Selected Poems* by Czeslaw Milosz, The Ecco Press.
11 'To Posterity' from *Selected Poems* by Bertolt Brecht, translated by H.-R.-Hays, Grove Press, page 173.
12 *Report to Greco* by Nikos Kazantzakis, Faber & Faber.
13 *A Tough Tale* by Mongane Wally Serote, Kliptown Books.

Octavio Paz

In Search of the Present
1990

Octavio Paz, poet and essayist, was born in Mexico City in 1914. His paternal grandfather was a prominent liberal intellectual and his father a political journalist who took part in the agrarian uprisings led by Emiliano Zapata. Paz wrote from an early age, and his first collection of poetry, Luna Silvestre *(Rustic Moon), was published when he was nineteen.*

Paz entered the Mexican diplomatic service in 1945 and became the Mexican ambassador to India in 1962. He resigned from the service six years later in protest at the government's violent suppression of student demonstrations in Tlatelolco during the Olympic Games in Mexico. Paz then worked as an editor and publisher, founding two important magazines dedicated to arts and politics, Plural *(1971–76) and* Vuelta, *which began in 1976.*

Paz's work was nourished by the belief that poetry is 'the secret religion of the modern age', able to revolutionise the world. His early poetry was influenced by surrealism, Marxism, existentialism and the Hindu and Buddhist religions, while his later work often explored the work of artists such as Joan Miró, Marcel Duchamp and Roberto Matta. He was a prolific writer who wrote many essays on poetics, literary and art criticism, as well as Mexican history, politics and culture.

The Academy praised Paz 'for impassioned writing with wide horizons, characterized by sensuous intelligence and humanistic integrity'. He died in 1998.

I begin with two words that all men have uttered since the dawn of humanity: thank you. The word gratitude has equivalents in every language and in each tongue the range of meanings is abundant. In the Romance languages this breadth spans the spiritual and the physical, from the divine grace conceded to men to save them from error and death, to the bodily grace of the dancing girl or the feline leaping through the undergrowth. Grace means pardon, forgiveness, favour, benefice, inspiration; it is a form of address, a pleasing style of speaking or painting, a gesture expressing politeness, and, in short, an act that reveals spiritual goodness. Grace is gratuitous; it is a gift. The person who receives it, the favoured one, is grateful for it; if he is not base, he expresses gratitude. That is what I am doing at this very moment with these weightless words. I hope my emotion compensates their weightlessness. If each of my words were a drop of water, you would see through them and glimpse what I feel: gratitude, acknowledgment. And also an indefinable mixture of fear, respect and surprise at finding myself here before you, in this place which is the home of both Swedish learning and world literature.

Languages are vast realities that transcend those political and historical entities we call nations. The European languages we speak in the Americas illustrate this. The special position of our literatures when compared to those of England, Spain, Portugal and France depends precisely on this fundamental fact: they are literatures written in transplanted tongues. Languages are born and grow from the native soil, nourished by a common history. The European languages were rooted out from their native soil and their own tradition, and then planted in an unknown and unnamed world: they took root in the new lands and, as they grew within the societies of America, they were transformed. They are the same plant yet also a different plant. Our literatures did not passively accept the changing fortunes of the transplanted languages: they participated in the process and even accelerated it. They very soon ceased to be mere transatlantic reflections: at times they have been the negation of the literatures of Europe; more often, they have been a reply.

In spite of these oscillations the link has never been broken. My classics are those of my language and I consider myself to be a descendant of Lope and Quevedo, as any Spanish writer would ... yet I am not a Spaniard. I think that most writers of Spanish America, as well as those from the United States, Brazil and Canada, would say the same as regards the English, Portuguese and French traditions. To understand more clearly the special position of writers in the Americas, we should think of the dialogue maintained by Japanese, Chinese or Arabic writers with the different literatures of Europe. It is a dialogue that cuts across multiple languages and civilizations. Our dialogue, on the other hand, takes place within the same language. We are Europeans yet we are not Europeans. What are we then? It is difficult to define what we are, but our works speak for us.

In the field of literature, the great novelty of the present century has been the appearance of the American literatures. The first to appear was that of the English-speaking part and then, in the second half of the twentieth century, that of Latin America in its two great branches: Spanish America and Brazil. Although they are very different, these three literatures have one common feature: the conflict, which is more ideological than literary, between the cosmopolitan and nativist tendencies, between Europeanism and Americanism. What is the legacy of this dispute? The polemics have disappeared; what remain are the works. Apart from this general resemblance, the differences between the three literatures are multiple and profound. One of them belongs more to history than to literature: the development of Anglo-American literature coincides with the rise of the United States as a world power whereas the rise of our literature coincides with the political and social misfortunes and upheavals of our nations. This proves once more the limitations of social and historical determinism: the decline of empires and social disturbances sometimes coincide with moments of artistic and literary splendour. Li-Po and Tu Fu witnessed the fall of the Tang dynasty; Velázquez painted for Felipe IV; Seneca and Lucan were contemporaries and also victims of Nero. Other differences are of a literary nature and apply more to particular works than to the character of each literature. But can we say that literatures have a *character*? Do they possess a set of shared features that distinguish them from other literatures? I doubt it. A literature is not defined by some fanciful, intangible character; it is a society of unique works united by relations of opposition and affinity.

The first basic difference between Latin-American and Anglo-American literature lies in the diversity of their origins. Both begin as projections of Europe. The projection of an island in the case of North America; that of a peninsula in our case. Two regions that are geographically, historically and culturally eccentric. The origins of North America are in England and the Reformation; ours are in Spain, Portugal and the Counter-Reformation. For the case of Spanish America I should briefly mention what distinguishes Spain from other European countries, giving it a particularly original historical identity. Spain is no less eccentric than England but its eccentricity is of a different kind. The eccentricity of the English is insular and is characterized by isolation: an eccentricity that excludes. Hispanic eccentricity is peninsular and consists of the coexistence of different civilisations and different pasts: an inclusive eccentricity. In what would later be Catholic Spain, the Visigoths professed the heresy of Arianism, and we could also speak about the centuries of domination by Arabic civilisation, the influence of Jewish thought, the Reconquest and other characteristic features.

Hispanic eccentricity is reproduced and multiplied in America, especially in those countries such as Mexico and Peru, where ancient and splendid civilisations had existed. In Mexico, the Spaniards encountered history as well as geography. That history is still alive: it is a present rather than a past. The temples and gods of pre-Columbian Mexico are a pile of ruins, but the spirit that breathed life into that world has not disappeared; it speaks to us in the hermetic language of myth, legend, forms of social coexistence, popular art, customs. Being a Mexican writer means listening to the voice of that present, that presence. Listening to it, speaking with it, deciphering it: expressing it ... After this brief digression we may be able to perceive the peculiar relation that simultaneously binds us to and separates us from the European tradition.

This consciousness of being separate is a constant feature of our spiritual history. Separation is sometimes experienced as a wound that marks an internal division, an anguished awareness that invites self-examination; at other times it appears as a challenge, a spur that incites us to action, to go forth and encounter others and the outside world. It is true that the feeling of separation is universal and not peculiar to Spanish Americans. It is born at the very moment of our birth: as we are wrenched from the Whole we fall into an alien land. This experience becomes a wound that never heals. It is the unfathomable depth of every man; all our ventures and exploits, all our acts and dreams, are bridges designed to overcome the separation and reunite us with the world and our fellow-beings. Each man's life and the collective history of mankind can thus be seen as attempts to reconstruct the original situation. An unfinished and endless cure for our divided condition. But it is not my intention to provide yet another description of this feeling. I am simply stressing the fact that for us this existential condition expresses itself in historical terms. It thus becomes an awareness of our history. How and when does this feeling appear and how is it transformed into consciousness? The reply to this double-edged question can be given in the form of a theory or a personal testimony. I prefer the latter: there are many theories and none is entirely convincing.

The feeling of separation is bound up with the oldest and vaguest of my memories: the first cry, the first scare. Like every child I built emotional bridges in the imagination to link me to the world and to other people. I lived in a town on the outskirts of Mexico City, in an old dilapidated house that had a jungle-like garden and a great room full of books. First games and first lessons. The garden soon became the centre of my world; the library, an enchanted cave. I used to read and play with my cousins and schoolmates. There was a fig tree, temple of vegetation, four pine trees, three ash trees, a nightshade, a pomegranate tree, wild grass and prickly plants that produced purple grazes. Adobe walls. Time was elastic; space was a spinning wheel. All time, past or future, real or imaginary, was pure presence. Space transformed itself ceaselessly. The beyond was here, all was here: a valley, a mountain, a distant country, the neighbours' patio. Books with pictures, especially history books, eagerly leafed through, supplied images of deserts and jungles, palaces and hovels, warriors and princesses, beggars and kings. We were shipwrecked with Sinbad and with Robinson, we fought with d'Artagnan, we took Valencia with the Cid. How I would have liked to stay forever on the Isle of Calypso! In summer the green branches of the fig tree would sway like the sails of a caravel or a pirate ship. High up on the mast, swept by the wind, I could make out islands and continents, lands that vanished as soon as they became tangible. The world was limitless yet it was always within reach; time was a pliable substance that weaved an unbroken present.

When was the spell broken? Gradually rather than suddenly. It is hard to accept being betrayed by a friend, deceived by the woman we love, or that the idea of freedom is the mask of a tyrant. What we call 'finding out' is a slow and tricky process because we ourselves are the accomplices of our errors and deceptions. Nevertheless, I can remember fairly clearly an incident that was the first sign, although it was quickly forgotten. I must have been about six when one of my cousins who was a little older showed me a North American magazine with a photograph of soldiers marching along a huge avenue, probably in New York. 'They've returned from the war,' she said. This handful of words disturbed me, as if they foreshadowed the end of the world or the Second Coming of Christ. I vaguely knew that somewhere far away a war had ended a few years earlier and that the soldiers were marching to celebrate their victory. For me, that war had taken place in another time, not here and now. The photo refuted me. I felt literally dislodged from the present.

From that moment time began to fracture more and more. And there was a plurality of spaces. The experience repeated itself more and more frequently. Any piece of news, a harmless phrase, the headline in a newspaper: everything proved the outside world's existence and my own unreality. I felt that the world was splitting and that I did not inhabit the present. My present was disintegrating: real time was somewhere else. My time, the time of the garden, the fig tree, the games with friends, the drowsiness among the plants at three in the afternoon under the sun, a fig torn open (black and red like a live coal but one that is sweet and fresh): this was a fictitious time. In spite of what my senses told me, the time from over there, belonging to the others, was the real one, the time of the real present. I accepted the inevitable: I became an adult. That was how my expulsion from the present began.

It may seem paradoxical to say that we have been expelled from the present, but it is a feeling we have all had at some moment. Some of us experienced it first as a condemnation, later transformed into consciousness and action. The search for the present is neither the pursuit of an earthly paradise nor that of a timeless eternity: it is the search for a real reality. For us, as Spanish Americans, the real present was not in our own countries: it was the time lived by others, by the English, the

French and the Germans. It was the time of New York, Paris, London. We had to go and look for it and bring it back home. These years were also the years of my discovery of literature. I began writing poems. I did not know what made me write them: I was moved by an inner need that is difficult to define. Only now have I understood that there was a secret relationship between what I have called my expulsion from the present and the writing of poetry. Poetry is in love with the instant and seeks to relive it in the poem, thus separating it from sequential time and turning it into a fixed present. But at that time I wrote without wondering why I was doing it. I was searching for the gateway to the present: I wanted to belong to my time and to my century. A little later this obsession became a fixed idea: I wanted to be a modern poet. My search for modernity had begun.

What is modernity? First of all it is an ambiguous term: there are as many types of modernity as there are societies. Each has its own. The word's meaning is uncertain and arbitrary, like the name of the period that precedes it, the Middle Ages. If we are modern when compared to medieval times, are we perhaps the Middle Ages of a future modernity? Is a name that changes with time a real name? Modernity is a word in search of its meaning. Is it an idea, a mirage or a moment of history? Are we the children of modernity or its creators? Nobody knows for sure. It doesn't matter much: we follow it, we pursue it. For me at that time modernity was fused with the present or rather produced it: the present was its last supreme flower. My case is neither unique nor exceptional: from the Symbolist period, all modern poets have chased after that magnetic and elusive figure that fascinates them. Baudelaire was the first. He was also the first to touch her and discover that she is nothing but time that crumbles in one's hands. I am not going to relate my adventures in pursuit of modernity: they are not very different from those of other twentieth-century poets.

Modernity has been a universal passion. Since 1850 she has been our goddess and our demoness. In recent years, there has been an attempt to exorcise her and there has been much talk of 'postmodernism'. But what is postmodernism if not an even more modern modernity?

For us, as Latin Americans, the search for poetic modernity runs historically parallel to the repeated attempts to modernize our countries. This tendency begins at the end of the eighteenth century and includes Spain herself. The United States was born into modernity and by 1830 was already, as de Tocqueville observed, the womb of the future; we were born at a moment when Spain and Portugal were moving away from modernity. This is why there was frequent talk of 'Europeanising' our countries: the modern was outside and had to be imported. In Mexican history this process begins just before the War of Independence. Later it became a great ideological and political debate that passionately divided Mexican society during the nineteenth century. One event was to call into question not the legitimacy of the reform movement but the way in which it had been implemented: the Mexican Revolution. Unlike its twentieth-century counterparts, the Mexican Revolution was not really the expression of a vaguely utopian ideology but rather the explosion of a reality that had been historically and psychologically repressed. It was not the work of a group of ideologists intent on introducing principles derived from a political theory; it was a popular uprising that unmasked what was hidden. For this very reason it was more of a revelation than a revolution. Mexico was searching for the present outside only to find it within, buried but alive. The search for modernity led us to discover our antiquity, the hidden face of the nation. I am not sure whether this unexpected historical lesson has been learnt by all: between tradition and modernity there is a bridge. When they are mutually isolated, tradition stagnates and modernity vaporises; when in conjunction, modernity breathes life into tradition, while the latter replies with depth and gravity.

The search for poetic modernity was a Quest, in the allegorical and chivalric sense this word had in the twelfth century. I did not find any Grail although I did cross several *waste lands* visiting castles of mirrors and camping among ghostly tribes. But I did discover the modern tradition. For modernity is not a poetic school but a lineage, a family dispersed over several continents and which for two centuries has survived many sudden changes and misfortunes: public indifference, isolation and tribunals in the name of religious, political, academic and sexual orthodoxy. Because it is a tradition and not a doctrine, it has been able to persist and to change at the same time. This is also why it is so diverse: each poetic adventure is distinct and each poet has sown a different plant in the miraculous forest of speaking trees. Yet if the works are diverse and each route is distinct, what is it that unites all these poets? Not an aesthetic but a search. My search was not fanciful, even though the idea of modernity is a mirage, a bundle of reflections. One day I discovered I was going back to the starting point instead of advancing: the search for modernity was a descent to the origins. Modernity led me to the source of my beginning, to my antiquity. Separation had now become reconciliation. I thus found out that the poet is a pulse in the rhythmic flow of generations.

THE IDEA OF modernity is a by-product of our conception of history as a unique and linear process of succession. Although its origins are in Judaeo-Christianity, it breaks with Christian doctrine. In Christianity, the cyclical time of pagan cultures is supplanted by unrepeatable history, something that has a beginning and will have an end. Sequential time was the profane time of history, an arena for the actions of fallen men, yet still governed by a sacred time which had neither beginning nor end. After Judgment Day there will be no future either in heaven or in hell. In the realm of eternity there is no succession because everything is. Being triumphs over becoming. The now time, our concept of time, is linear like that of Christianity but open to infinity with no reference to Eternity. Ours is the time of profane history, an irreversible and perpetually unfinished time that marches towards the future and not towards its end. History's sun is the future and Progress is the name of this movement towards the future.

Christians see the world, or what used to be called the *siècle* or worldly life, as a place of trial: souls can be either lost or saved in this world. In the new conception the historical subject is not the individual soul but the human race, sometimes viewed as a whole and sometimes through a chosen group that represents it: the developed nations of the West, the proletariat, the white race or some other entity. The pagan and Christian philosophical tradition had exalted Being as changeless perfection overflowing with plenitude; we adore Change, the motor of progress and the model for our societies. Change articulates itself in two privileged ways: as evolution and as revolution. The trot and the leap. Modernity is the spearhead of historical movement, the incarnation of evolution or revolution, the two faces of progress. Finally, progress takes place thanks to the dual action of science and technology, applied to the realm of nature and to the use of her immense resources.

Modern man has defined himself as a historical being. Other societies chose to define themselves in terms of values and ideas different from change: the Greeks venerated the *polis* and the circle yet were unaware of progress; like all the Stoics, Seneca was much concerned about the eternal return; Saint Augustine believed that the end of the world was imminent; Saint Thomas constructed a scale of the degrees of being, linking the smallest creature to the Creator, and so on. One after the other these ideas and beliefs were abandoned. It seems to me that the same decline is beginning to affect our idea of Progress and, as a result, our vision of time, of history and of ourselves. We are witnessing the twilight of the future. The decline of the idea of modernity and the popularity of a notion as dubious as that of 'postmodernism' are phenomena that affect not only literature and the arts: we are experiencing the crisis of the essential ideas and beliefs that have guided mankind for over two centuries. I have dealt with this matter at length elsewhere. Here I can only offer a brief summary.

In the first place, the concept of a process open to infinity and synonymous with endless progress has been called into question. I need hardly mention what everybody knows: natural resources are finite and will run out one day. In addition, we have inflicted what may be irreparable damage on the natural environment and our own species is endangered. Finally, science and technology, the instruments of progress, have shown with alarming clarity that they can easily become destructive forces. The existence of nuclear weapons is a refutation of the idea that progress is inherent in history. This refutation, I add, can only be called devastating.

In the second place, we have the fate of the historical subject, mankind, in the twentieth century. Seldom have nations or individuals suffered so much: two world wars, tyrannies spread over five continents, the atomic bomb and the proliferation of one of the cruelest and most lethal institutions known by man: the concentration camp. Modern technology has provided countless benefits, but it is impossible to close our eyes when confronted by slaughter, torture, humiliation, degradation and other wrongs inflicted on millions of innocent people in our century.

In the third place, the belief in the necessity of progress has been shaken. For our grandparents and our parents, the ruins of history (corpses, desolate battlefields, devastated cities) did not invalidate the underlying goodness of the historical process. The scaffolds and tyrannies, the conflicts and savage civil wars were the price to be paid for progress, the blood money to be offered to the god of history. A god? Yes, reason itself deified and prodigal in cruel acts of cunning, according to Hegel. The alleged rationality of history has vanished. In the very domain of order, regularity and coherence (in pure sciences like physics) the old notions of accident and catastrophe have reappeared. This disturbing resurrection reminds me of the terrors that marked the advent of the millennium, and the anguish of the Aztecs at the end of each cosmic cycle.

The last element in this hasty enumeration is the collapse of all the philosophical and historical hypotheses that claimed to reveal the laws governing the course of history. The believers, confident that they held the keys to history, erected powerful states over pyramids of corpses. These arrogant constructions, destined in theory to liberate men, were very quickly transformed into gigantic prisons. Today we have seen them fall, overthrown not by their ideological enemies but by the impatience and the desire for freedom of the new generations. Is this the end of all Utopias? It is rather the end of the idea of history as a phenomenon, the outcome of which can be known in advance. Historical determinism has been a costly and bloodstained fantasy. History is unpredictable because its agent, mankind, is the personification of indeterminism.

This short review shows that we are very probably at the end of a historical period and at the beginning of another. The end of the Modern Age or just a mutation? It is difficult to tell. In any case, the collapse of Utopian schemes has left a great void, not in the countries where this ideology has proved to have failed but in those where many embraced it with enthusiasm and hope. For the first time in history mankind lives in a sort of spiritual wilderness and not, as before, in the shadow of those religious and political systems that consoled us at the same time as they oppressed us. Although all societies are historical, each one has lived under the guidance and inspiration of a set of metahistorical beliefs and ideas. Ours is the first age that is ready to live without a metahistorical doctrine; whether they be religious or philosophical, moral or aesthetic, our absolutes are not collective but private. It is a dangerous experience. It is also impossible to know whether the tensions and conflicts unleashed in this privatisation of ideas, practices and beliefs that belonged traditionally to the public domain will not end up by destroying the social fabric. Men could then become possessed once more by ancient religious fury or by fanatical nationalism. It would be terrible if the fall of the abstract idol of ideology were to foreshadow the resurrection of the buried passions of tribes, sects and churches. The signs, unfortunately, are disturbing.

The decline of the ideologies I have called metahistorical, by which I mean those that assign to history a goal and a direction, implies first the tacit abandonment of global solutions. With good sense, we tend more and more towards limited remedies to solve concrete problems. It is prudent to abstain from legislating about the future. Yet the present requires much more than attention to its immediate needs: it demands a more rigorous global reflection. For a long time I have firmly believed that the twilight of the future heralds the advent of the now. To think about the now implies first of all to recover the critical vision. For example, the triumph of the market economy (a triumph due to the adversary's default) cannot be simply a cause for joy. As a mechanism the market is efficient, but like all mechanisms it lacks both conscience and compassion. We must find a way of integrating it into society so that it expresses the social contract and becomes an instrument of justice and fairness. The advanced democratic societies have reached an enviable level of prosperity; at the same time they are islands of abundance in the ocean of universal misery. The topic of the market is intricately related to the deterioration of the environment. Pollution affects not only the air, the rivers and the forests but also our souls. A society possessed by the frantic need to produce more in order to consume more tends to reduce ideas, feelings, art, love, friendship and people themselves to consumer products. Everything becomes a thing to be bought, used and then thrown in the rubbish dump. No other society has produced so much waste as ours has. Material and moral waste.

Reflecting on the now does not imply relinquishing the future or forgetting the past: the present is the meeting place for the three directions of time. Neither can it be confused with facile hedonism. The tree of pleasure does not grow in the past or in the future but at this very moment. Yet death is also a fruit of the present. It cannot be rejected, for it is part of life. Living well implies dying well. We have to learn how to look death in the face. The present is alternatively luminous and sombre, like a sphere that unites the two halves of action and contemplation. Thus, just as we have had philosophies of the past and of the future, of eternity and of the void, tomorrow we shall have a philosophy of the present. The poetic experience could be one of its foundations. What do we know about the present? Nothing or almost nothing. Yet the poets do know one thing: the present is the source of presences.

In this pilgrimage in search of modernity I lost my way at many points only to find myself again. I returned to the source and discovered that modernity is not outside but within us. It is today and the most ancient antiquity; it is tomorrow and the beginning of the world; it is a thousand years old and yet newborn. It speaks in Nahuatl, draws Chinese ideograms from the ninth century, and appears on the television screen. This intact present, recently unearthed, shakes off the dust of centuries, smiles and suddenly starts to fly, disappearing through the window. A simultaneous plurality of time and presence:

modernity breaks with the immediate past only to recover an age-old past and transform a tiny fertility figure from the neolithic into our contemporary. We pursue modernity in her incessant metamorphoses yet we never manage to trap her. She always escapes: each encounter ends in flight. We embrace her and she disappears immediately: it was just a little air. It is the instant, that bird that is everywhere and nowhere. We want to trap it alive but it flaps its wings and vanishes in the form of a handful of syllables. We are left empty-handed. Then the doors of perception open slightly and the other time appears, the real one we were searching for without knowing it: the present, the presence.

Translated from Spanish by Anthony Stanton

Camilo José Cela

Eulogy to the Fable
1989

Camilo José Cela was born in 1916 in Iria Flavia in the district of Padron, north-western Spain. He wrote and published poetry, prose fiction, plays, travel books and essays, with his first novel published in 1942. Titled La familia de Pascual Duarte *(The Family of Pascual Duarte), this work, with its morally ambiguous protagonist, was of great importance in the development of the Spanish novel in the years after the Second World War. But it was the novel* La colmena *(The Hive) that exemplified Cela's sarcastic, grotesque style of realism. Published in 1951, it showed the influence of the work of writers such as Miguel de Cervantes, Jean-Paul Sartre and James Joyce.*

Cela's fiction began to move toward the experimental after the publication of San Camilo 1936 *in 1969, reaching its culmination in the novel* Cristo versus Arizona *(Christ versus Arizona)—this work contains a sentence that is more than a hundred pages long. His poetry includes the collection* Pisando la dudosa luz del dia, *and his articles have been collected in the volumes* Mesa revuelta, Las companies convenientes *and* El asno de Buridán, *among others.*

The Academy described Cela's writing as 'a rich and intensive prose, which with restrained compassion forms a challenging vision of man's vulnerability'. He died in 2002.

My old friend and mentor Pío Baroja—who did not receive the Nobel Prize because the bright light of success does not always fall on the righteous—had a clock on his wall. Around the face of that clock there were words of enlightenment, a saying that made you tremble as the hands of the clock moved round. It said 'Each hour wounds; the last hour kills.' In my case, many chimes have been rung in my heart and soul by the hands of that clock—which never goes back—and today, with one foot in the long life behind me and the other in hope for the future, I come before you to say a few words about the spoken word and to reflect in a spirit of goodwill and hopefully to good avail on liberty and literature. I do not rightly know at what point one crosses the threshold into old age but to be on the safe side I take refuge in the words of Don Francisco de Quevedo who said: 'We all wish to reach a ripe old age, but none of us are prepared to admit that we are already there.'

However, one cannot ignore the obvious. I also know that time marches inexorably onwards. So I will say what I have to say here and now without resorting to either inspiration or improvisation, since I dislike both.

Finding myself here today, addressing you from this dais which is so difficult to reach, I begin to wonder whether the glitter of words—my words in this case—has not dazzled you as to my real merit which I feel is a poor thing compared to the high honour you have conferred upon me. It is not difficult to write in Spanish; the Spanish language is a gift from the gods that we Spaniards take for granted. I take comfort therefore in the belief that you wished to pay tribute to a glorious language and not to the humble writer who uses it for everything it can express: the joy and the wisdom of Mankind, since literature is an art form of all and for all, although written without deference, heeding only the voiceless, anonymous murmur of a given place and time.

I write from solitude and I speak from solitude. Mateo Alemán in his *Cuzmán de Alfarache* and Francis Bacon in his essay *Of Solitude*—both writing more or less at the same period—said that the man who seeks solitude has much of the divine and much of the beast in him. However, I did not seek solitude. I found it. And from my solitude I think, work and live—and I believe that I write and speak with almost infinite composure and resignation. In my solitude I constantly keep in mind the principle expounded by Picasso, another old friend and mentor, that no lasting work of art can be achieved without great solitude. As I go through life giving the impression that I am belligerent, I can speak of solitude without embarrassment and even with a certain degree of thankful, if painful, acceptance.

The greatest reward is to know that one can speak and emit articulate sounds and utter words that describe things, events and emotions.

When defining man, philosophers have traditionally used the standard medium of close genus and specific difference, that is to say reference to our animal status and the origin of differences. From Aristotle's *zoon politikon* to Descartes' *res cogitans* such reference has been an essential means of distinguishing man from beast. But however much moral philosophers may challenge what I'm going to say, I maintain that it would not be difficult to find abundant evidence identifying language as the definitive source of human nature which, for better or worse, sets us apart from all other animals.

We are different from other animals, although since Darwin we know that we have evolved from them. The evolution of language is thus a fundamental fact that we cannot ignore.

The phylogenesis of the human species covers a process of evolution in which the organs that produce and identify sounds and the brain that makes sense of those sounds develop over a long period of time, which includes the birth of Mankind. No subsequent phenomena, neither *El Cantar de Mío Cid* nor *El Quijote*, nor quantum theory, can compare in importance to the first time that the most basic things were given a name. However, for obvious reasons I am not going to dwell here on the evolution of language in its primeval and fundamental sense. Rather I will deal with its secondary and accidental but relatively more important meaning for those of us who were born into a society whose tradition is more literary than secular.

Ethnologists such as the distinguished A. S. Diamond believe that the history of language, of all languages, follows a pattern in which at the very beginning sentences are simple and primitive but go on to become more complicated in terms of syntactic and semantic variations. By extrapolating from this historically verifiable trend, it can be deduced that this increasing complexity evolves from the initial stage where communication relies mainly on the verb, building up to the present situation where it is nouns, adjectives and adverbs that give flavor and depth to the sentence. If this theory is correct and if we apply a little imagination, we might conclude that the first word to be used was a verb in its most immediate and urgent tense, namely the imperative.

And indeed the imperative still retains considerable importance in communication. It is a difficult tense to use. It must be handled with care since it requires a highly detailed knowledge of the rules of the game, which are not always straightforward. A badly placed imperative can bring about the exact opposite of the desired objective. John Langshaw Austin's famous triple distinction (locutionary, illocutionary and perlocutionary language) is an erudite demonstration of the thesis that perlocutionary language tends to provoke specific behaviour on the part of the interlocutor. It is useless to issue an order if the person to whom it is addressed dissembles and ends up doing whatever he likes.

Thus from *zoon politikon* to *res cogitans* sufficient distinctions have been drawn between the beast that grazes and the man that sings, albeit not always in well-measured tones.

In Plato's *Dialogue* that bears his name, Cratylus hides Heraclitus among the folds of his tunic. The philosopher Democritus through his interlocutor Hermogenes speaks of the concepts of fullness and emptiness. The same can be said of Protagoras the anti-geometrician who irreverently maintained that 'Man is the measure of all things': what they are and how they are, what they are not and how they are not.

Cratylus was concerned with language—what it is and what it is not—and developed those ideas at some length in his discourse with Hermogenes. Cratylus believes that what things are called is naturally related to what they are. Things are born or created or are discovered or invented. From their very beginning they contain essentially the exact term which identifies them and distinguishes them from everything else. He seems to be trying to tell us that this distinction is unique and comes from the same ovum as the thing itself. Except in the reasoned world of the etymologist, a dog has always been a dog in all the ancient languages and love has been love since first it was felt. The boundaries of paradox in the thoughts of Cratylus in contrast to Heraclitus' hypotheses are hidden in the dovetailed indivisibility or unity of opposites, their harmony (day and night), the constant movement and reaffirmation of their substance. The same is true of words as things in their own right (there is no dog without the cat and no love without hate).

Conversely, Hermogenes thought that words were mere conventions established by humans for the reasonable purpose of understanding one another. Man is confronted with things or they are presented to him. Faced with something new, man gives it a name. The significance of things is not the spring in the woods but the well dug by man. The parabolic frontier of the senses, and of expression, as expounded by Hermogenes and concealed by Democritus and at times by Protagoras, comes up time and again: is man who measures and designates all things generic or individual? Is the measurement of those things a mere epistemological concept? Are things only physical matter or are they also feelings and concepts? By reducing being to illusion, Hermogenes kills off truth in the cradle; the contradictory conclusion that the only possible propositions are those which man formulates by himself and to himself, renders real what is true and what is not true. You will recall that according to Victor Henry's famous aporia man can give a name to things but he cannot take them over; he can change the language but he cannot change it any way he wishes. Referring in perhaps overcautious terms to the exactitude of names Plato seems to sympathize obliquely with Cratylus' position: things are called what they have to be called (an organic and valid theory that is on the verge of being acknowledged in pure reason as a principle) and not what man decides they should be called according to which way the wind is blowing at any given time (this being a changing or even fluctuating corollary, dependent on the changing suppositions present at the same time as, or prior to, a given thing).

This attitude, originally romantic and consequently demagogical, was the starting point for the Latin poets, headed by Horace. It gave rise to all the ills which have afflicted us in this field since that time and which we have not been able to remedy. *Ars Poetica*, verses 70 to 72, sings of the prevalence of usage in the evolution of language (not always a welcome development):

> Multa renascentur quae iam cecidere cadentque
> quae nunc sunt in honore vocabula, si volet usus,
> quem penes arbitrium est et ius et norma loquendi.

This time-bomb, however pleasing in its charity, had several complex consequences leading finally to the supposition that language is made by the people—and inevitably by the people alone—and that it is futile to try and subject language to the precise and reasonable rules of logic. This dangerous assertion by Horace that usage determines what is right and acceptable in language created a rubbish-dump clogged with overgrown efforts in which the shortcut became the highway along which man progressed bearing the banner of language blowing freely and trembling in the breeze, obstinately continuing to confuse victory with the subservience inherent in its very image.

While Horace was partly right (and we should not deny that), he was also wrong in a number of ways and we should not try to hide that either. But we should also acknowledge the contribution of Cratylus and Hermogenes by refining their principles. Cratylus' position falls within what is referred to as natural or ordinary or spoken language, which is the product of the constant use of a historical and psychological path, while Hermogenes' proposition fits into what we understand as artificial or specialized language or jargon, deriving from a more or less formal arrangement or from some formal method based on logic but with no historical or psychological tradition behind it—at least at the time it is conceived. The first Wittgenstein, the author of the *Tractatus*, is a celebrated modern exponent of Hermogenes' proposition. Thus in that sense it would not be illogical to talk of Cratylian or natural or human language and of Hermogenean or artificial or para-human language. Like Horace my point of reference is obviously the former, the language of life and literature, without technical or defensive obstacles. Max Scheler—and indeed phenomenologists generally—is also referring to what I will now call Cratylian language when he talks about language as an indication or announcement or expression, as is Karl Bühler when he classifies the three functions of language as symptom, signal and symbol.

It goes without saying that Hermogenean language naturally accommodates its original artificiality. On the other hand, Cratylian language does not adapt to extraneous territory where there are often hidden pitfalls alien to its essential transparency.

It is dangerous to admit that in the final analysis natural, Cratylian language is the offspring of a magical marriage between the people and chance. Because people do not create language they determine its development. We can say, albeit with considerable reservations, that people solve to a certain extent the puzzle of language by giving names to things; but they also adulterate and hybridise it. If people were not subject to those hidden pitfalls referred to earlier this issue would be much more urgent and linear. What is not put forward but which nevertheless lies hidden within the true heart of the matter is one and the same and already determined; and neither I nor anyone else can change that.

The Cratylian language, the structure or system described by Ferdinand de Saussure as 'langue', is the common language of a community (or rather more *in* than of *a* community), is formed and authenticated by writers and regulated and generally orientated by Academies. These three estates—the community, the writer and the Academies—do not always fulfill their respective duties. Very often they invade and interfere in other areas. It would appear that neither the Academies, nor the writers nor the community are happy with their own roles. While not competent to do so they prefer to define the role of others which, perhaps even rightly in principle, will always be unclear and ill-defined and, even worse, end up dissipating and obscuring the subject of their attention, namely the language and the verb which should be essentially transparent. The algebraic and mere instrument with no value other than its usefulness, in the final analysis, as in Unamuno's *Love and Pedagogy*.

The final determining factor, the state, which is neither the community nor the writers nor the Academies, conditions and constrains everything, intervenes in a thousand different ways (administrative jargon, government pronouncements, television etc.) compounding, more by bad example than by inhibition, disorder and disarray, chaos and confusion.

But no one says anything about popular, literary, academic, state and other excesses. Language evolves not in its own way, which in principle would be appropriate, but is rather pushed around by the opposing forces surrounding it.

The community to whom Horace's lines are recited eventually believe that this is how a language should evolve and tries to incorporate phrases, styles and expressions that are neither intuitive nor the product of their subconscious—which at least might produce something valid or plausible—but rather deliberately and consciously invented, or, even worse, imported (at the wrong time and against sound common sense).

Writers, obviously with some exceptions, follow the often defective usage in their own environment and introduce and sanction expressions that are cumbersome and, worse still, divorced from the essential spirit of the language.

The Academies' problems stem from the basis on which they operate: as institutions they tend to be conservative and afraid of being challenged.

The erosion of the Cratylian language by Hermogenean influences is becoming more pronounced and there is a danger that it will desiccate that living language and render the natural language artificial. As I have already said, this threat is caused by invented, gratuitously incorporated or inopportunely resurrected or revitalized language.

There seems to be some political reason behind the impetus that now leads, as it has in the past, gaily to abandon the principles of a language in the face of a blunt attack by those besieging it. In my view the risks outweigh the possible benefits—which are somewhat Utopian—that might accrue at some future unspecified date. While I am far from being a purist, I would like to call on writers in the first instance and then on academies and on states to a lesser degree to put an end to the chaos. There is undoubtedly a continuity in language that supersedes any classifications we wish to establish but that does not constitute grounds for tearing down the natural frontiers of language. If we allow that we would be admitting to a defeat that has not yet taken place.

Let us rally our genius in defence of language, all languages, and let us never forget that confusing procedure with the rule of Law, just as observing the letter rather than the spirit of the Law, always leads to injustice that is both the source and consequence of disorder.

Thought is intrinsically linked to language. Moreover, freedom is also probably linked to certain linguistic and conceptual patterns. Together they provide the broad framework for all human endeavour; those that seek to explore and expand human frontiers, also those that seek to undermine the status of man. Thought and liberty are found in the minds of heroes and villains alike.

But this generalisation obscures the need for greater precision if we are to arrive at an understanding of the real meaning of what it is to think and to be free. Insofar as we are able to identify the phenomena that take place in the mind, thinking for man means thinking about being free. There has been much argument regarding the extent to which this freedom or liberty is something concrete or whether it is just another slick phenomenon produced by the human mind. But such argument is probably futile. A wise Spanish philosopher has pointed out that the illusion and the real image of freedom are one and the same thing. If man is not free, if he is bound by chains that psychology, biology, sociology and history seek to identify, as a human being he also carries within himself the idea, which may be an illusion but which is absolutely universal, that he is free. And if we wish to be free we will organize our world in much the same way as we would if we were free.

The architectural design on which we have tried to build successfully or otherwise the complex framework of our societies contains the basic principle of human freedom, and it is in the light of that principle that we value, exalt, denigrate, castigate and suffer: the aura of liberty is the spirit enshrined in our moral codes, political principles and legal systems.

We know that we think. We think because we are free. The link between thought and freedom is like a fish biting its own tail or rather a fish that wants to get hold of its own tail; because being free is both a direct consequence of and an essential condition for thought. Through thought man can detach himself as much as he wants from the laws of nature; he can accept and submit to those laws, for example like the chemist who has gone beyond the boundaries of phlogiston theory will base his success and prestige on such acceptance and submission. In thought, however, the realms of the absurd lie side by side with the empire of logic because man does not think only in terms of the real and the possible. The mind can shatter its own machinations into a thousand pieces and rearrange them into a totally different image.

Thus one can have as many rational interpretations of the world based on empirical principles as the thinker wishes primarily on the basis of the promise of freedom. Free thinking in this narrow sense is that antithesis of the empirical world and finds expression in the fable. Thus the capacity to create fables would appear to be the third element in the human status—the others being thought and freedom—and this capacity can turn things round in such a way that things which before they became the subject of a fable were not even untruths become truths.

Through the process of thought man begins to discover hidden truth in the world, he can aim to create his own different world in whatever terms he wishes through the medium of the fable. Thus truth, thought, freedom and fable are interlinked in a complicated and on occasion suspect relationship. It is like a dark passageway with several side-turnings going off in the wrong direction; a labyrinth with no way out. But the element of risk has always been the best justification for embarking on an adventure.

The fable and scientific truth are not forms of thought. They are rather heterogeneous entities that cannot possibly be compared with one another since they are subject to completely different rules and techniques. Consequently, it is not appropriate to brandish the standard of literature in the struggle to free men's minds. Literature should rather be regarded as a counterweight to the newfound slavish submission to science. I would go further and say that I believe that a prudent and careful distinction must be drawn between those forms of science and literature that join together to confine man within rigid limits which deny all ideas of freedom, and that we must be daring and offset those forms by other scientific and literary experiences aimed at engendering hope. By unreservedly trusting in the superiority of human freedom and dignity, rather than suspect truths that dissolve in a sea of presumption, would be an indication that we have progressed. However, in itself it is not enough. If we have learned anything it is that science is incapable of justifying aspirations to freedom and that on the contrary it rests on crutches that tilt it in exactly the opposite direction. Science should be based solely on the most profound exigencies of human freedom and will. That is the only means of enabling science to break away from utilitarianism that cannot withstand the pitfalls of quantity and measurement. This leads us to the need to recognize that literature and science, although heterogeneous, cannot remain isolated in a prophylactic endeavour to define areas of influence and this for two reasons, namely the status of language (that basic instrument of thought) as well as the need to define the limits of and distinguish between that which is commendable and laudable and that which must be denounced by all committed individuals.

I believe that literature as an instrument for creating fables is founded on two basic pillars that provide it with strength to ensure that literary endeavour is worthwhile. Firstly aesthetics, which impose a requirement on an essay, poem, drama or comedy to maintain certain minimum standards that distinguish it from the sub-literary world in which creativity cannot keep pace with the readers' emotions. From socialist reality to the innumerable inconstancies of would-be experimentalists, wherever aesthetic talent is lacking the resulting sub-literature becomes a monotonous litany of words incapable of creating a genuine worthwhile fable.

The second pillar on which literary endeavour rests is ethics, which complements aesthetics and which has a lot to do with all that has been said up to now regarding thought and freedom. Of course, ethics and aesthetics are in no way synonymous, nor do they have the same value. Literature can balance itself precariously on aesthetics alone—art for art's sake—and it could be that aesthetics in the long run may be a more comprehensive concept than ethical commitment. We can still appreciate Homer's verses and medieval epic canticles although we may have forgotten or at least no longer automatically link them with ethical behaviour in ancient Greek cities or in feudal Europe. However, art for art's sake is by definition an extremely difficult undertaking and one that always runs the risk of being used for purposes that distort its real meaning.

I do believe that ethical principle is the element that makes a work of literature worthy of playing the noble role of creating a fable. But I must explain clearly what I mean because the literary fable as a means of expressing the links between man's capacity to think and the perhaps Utopian idea of being free cannot be based on just any kind of ethical commitment. My understanding is that a work of literature can only be subject to the ethical commitment of the person, the author, to his own idea of freedom. Of course no one, not even the cleverest and most balanced literary author, can ever (or rather cannot always) overcome his humanity; anyone can have a blind spot, and freedom is a sufficiently ambiguous concept and many blinding errors can be committed in its name. Nor can an aesthetic sense be acquired from a textbook. Thus, the literary fable must be based on both a sense of ethics and a commitment to aesthetics. That is the only way it can acquire a significance that will transcend ephemeral fashions or confused appreciation that can quickly change. The history of man is changing and tortuous. Consequently, it is difficult to anticipate ethical or aesthetic sensibilities. There are writers who are so tuned in to the feeling of their time that they become magnificent exponents of the prevailing collective trend and whose work is a conditional reflex. Others take on the thankless and not sufficiently applauded task of carrying freedom and human creativity further along the road, even if in the end that too may lead nowhere.

This is the only way in which literature can fulfill its role of closely identifying its commitment to the human status and, if we wish to be absolutely precise in this thesis, the only endeavor that can unreservedly be called true literature. However, human society cannot be linked to geniuses, saints and heroes alone.

In this task of seeking out freedom, the fable has the benefit of the well-known characteristic of the intrinsic malleability of the literary story. The fable does not need to subject itself to anything that might restrict its scope, novelty and element of surprise. Thus, unlike any other form of thought, it can wave the Utopian banner high. Perhaps that is why the most avid authors of treatises of political philosophy have opted to use the literary story to convey Utopian propositions that would not have found ready acceptance outside the realms of fiction at the time they were written. There are no limits to the Utopianism that the fable can express since by its very nature the fable itself is based on Utopianism.

However, the advantages of literary expression are not confined to the ease with which it can convey Utopian propositions. The intrinsic plasticity of the story, the malleability of the situations, personalities and events it creates provide a superb foundry from which one can, without undue risk, set up an entire factory, or, to put it another way, a laboratory in which men conduct experiments on human behavior in optimum conditions. But the fable does not restrict itself to expressing the Utopian. It can also analyse carefully what it means and what its consequences are in the myriad different alternative situations ranging from learned prediction to the absurd that creative thought can produce.

The role of literature as an experimental laboratory has been often highlighted in science fiction; speculation about the future that has subsequently been realized. Critics have heaped praise on novelists who have a talent for predicting in their fables the basic coordinates that subsequently have been substantiated. But the real usefulness of the fable as a test tube lies not in its anecdotal capacity for accurately predicting something technical but as a means of conveying in a timely, direct or negative fashion all possible facets of a world that may be possible now or in the future. It is the search for human commitment, for tragic experiences, that can shed light on the ambiguity of blindly choosing options in the face of the demands placed upon us by our world, now or in the future, that turns the fresco of literature into an experimental laboratory. The value of literature as a means of carrying out experiments on behaviour has little to do with prediction since human behaviour only has a past, present and future in a very specific, narrow sense. There are, however, basic aspects of our nature which have an impressive permanency about them and which cause us to be deeply moved by an emotional story from a completely different age to the one we live in. It is this 'universal man' that is the most prized figure in literary fable, an experimental workshop in which there are no frontiers and no ages. It is the Quixotes, the Othellos, the Don Juans that illustrate to us that the fable is a game of chess played over and over again, a thousand times, with whatever pieces destiny throws up at any given time.

In absolute terms it might appear that this detracts from the so-called freedom I am advocating, and indeed that would be the case if one did not take account of the role of that imperfect, voluble and confused personality, the author, the man. The magic of Shylock would never have emerged without the genius of Bard, whose unreliable memory was of course far more inconsistent than that of the characters to whom he gave life and to whom in the end he denied death. And what of those anonymous scholars and jugglers whom we remember only for the result produced by their talents? There is undoubtedly something that must be remembered over whatever sociology or history tries to impose upon us, and that is that thus far, and insofar as we can conceive of the future of mankind, works of literature are very much subject to the needs of the author; that is to say to a single source of those ethical and aesthetic insights I referred to earlier, an author who acts as a filter for the current which undoubtedly emanates from the whole surrounding society. It is perhaps this link between Man and Society that best expresses the very paradox of being a human being proud of his individuality, and at the same time tied to the community that surrounds him and from which he cannot disengage himself without risking madness. There is a moral here; the limitations of literature are precisely those of human nature and they show us that there is another status, identical in other ways, which is that of gods and demons. Our mind can imagine demiurges and the ease with which human beings invent religions clearly demonstrates that this is so. Our capacity to create fables provides a useful literary means of illustrating those demiurges, as indeed we have done constantly since Homer wrote his verses. But even that cannot lead us to mistake our nature or put out once and for all the tenuous flame of freedom that burns in the innermost being of the slave who can be forced to obey but not to love, to suffer and die but not to change his most profound thoughts.

When the proud, blind rationalist renewed in enlightened minds the biblical temptation, the last maxim of which promised 'You will be as gods', he did not take account of the fact that Man had already gone much further down that road. The misery and the pride that for centuries had marked Man's efforts to be like the gods had already taught Man a better reason; that through effort and imagination they could become Men. For my part, I must say proudly that in this latter task, much of which still remains to be accomplished, the literary fable has always been, and in all circumstances proved to be, a decisive tool; a weapon that can cleave the way forward in the endless march to freedom.

Translated from Spanish by Mary Penney

Naguib Mahfouz

Mankind's Coming of Age
1988

Naguib Mahfouz began to write at seventeen. Born in Cairo in 1911, he has long been regarded as a cultural icon in his home country. His first novel was published in 1939, and he wrote ten more before the Egyptian Revolution of July 1952. The year 1959 saw the publication of the Cairo Trilogy—Bayn al Qasrayn (Between the Palaces), Qasr al Shawq (Palace of Longing) and Sukkariya (Sugarhouse)—and these depictions of traditional urban life made him famous throughout the Arab world. The novel The Children of Gebelawi *signaled a new phase in his work, where political judgments were often hidden within allegory and symbolism.*

Mahfouz worked for many years as a civil servant in various departments of the Egyptian government, including as a consultant on Cultural Affairs to the Ministry of Culture. Since his retirement in 1972, his work has become increasingly experimental and prolific. In total, he has written thirty novels, more than a hundred short stories and over two hundred articles. Many of his novels have been made into films for the Arabic-speaking world. Mahfouz has lived under constant bodyguard protection since an assassination attempt by Islamic extremists in 1994.

The Academy praised Mahfouz as a writer 'who, through works rich in nuance—now clear-sightedly realistic, now evocatively ambiguous—has formed an Arabian narrative art that applies to all mankind'. His speech was read at the Academy by Mr Mohamed Salmawy, first in Arabic, then in English. Mahfouz died in 2006.

To begin with I would like to thank the Swedish Academy and its Nobel committee for taking notice of my long and perseverant endeavours, and I would like you to accept my talk with tolerance. For it comes in a language unknown to many of you. But it is the real winner of the prize. It is, therefore, meant that its melodies should float for the first time into your oasis of culture and civilisation. I have great hopes that this will not be the last time either, and that literary writers of my nation will have the pleasure to sit with full merit among your international writers who have spread the fragrance of joy and wisdom in this grief-ridden world of ours.

I was told by a foreign correspondent in Cairo that the moment my name was mentioned in connection with the prize silence fell, and many wondered who I was. Permit me, then, to present myself in as objective a manner as is humanly possible. I am the son of two civilisations that at a certain age in history have formed a happy marriage. The first of these, seven thousand years old, is the Pharaonic civilisation; the second, one thousand, four hundred years old, is the Islamic one. I am perhaps in no need to introduce to any of you either of the two, you being the elite, the learned ones. But there is no harm, in our present situation of acquaintance and communion, in a mere reminder.

As for Pharaonic civilisation, I will not talk of the conquests and the building of empires. This has become a worn-out pride the mention of which modern conscience, thank God, feels uneasy about. Nor will I talk about how it was guided for the first time to the existence of God and its ushering in the dawn of human conscience. This is a long history and there is not one of you who is not acquainted with the prophet-king Akhenaton. I will not even speak of this civilisation's achievements in art and literature, and its renowned miracles: the Pyramids and the Sphinx and Karnak. For he who has not had the chance to see these monuments has read about them and pondered over their forms.

Let me, then, introduce Pharaonic civilisation with what seems like a story since my personal circumstances have ordained that I become a storyteller. Hear, then, this recorded historical incident: Old papyri relate that Pharaoh had learned of the existence of a sinful relation between some women of the harem and men of his court. It was expected that he should finish them off in accordance with the spirit of his time. But he, instead, called to his presence the choice men of law and asked them to investigate what he had come to learn. He told them that he wanted the Truth so that he could pass his sentence with Justice.

This conduct, in my opinion, is greater than founding an empire or building the Pyramids. It is more telling of the superiority of that civilisation than any riches or splendour. Gone now is that civilisation—a mere story of the past. One day the great Pyramid will disappear too. But Truth and Justice will remain for as long as Mankind has a ruminative mind and a living conscience.

As for Islamic civilisation, I will not talk about its call for the establishment of a union between all Mankind under the guardianship of the Creator, based on freedom, equality and forgiveness. Nor will I talk about the greatness of its prophet. For among your thinkers there are those who regard him the greatest man in history. I will not talk of its conquests which have planted thousands of minarets calling for worship, devoutness and good throughout great expanses of land from the environs of India and China to the boundaries of France. Nor will I talk of the fraternity between religions and races that has been achieved in its embrace in a spirit of tolerance unknown to Mankind neither before nor since.

I will, instead, introduce that civilisation in a moving dramatic situation summarising one of its most conspicuous traits: In one victorious battle against Byzantium it has given back its prisoners of war in return for a number of books of the ancient Greek heritage in philosophy, medicine and mathematics. This is a testimony of value for the human spirit in its demand for knowledge, even though the demander was a believer in God and the demanded a fruit of a pagan civilisation.

It was my fate to be born in the lap of these two civilisations, and to absorb their milk, to feed on their literature and art. Then I drank the nectar of your rich and fascinating culture. From the inspiration of all this—as well as my own anxieties—words bedewed from me. These words had the fortune to merit the appreciation of your revered Academy, which has crowned my endeavour with the great Nobel Prize. Thanks be to it in my name and in the name of those great departed builders who have founded the two civilisations.

You may be wondering: This man coming from the third world, how did he find the peace of mind to write stories? You are perfectly right. I come from a world labouring under the burden of debts whose paying back exposes it to starvation or very close to it. Some of its people perish in Asia from floods, others do so in Africa from famine. In South Africa millions have been undone with rejection and with deprivation of all human rights in the age of human rights, as though they were not counted among humans. In the West Bank and Gaza there are people who are lost in spite of the fact that they are living on their own land; land of their fathers, grandfathers and great grandfathers. They have risen to demand the first right secured by primitive Man; namely, that they should have their proper place recognised by others as their own. They were paid back for their brave and noble move—men, women, youths and children alike—by the breaking of bones, killing with bullets, destroying of houses and torture in prisons and camps. Surrounding them are 150 million Arabs following what is happening in anger and grief. This threatens the area with a disaster if it is not saved by the wisdom of those desirous of a just and comprehensive peace.

Yes, how did the man coming from the Third World find the peace of mind to write stories? Fortunately, art is generous and sympathetic. In the same way that it dwells with the happy ones it does not desert the wretched. It offers both alike the convenient means for expressing what swells up in their bosom.

In this decisive moment in the history of civilisation it is inconceivable and unacceptable that the moans of Mankind should die out in the void. There is no doubt that Mankind has at last come of age, and our era carries the expectations of *entente* between the Super Powers. The human mind now assumes the task of eliminating all causes of destruction and annihilation. And just as scientists exert themselves to cleanse the environment of industrial pollution, intellectuals ought to exert themselves to cleanse humanity of moral pollution. It is both our right and duty to demand of the big leaders in the countries of civilisation as well as their economists to affect a real leap that would place them into the focus of the age.

In the olden times every leader worked for the good of his own nation alone. The others were considered adversaries, or subjects of exploitation. There was no regard to any value but that of superiority and personal glory. For the sake of this, many morals, ideals and values were wasted; many unethical means were justified; many uncounted souls were made to perish. Lies, deceit, treachery, cruelty reigned as the signs of sagacity and the proof of greatness. Today, this view needs to be changed from its very source. Today, the greatness of a civilised leader ought to be measured by the universality of his vision and his sense of responsibility towards all humankind. The developed world and the Third World are but one family. Each human being bears responsibility towards it by the degree of what he has obtained of knowledge, wisdom and civilisation. I would not be exceeding the limits of my duty if I told them in the name of the Third World: Be not spectators to our miseries. You have to play therein a noble role befitting your status. From your position of superiority you are responsible for any misdirection of animal, or plant, to say nothing of Man, in any of the four corners of the world. We have had enough of words. Now is the time for action. It is time to end the age of brigands and usurers. We are in the age of leaders responsible for the whole globe. Save the enslaved in the African south! Save the famished in Africa! Save the Palestinians from the bullets and the torture! Nay, save the Israelis from profaning their great spiritual heritage! Save the ones in debt from the rigid laws of economy! Draw their attention to the fact that their responsibility to Mankind should precede their commitment to the laws of a science that Time has perhaps overtaken.

I beg your pardon; I feel I may have somewhat troubled your calm. But what do you expect from one coming from the Third World? Is not every vessel coloured by what it contains? Besides, where can the moans of Mankind find a place to resound if not in your oasis of civilisation planted by its great founder for the service of science, literature and sublime human values? And as he did one day by consecrating his riches to the service of good, in the hope of obtaining forgiveness, we, children of the Third World, demand of the able ones, the civilised ones, to follow his example, to imbibe his conduct, to meditate upon his vision.

IN SPITE OF all that goes on around us I am committed to optimism until the end. I do not say with Kant that Good will be victorious in the other world. Good is achieving victory every day. It may even be that Evil is weaker than we imagine. In front of us is an indelible proof: were it not for the fact that victory is always on the side of Good, hordes of wandering humans would not have been able in the face of beasts and insects, natural disasters, fear and egotism, to grow and multiply. They would not have been able to form nations, to excel in creativeness and invention, to conquer outer space, and to declare Human Rights. The truth of the matter is that Evil is a loud and boisterous debaucherer, and that Man remembers what hurts more than what pleases. Our great poet Abul-'Alaa' Al-Ma'ari was right when he said:

> A grief at the hour of death
> Is more than a hundred-fold
> Joy at the hour of birth.

I finally reiterate my thanks and ask your forgiveness.

Translated from Arabic by Mohammed Salmawy

Joseph Brodsky

Aesthetics and Language
1987

For much of his life, Joseph Brodsky lived in exile. Born in Leningrad in 1940, he began to write poetry at the age of eighteen. He was sentenced to five years' hard labour by the Soviet authorities in March 1964 for 'social parasitism', and lived in exile in the Archangelsk region of northern Russia for eighteen months before his sentence was commuted following pressure from prominent Soviet and international literary figures.

The majority of Brodsky's work has appeared only in the West, as he refused to censor his writing. Brodsky was exiled from the USSR on June 4, 1972, and after living for a short while in Vienna and London, eventually settled in the US. There he held numerous positions at universities around the country, including Poet-in-Residence and Visiting Professor at the University of Michigan and Columbia University, and in the UK at Cambridge University. His poetry has been translated into more than ten languages. His volumes of poetry include A Part of Speech, To Urania, So Forth *and* Nativity Poems, *and his essays have been collected in* Less Than One *and* On Grief and Reason.

Brodsky received the prize 'for an all-embracing authorship, imbued with clarity of thought and poetic intensity'. He died in 1996.

I

For someone rather private, for someone who all his life has preferred his private condition to any role of social significance, and who went in this preference rather far—far from his motherland to say the least, for it is better to be a total failure in democracy than a martyr or the crème de la crème in tyranny—for such a person to find himself all of a sudden on this rostrum is a somewhat uncomfortable and trying experience.

This sensation is aggravated not so much by the thought of those who stood here before me as by the memory of those who have been bypassed by this honour, who were not given this chance to address 'urbi et orbi', as they say, from this rostrum and whose cumulative silence is sort of searching, to no avail, for release through this speaker.

The only thing that can reconcile one to this sort of situation is the simple realisation that—for stylistic reasons, in the first place—one writer cannot speak for another writer, one poet for another poet especially; that had Osip Mandelstam, or Marina Tsvetaeva, or Robert Frost, or Anna Akhmatova, or Wystan Auden stood here, they couldn't have helped but speak precisely for themselves, and that they, too, might have felt somewhat uncomfortable.

These shades disturb me constantly; they are disturbing me today as well. In any case, they do not spur one to eloquence. In my better moments, I deem myself their sum total, though invariably inferior to any one of them individually. For it is not possible to better them on the page; nor is it possible to better them in actual life. And it is precisely their lives, no matter how tragic or bitter they were, that often move me—more often perhaps than the case should be—to regret the passage of time. If the next life exists—and I can no more deny them the possibility of eternal life than I can forget their existence in this one—if the next world does exist, they will, I hope, forgive me and the quality of what I am about to utter: after all, it is not one's conduct on the podium which dignity in our profession is measured by.

I have mentioned only five of them, those whose deeds and whose lot matter so much to me, if only because if it were not for them, I, both as a man and a writer, would amount to much less; in any case, I wouldn't be standing here today.

There were more of them, those shades—better still, sources of light: lamps? stars?—more, of course, than just five. And each one of them is capable of rendering me absolutely mute. The number of those is substantial in the life of any conscious man of letters; in my case, it doubles, thanks to the two cultures to which fate has willed me to belong. Matters are not made easier by thoughts about contemporaries and fellow writers in both cultures, poets and fiction writers whose gifts I rank above my own, and who, had they found themselves on this rostrum, would have come to the point long ago, for surely they have more to tell the world than I do.

I will allow myself, therefore, to make a number of remarks here—disjointed, perhaps stumbling, and perhaps even perplexing in their randomness. However, the amount of time allotted to me to collect my thoughts, as well as my very occupation, will, or may, I hope, shield me, at least partially, against charges of being chaotic. A man of my occupation seldom claims a systematic mode of thinking; at worst, he claims to have a system—but even that, in his case, is borrowing from a milieu, from a social order, or from the pursuit of philosophy at a tender age. Nothing convinces an artist more of the arbitrariness of the means to which he resorts to attain a goal—however permanent it may be—than the creative process itself, the process of composition. Verse really does, in Akhmatova's words, grow from rubbish; the roots of prose are no more honorable.

II

If art teaches anything (to the artist, in the first place), it is the privateness of the human condition. Being the most ancient as well as the most literal form of private enterprise, it fosters in a man, knowingly or unwittingly, a sense of his uniqueness, of individuality, of separateness—thus turning him from a social animal into an autonomous 'I'. Lots of things can be shared: a bed, a piece of bread, convictions, a mistress, but not a poem by, say, Rainer Maria Rilke. A work of art, of literature especially, and a poem in particular, addresses a man tete-a-tete, entering with him into direct—free of any go-betweens—relations.

It is for this reason that art in general, literature especially, and poetry in particular, is not exactly favored by the champions of the common good, masters of the masses, heralds of historical necessity. For there, where art has stepped, where a poem has been read, they discover, in place of the anticipated consent and unanimity, indifference and polyphony; in place of the resolve to act, inattention and fastidiousness. In other words, into the little zeros with which the champions of the common good and the rulers of the masses tend to operate, art introduces a 'period, period, comma and a minus', transforming each zero into a tiny human, albeit not always pretty, face.

The great Baratynsky, speaking of his Muse, characterised her as possessing an 'uncommon visage'. It's in acquiring this 'uncommon visage' that the meaning of human existence seems to lie, since for this uncommonness we are, as it were, prepared genetically. Regardless of whether one is a writer or a reader, one's task consists first of all in mastering a life that is one's own, not imposed or prescribed from without, no matter how noble its appearance may be. For each of us is issued but one life, and we know full well how it all ends. It would be regrettable to squander this one chance on someone else's appearance, someone else's experience, on a tautology—regrettable all the more because the heralds of historical necessity, at whose urging a man may be prepared to agree to this tautology, will not go to the grave with him or give him so much as a thank-you.

Language and, presumably, literature are things that are more ancient and inevitable, more durable than any form of social organisation. The revulsion, irony or indifference often expressed by literature towards the state is essentially a reaction of the permanent—better yet, the infinite—against the temporary, against the finite. To say the least, as long as the state permits itself to interfere with the affairs of literature, literature has the right to interfere with the affairs of the state. A political system, a form of social organisation, as any system in general, is by definition a form of the past tense that aspires to impose itself upon the present (and often on the future as well); and a man whose profession is language is the last one who can afford to forget this. The real danger for a writer is not so much the possibility (and often the certainty) of persecution on the part of the state, as it is the possibility of finding oneself mesmerised by the state's features, which, whether monstrous or undergoing changes for the better, are always temporary.

The philosophy of the state, its ethics—not to mention its aesthetics—are always 'yesterday'. Language and literature are always 'today', and often—particularly in the case where a political system is orthodox—they may even constitute 'tomorrow'. One of literature's merits is precisely that it helps a person to make the time of his existence more specific, to distinguish himself from the crowd of his predecessors as well as his like numbers, to avoid tautology—that is, the fate otherwise known by the honorific term, 'victim of history'. What makes art in general, and literature in particular, remarkable, what distinguishes them from life, is precisely that they abhor repetition. In everyday life you can tell the same joke thrice and, thrice getting a laugh, become the life of the party. In art, though, this sort of conduct is called 'cliché'.

Art is a recoilless weapon, and its development is determined not by the individuality of the artist, but by the dynamics and the logic of the material itself, by the previous fate of the means that each time demand (or suggest) a qualitatively new aesthetic solution. Possessing its own genealogy, dynamics, logic and future, art is not synonymous with, but at best parallel to history; and the manner by which it exists is by continually creating a new aesthetic reality. That is why it is often found 'ahead of progress', ahead of history, whose main instrument is—should we not, once more, improve upon Marx—precisely the cliché.

Nowadays, there exists a rather widely held view, postulating that in his work a writer, in particular a poet, should make use of the language of the street, the language of the crowd. For all its democratic appearance, and its palpable advantages for a writer, this assertion is quite absurd and represents an attempt to subordinate art, in this case, literature, to history. It is only if we have resolved that it is time for Homo sapiens to come to a halt in his development that literature should speak the language of the people. Otherwise, it is the people who should speak the language of literature.

On the whole, every new aesthetic reality makes man's ethical reality more precise. For aesthetics is the mother of ethics; the categories of 'good' and 'bad' are, first and foremost, aesthetic ones, at least etymologically preceding the categories of 'good' and 'evil'. If in ethics not 'all is permitted', it is precisely because not 'all is permitted' in aesthetics, because the number of colours in the spectrum is limited. The tender babe who cries and rejects the stranger or who, on the contrary, reaches out to him, does so instinctively, making an aesthetic choice, not a moral one.

Aesthetic choice is a highly individual matter, and aesthetic experience is always a private one. Every new aesthetic reality makes one's experience even more private; and this kind of privacy, assuming at times the guise of literary (or some other) taste, can in itself turn out to be, if not as guarantee, then a form of defence against enslavement. For a man with taste, particularly literary taste, is less susceptible to the refrains and the rhythmical incantations peculiar to any version of political demagogy. The point is not so much that virtue does not constitute a guarantee for producing a masterpiece, as that evil, especially political evil, is always a bad stylist. The more substantial an individual's aesthetic experience is, the sounder his taste, the sharper his moral focus, the freer—though not necessarily the happier—he is.

It is precisely in this applied, rather than Platonic, sense that we should understand Dostoevsky's remark that beauty will save the world, or Matthew Arnold's belief that we shall be saved by poetry. It is probably too late for the world, but for the individual man there always remains a chance. An aesthetic instinct develops in man rather rapidly, for, even without fully realising who he is and what he actually requires, a person instinctively knows what he doesn't like and what doesn't suit him. In an anthropological respect, let me reiterate, a human being is an aesthetic creature before he is an ethical one. Therefore, it is not that art, particularly literature, is a by-product of our species' development, but just the reverse. If what distinguishes us from other members of the animal kingdom is speech, then literature—and poetry in particular, being the highest form of locution—is, to put it bluntly, the goal of our species.

I am far from suggesting the idea of compulsory training in verse composition; nevertheless, the subdivision of society into intelligentsia and 'all the rest' seems to me unacceptable. In moral terms, this situation is comparable to the subdivision of society into the poor and the rich; but if it is still possible to find some purely physical or material grounds for the existence of social inequality, for intellectual inequality these are inconceivable. Equality in this respect, unlike in anything else, has been guaranteed to us by nature. I am speaking not of education, but of the education in speech, the slightest imprecision in which may trigger the intrusion of false choice into one's life. The existence of literature prefigures existence on literature's plane of regard—and not only in the moral sense, but lexically as well. If a piece of music still allows a person the possibility of choosing between the passive role of listener and the active one of performer, a work of literature—of the art which is, to use Montale's phrase, hopelessly semantic—dooms him to the role of performer only.

In this role, it would seem to me, a person should appear more often than in any other. Moreover, it seems to me that, as a result of the population explosion and the attendant, ever-increasing atomisation of society (i.e., the ever-increasing isolation of the individual), this role becomes more and more inevitable for a person. I don't suppose that I know more about life than anyone of my age, but it seems to me that, in the capacity of an interlocutor, a book is more reliable than a friend or a beloved. A novel or a poem is not a monologue, but the conversation of a writer with a reader, a conversation, I repeat, that is very private, excluding all others—if you will, mutually misanthropic. And in the moment of this conversation a writer is equal to a reader, as well as the other way around, regardless of whether the writer is a great one or not. This equality is the equality of consciousness. It remains with a person for the rest of his life in the form of memory, foggy or distinct; and, sooner or later, appropriately or not, it conditions a person's conduct. It's precisely this that I have in mind in speaking of the role of the performer, all the more natural for one because a novel or a poem is the product of mutual loneliness—of a writer or a reader.

In the history of our species, in the history of Homo sapiens, the book is anthropological development, similar essentially to the invention of the wheel. Having emerged in order to give us some idea not so much of our origins as of what that sapiens is capable of, a book constitutes a means of transportation through the space of experience, at the speed of a turning page. This movement, like every movement, becomes a flight from the common denominator, from an attempt to elevate this denominator's line, previously never reaching higher than the groin, to our heart, to our consciousness, to our imagination. This flight is the flight in the direction of 'uncommon visage', in the direction of the numerator, in the direction of autonomy, in the direction of privacy. Regardless of whose image we are created in, there are already five billion of us, and for a human being there is no other future save that outlined by art. Otherwise, what lies ahead is the past—the political one, first of all, with all its mass police entertainments.

In any event, the condition of society in which art in general, and literature in particular, are the property or prerogative of a minority appears to me unhealthy and dangerous. I am not appealing for the replacement of the state with a library, although this thought has visited me frequently; but there is no doubt in my mind that, had we been choosing our leaders on the basis of their reading experience and not their political programs, there would be much less grief on earth. It seems to me that a potential master of our fates should be asked, first of all, not about how he imagines the course of his foreign policy, but about his attitude toward Stendhal, Dickens, Dostoevsky. If only because the lock and stock of literature is indeed human diversity and perversity, it turns out to be a reliable antidote for any attempt—whether familiar or yet to be invented—toward a total mass solution to the problems of human existence. As a form of moral insurance, at least, literature is much more dependable than a system of beliefs or a philosophical doctrine.

Since there are no laws that can protect us from ourselves, no criminal code is capable of preventing a true crime against literature; though we can condemn the material suppression of literature—the persecution of writers, acts of censorship, the burning of books—we are powerless when it comes to its worst violation: that of not reading the books. For that crime, a person pays with his whole life; if the offender is a nation, it pays with its history. Living in the country I live in, I would be the first prepared to believe that there is a set dependency between a person's material wellbeing and his literary ignorance. What keeps me from doing so is the history of that country in which I was born and grew up. For, reduced to a cause-and-effect minimum, to a crude formula, the Russian tragedy is precisely the tragedy of a society in which literature turned out to be the prerogative of the minority: of the celebrated Russian intelligentsia.

I have no wish to enlarge upon the subject, no wish to darken this evening with thoughts of the tens of millions of human lives destroyed by other millions, since what occurred in Russia in the first half of the twentieth century occurred before the introduction of automatic weapons—in the name of the triumph of a political doctrine whose unsoundness is already manifested in the fact that it requires human sacrifice for its realisation. I'll just say that I believe—not empirically, alas, but only theoretically—that, for someone who has read a lot of Dickens, to shoot his like in the name of some idea is more problematic than for someone who has read no Dickens. And I am speaking precisely about reading Dickens, Sterne, Stendhal, Dostoevsky, Flaubert, Balzac, Melville, Proust, Musil and so forth; that is, about literature, not literacy or education. A literate, educated person, to be sure, is fully capable, after reading this or that political treatise or tract, of killing his like, and even of experiencing, in so doing, a rapture of conviction. Lenin was literate, Stalin was literate, so was Hitler; as for Mao Zedong, he even wrote verse. What all these men had in common, though, was that their hit list was longer than their reading list.

However, before I move on to poetry, I would like to add that it would make sense to regard the Russian experience as a warning, if for no other reason than that the social structure of the West up to now is, on the whole, analogous to what existed in Russia prior to 1917. (This, by the way, is what explains the popularity in the West of the nineteenth-century Russian psychological novel, and the relative lack of success of contemporary Russian prose. The social relations that emerged in Russia in the twentieth century presumably seem no less exotic to the reader than do the names of the characters, which prevent him from identifying with them.) For example, the number of political parties, on the eve of the October coup in 1917, was no fewer than what we find today in the United States or Britain. In other words, a dispassionate observer might remark that in a certain sense the nineteenth century is still going on in the West, while in Russia it came to an end; and if I say it ended in tragedy, this is, in the first place, because of the size of the human toll taken in course of that social—or chronological—change. For in a real tragedy, it is not the hero who perishes; it is the chorus.

III

Although for a man whose mother tongue is Russian to speak about political evil is as natural as digestion, I would here like to change the subject. What's wrong with discourses about the obvious is that they corrupt consciousness with their easiness, with the quickness with which they provide one with moral comfort, with the sensation of being right. Herein lies their temptation, similar in its nature to the temptation of a social reformer who begets this evil. The realisation, or rather the comprehension, of this temptation, and rejection of it, are perhaps responsible to a certain extent for the destinies of many of my contemporaries, responsible for the literature that emerged from under their pens. It, that literature, was neither a flight from history nor a muffling of memory, as it may seem from the outside. 'How can one write music after Auschwitz?' inquired Adorno; and one familiar with Russian history can repeat the same question by merely changing the name of the camp—and repeat it perhaps with even greater justification, since the number of people who perished in Stalin's camps far surpasses the number of German prison-camp victims. 'And how can you eat lunch?' the American poet Mark Strand once retorted. In any case, the generation to which I belong has proven capable of writing that music.

That generation—the generation born precisely at the time when the Auschwitz crematoria were working full blast, when Stalin was at the zenith of his Godlike, absolute power, which seemed sponsored by Mother Nature herself—that generation came into the world, it appears, in order to continue what, theoretically, was supposed to be interrupted in those crematoria and in the anonymous common graves of Stalin's archipelago. The fact that not everything got interrupted, at least not in Russia, can be credited in no small degree to my generation, and I am no less proud of belonging to it than I am of standing here today. And the fact that I am standing here is a recognition of the services that generation has rendered to culture; recalling a phrase from Mandelstam, I would add, to world culture. Looking back, I can say again that we were beginning in an empty—indeed, a terrifyingly wasted—place, and that, intuitively rather than consciously, we aspired precisely to the recreation of the effect of culture's continuity, to the reconstruction of its forms and tropes, toward filling its few surviving, and often totally compromised, forms, with our own new, or appearing to us as new, contemporary content.

There existed, presumably, another path: the path of further deformation, the poetics of ruins and debris, of minimalism, of choked breath. If we rejected it, it was not at all because we thought that it was the path of self-dramatisation, or because we were extremely animated by the idea of preserving the hereditary nobility of the forms of culture we knew, the forms that were equivalent, in our consciousness, to forms of human dignity. We rejected it because in reality the choice wasn't ours, but, in fact, culture's own—and this choice, again, was aesthetic rather than moral.

To be sure, it is natural for a person to perceive himself not as an instrument of culture, but, on the contrary, as its creator and custodian. But if today I assert the opposite, it's not because toward the close of the twentieth century there is a certain charm in paraphrasing Plotinus, Lord Shaftesbury, Schelling or Novalis, but because, unlike anyone else, a poet always knows that what in the vernacular is called the voice of the Muse is, in reality, the dictate of the language; that it's not that the language happens to be his instrument, but that he is language's means toward the continuation of its existence. Language, however, even if one imagines it as a certain animate creature (which would only be just), is not capable of ethical choice.

A person sets out to write a poem for a variety of reasons: to win the heart of his beloved; to express his attitude toward the reality surrounding him, be it a landscape or a state; to capture his state of mind at a given instant; to leave—as he thinks at that moment—a trace on the earth. He resorts to this form—the poem—most likely for unconsciously mimetic reasons: the black vertical clot of words on the white sheet of paper presumably reminds him of his own situation in the world, of the balance between space and his body. But regardless of the reasons for which he takes up the pen, and regardless of the effect produced by what emerges from beneath that pen on his audience—however great or small it may be—the immediate consequence of this enterprise is the sensation of coming into direct contact with language or, more precisely, the sensation of immediately falling into dependence on it, on everything that has already been uttered, written and accomplished in it.

This dependence is absolute, despotic; but it unshackles as well. For, while always older than the writer, language still possesses the colossal centrifugal energy imparted to it by its temporal potential—that is, by all time lying ahead. And this potential is determined not so much by the quantitative body of the nation that speaks it (though it is determined by that, too), as by the quality of the poem written in it. It will suffice to recall the authors of Greek or Roman antiquity; it will suffice to recall Dante. And that which is being created today in Russian or English, for example, secures the existence of these languages over the course of the next millennium also. The poet, I wish to repeat, is language's means for existence—or, as my beloved Auden said, he is the one by whom it lives. I who write these lines will cease to be; so will you who read them. But the language in which they are written and in which you read them will remain not merely because language is more lasting than man, but because it is more capable of mutation.

One who writes a poem, however, writes it not because he courts fame with posterity, although often he hopes that a poem will outlive him, at least briefly. One who writes a poem writes it because the language prompts, or simply dictates, the next line. Beginning a poem, the poet as a rule doesn't know the way it's going to come out, and at times he is very surprised by the way it turns out, since often it turns out better than he expected, often his thought carries further than he reckoned. And that is the moment when the future of language invades its present.

There are, as we know, three modes of cognition: analytical, intuitive and the mode that was known to the Biblical prophets, revelation. What distinguishes poetry from other forms of literature is that it uses all three of them at once (gravitating primarily toward the second and the third). For all three of them are given in the language; and there are times when, by means of a single word, a single rhyme, the writer of a poem manages to find himself where no one has ever been before him, further, perhaps, than he himself would have wished for. The one who writes a poem writes it above all because verse writing is an extraordinary accelerator of conscience, of thinking, of comprehending the universe. Having experienced this acceleration once, one is no longer capable of abandoning the chance to repeat this experience; one falls into dependency on this process, the way others fall into dependency on drugs or on alcohol. One who finds himself in this sort of dependency on language is, I guess, what they call a poet.

Translated from Russian by Barry Rubin

Wole Soyinka

This Past Must Address Its Present
1986

Wole Soyinka was born at Abeokuta, near Ibadan in western Nigeria. He spent a number of years in England in the 1950s, before returning to Nigeria in 1960 to study African drama. During the civil war Soyinka wrote in support of a ceasefire, which lead to his arrest in 1967 for allegedly conspiring with the Biafra rebels. He was held for 22 months as a political prisoner.

Soyinka has published more than twenty works, including plays, novels and poetry. Much of his writing has focused on social and political oppression, and he has been a vocal critic of several Nigerian regimes. He writes in English, and his work is marked by the richness and scope of his word choice. Many of his plays draw on the African tradition of incorporating dance, music and action, and are based on the mythology of his tribe, the Yoruba. Soyinka's plays include The Swamp Dwellers, The Trial of Brother Jero, Death and the King's Horseman *and* The Bacchae of Euripides. *He has written two novels,* The Interpreters *and* Season of Anomy, *and among his autobiographical works are* The Man Died: Prison Notes *and* Aké. *His poems are collected in* Poems from Prison, A Shuttle in the Crypt *and* Mandela's Earth and Other Poems.

The Academy honoured Soyinka, 'who in a wide cultural perspective and with poetic overtones fashions the drama of existence'.

A rather curious scene, unscripted, once took place in the wings of a London theatre at the same time as the scheduled performance was being presented on the actual stage, before an audience. What happened was this: an actor refused to come on stage for his allocated role. Action was suspended. A fellow actor tried to persuade him to emerge, but he stubbornly shook his head. Then a struggle ensued. The second actor had hoped that, by suddenly exposing the reluctant actor to the audience in full glare of the spotlight, he would have no choice but to rejoin the cast. And so he tried to take the delinquent actor by surprise, pulling him suddenly towards the stage. He did not fully succeed, so a brief but untidy struggle began. The unwilling actor was completely taken aback and deeply embarrassed—some of that tussle was quite visible to a part of the audience.

The performance itself, it should be explained, was an improvisation around an incident. This meant that the actors were free, within the convention of the performance—to stop, re-work any part they wished, invite members of the audience on stage, assign roles and change costumes in full view of the audience. They therefore could also dramatise their wish to have that uncooperative actor join them—which they did with gusto. That actor had indeed left the stage before the contentious scene began. He had served notice during rehearsals that he would not participate in it. In the end, he had his way, but the incident proved very troubling to him for weeks afterwards. He found himself compelled to puzzle out this clash in attitudes between himself and his fellow writers and performers. He experienced, on the one hand, an intense rage that he had been made to appear incapable of confronting a stark reality, made to appear to suffer from interpretative coyness, to seem inhibited by a cruel reality or perhaps to carry his emotional involvement with an event so far as to interfere with his professional will. Of course, he knew that it was none of these things. The truth was far simpler. Unlike his colleagues together with whom he shared, unquestionably, the same political attitude towards the event which was being represented, he found the mode of presentation at war with the ugliness it tried to convey, creating an intense disquiet about his very presence on that stage, in that place, before an audience whom he considered collectively responsible for that dehumanising actuality.

And now let us remove some of the mystery and make that incident a little more concrete. The scene was the Royal Court Theatre, London, 1958. It was one of those Sunday nights which were given to experimentation, an innovation of that remarkable theatre manager-director, George Devine, whose creative nurturing radicalised British theater of that period and produced later icons like John Osborne, N.-F. Simpson, Edward Bond, Arnold Wesker, Harold Pinter, John Arden etc., and even forced the then conservative British palate to sample stylistic and ideological pariahs like Samuel Beckett and Bertold Brecht. On this particular occasion, the evening was devoted to a form of 'living' theatre, and the main fare was titled *Eleven Men Dead at Hola*. The actors were not all professional actors; indeed they were mostly writers who jointly created and performed these dramatic pieces. Those with a long political memory may recall what took place at Hola Camp, Kenya, during the Mau-Mau Liberation struggle. The British Colonial power believed that the Mau-Mau could be smashed by herding Kenyans into special camps, trying to separate the hard cases, the mere suspects and the potential recruits—oh, they had it all neatly worked out. One such camp was Hola Camp and the incident involved the death of eleven of the detainees who were simply beaten to death by camp officers and warders. The usual inquiry set up, and it was indeed the report which provided the main text on which the performance was based.

We need now only to identify the reluctant actor, if you have not guessed that by now—it was none other than this speaker. I recall the occasion as vividly as actors are wont to recollect for ever and ever the frightening moment of a blackout, when the lines are not only forgotten but even the moment in the play. The role which I had been assigned was that of a camp guard, one of the killers. We were equipped with huge nightsticks and, while a narrator read the testimony of one of the guards, our task was to raise the cudgels slowly and, almost ritualistically, bring them down on the necks and shoulders of the prisoners, under orders of the white camp officers. A surreal scene. Even in rehearsals, it was clear that the end product would be a surrealist tableau. The narrator at a lectern under a spot; a dispassionate reading, deliberately clinical, letting the stark facts reveal the states of mind of torturers and victims. A small ring of white officers, armed. One seizes a cudgel from one of the warders to demonstrate how to beat a human being without leaving visible marks. Then the innermost clump of detainees, their only weapon—non-violence. They had taken their decision to go on strike, refused to go to work unless they obtained better camp conditions. So they squatted on the ground and refused to move, locked their hands behind their knees in silent defiance. Orders were given. The inner ring of guards, the blacks, moved in, lifted the bodies by hooking their hands underneath the armpits of the detainees, carried them like toads in a state of petrification to one side, divided them in groups.

The faces of the victims are impassive; they are resolved to offer no resistance. The beatings begin: one to the left side, then the back, the arms—right, left, front, back. Rhythmically. The cudgels swing in unison. The faces of the white guards glow with professional satisfaction, their arms gesture languidly from time to time, suggesting it is time to shift to the next batch, or beat a little more severely on the neglected side. In terms of images, a fluid, near balletic scene.

Then the contrast, the earlier official version, enacting how the prisoners were supposed to have died. This claimed that the prisoners had collapsed, that they died after drinking from a poisoned water supply. So we staged that also. The prisoners filed to the water wagon, gasping with thirst. After the first two or three had drunk and commenced writhing with pain, these humane guards rushed to stop the others but no, they were already wild with thirst, fought their way past salvation and drank greedily the same source. The groans spread from one to the other, the writhing, the collapse—then agonised deaths. That was the version of the camp governors.

The motif was simple enough, the theatrical format a tried and tested one, faithful to a particular convention. What then was the problem? It was one, I believe, that affects most writers. When is playacting rebuked by reality? When is fictionalising presumptuous? What happens after playacting? One of the remarkable properties of the particular theatrical convention I have just described is that it gives off a strong odour of perenniality, that feeling of 'I have been here before.' 'I have been a witness to this.' 'The past enacts its presence.' In such an instance, that sense of perenniality can serve both as exorcism, a certificate of release or indeed—especially for the audience— a soporific. We must bear in mind that at the time of presentation, and to the major part of that audience, every death of a freedom fighter was a notch on a gun, the death of a fiend, an animal, a bestial mutant, not the martyrdom of a patriot.

We know also, however, that such efforts can provoke changes, that an actualisation of the statistical, journalistic footnote can arouse revulsion in the complacent mind, leading to the beginning of a commitment to change, redress. And on this occasion, angry questions had been raised in the houses of parliament. Liberals, humanitarians and reformists had taken up the cause of justice for the victims. Some had even travelled to Kenya to obtain details which exposed the official lie. This profound unease, which paralysed my creative will, therefore reached beyond the audience and, finally, I traced its roots to my own feelings of assaulted humanity, and its clamour for a different form of response. It provoked a feeling of indecency about that presentation, rather like the deformed arm of a leper which is thrust at the healthy to provoke a charitable sentiment. This, I believe, was the cause of that intangible, but totally visceral rejection which thwarted the demands of my calling, rendered it inadequate and mocked the empathy of my colleagues. It was as if the inhuman totality, of which that scene was a mere fragment, was saying to us: Kindly keep your comfortable sentiment to yourselves.

Of course, I utilise that episode only as illustration of the far deeper internalised processes of the creative mind, a process that endangers the writer in two ways: he either freezes up completely, or he abandons the pen for far more direct means of contesting unacceptable reality. And again, Hola Camp provides a convenient means of approaching that aspect of my continent's reality which, for us whom it directly affronts, constitutes the greatest threat to global peace in our actual existence. For there is a gruesome appropriateness in the fact that an African, a black man should stand here today, in the same year that the progressive prime minister of this host country was murdered, in the same year as Samora Machel was brought down on the territory of the desperate last-ditch guardians of the theory of racial superiority which has brought so much misery to our common humanity. Whatever the facts are about Olof Palme's death, there can be no question about his life. To the racial oppression of a large sector of humanity, Olof Palme pronounced, and acted, a decisive No! Perhaps it was those who were outraged by this act of racial 'treachery' who were myopic enough to imagine that the death of an individual would arrest the march of his convictions; perhaps it was simply yet another instance of the Terror Epidemic that feeds today on shock, not reason. It does not matter; an authentic conscience of the white tribe has been stilled, and the loss is both yours and mine. Samora Machel, the leader who once placed his country on a war footing against South Africa, went down in as yet mysterious circumstances. True, we are all still haunted by the Nkomati Accord which negated that earlier triumphant moment on the African collective will; nevertheless, his foes across the border have good reason to rejoice over his demise and, in that sense, his death is, ironically, a form of triumph for the black race.

Is that perhaps too stark a paradox? Then let me take you back to Hola Camp. It is cattle which are objects of the stick, or whip. So are horses, goats, donkeys etc. Their definition therefore involves being occasionally beaten to death. If, thirty years after Hola Camp, it is at all thinkable that it takes the ingenuity of the most sophisticated electronic interference to kill an African resistance fighter, the champions of racism are already admitting to themselves what they continue to deny to the world: that they, white supremacist breed, have indeed come a long way in their definition of their chosen enemy since Hola Camp. They have come an incredibly long way since Sharpeville when they shot unarmed, fleeing Africans in the back. They have come very far since 1930 when, at the first organised incident of the burning of passes, the South African blacks decided to turn Dingaan's Day, named for the defeat of the Zulu leader Dingaan, into a symbol of affirmative resistance by publicly destroying their obnoxious passes. In response to those thousands of passes burnt on Cartright Flats, the Durban police descended on the unarmed protesters killing some half dozen and wounding hundreds. They backed it up with a scorched earth campaign which dispersed thousands of Africans from their normal environment, victims of imprisonment and deportation. And even that 1930 repression was a quantum leap from that earlier, spontaneous protest against the Native Pass Law in 1919, when the police merely rode down the protesters on horseback, whipped and sjamboked them, chased and harried them, like stray goats and wayward cattle, from street corner to shanty lodge. Every act of racial terror, with its vastly increasing sophistication of style and escalation in human loss, is itself an acknowledgment of improved knowledge and respect for the potential of what is feared, an acknowledgment of the sharpening tempo of triumph by the victimised.

For there was this aspect which struck me most forcibly in that attempt to recreate the crime at Hola Camp: in the various testimonies of the white officers, it stuck out, whether overtly stated or simply through their efficient detachment from the ongoing massacre. It was this: at no time did these white overseers actually experience the human 'otherness' of their victims. They clearly did not experience the reality of the victims as human beings. Animals perhaps, a noxious form of vegetable life maybe, but certainly not human. I do not speak here of their colonial overlords, the ones who formulated and sustained the policy of settler colonialism, the ones who dispatched the Maxim guns and tuned the imperial bugle. They knew very well that empires existed which had to be broken, that civilisations had endured for centuries which had to be destroyed. The 'sub-human' denigration for which their 'civilising mission' became the altruistic remedy, was the mere rationalising icing on the cake of imperial greed. But yes indeed, there were the agents, those who carried out orders (like Eichmann, to draw parallels from the white continent); they—whether as bureaucrats, technicians or camp governors had no conceptual space in their heads which could be filled—except very rarely and exceptionally—by 'the black as also human'. It would be correct to say that this has remained the pathology of the average South African white since the turn of the last century to this moment. Here, for example, is one frank admission by an enlightened, even radical mind of that country:

> It was not until my last year in school that it had occurred to me that these black people, these voteless masses, were in any way concerned with the socialism which I professed or that they had any role to play in the great social revolution which in these days seemed to be imminent. The 'workers' who were

destined to inherit the new world were naturally the white carpenters and bricklayers, the tramworkers and miners who were organized in their trade unions and who voted for the Labour Party. I would no more have thought of discussing politics with a native youth than of inviting him home to play with me or to a meal or asking him to join the Carnarvon Football Club. The African was on a different plane, hardly human, part of the scene as were dogs and trees and, more remotely, cows. I had no special feelings about him, not interest nor hate nor love. He just did not come into my social picture. So completely had I accepted the traditional attitudes of the time.

Yes, I believe that this self-analysis by Eddie Roux, the Afrikaner political rebel and scientist, remains today the flat, unvarnished truth for the majority of Afrikaners. 'No special feelings, not interest nor hate nor love', the result of a complete acceptance of 'traditional attitudes'. That passage captures a mind's racial tabula rasa, if you like—in the first decade of this century—about the time, in short, when the Nobel series of prizes was inaugurated. But a slate, no matter how clean, cannot avoid receiving impressions once it is exposed to air—fresh or polluted. And we are now in the year 1986, that is after an entire century of direct, intimate exposure, since that confrontation, that first rejection of the dehumanising label implicit in the Native Pass Laws.

Eddie Roux, like hundreds, even thousands of his countrymen, soon made rapid strides. His race has produced its list of martyrs in the cause of nonracialism—one remembers, still with a tinge of pain, Ruth First, destroyed by a letter bomb delivered by the long arm of Apartheid. There are others—André Brink, Abram Fischer, Helen Suzman, Breyten Breytenbach—with the scars of martyrdom still seared into their souls. Intellectuals, writers, scientists, plain working men, politicians—they come to that point where a social reality can no longer be observed as a culture on a slide beneath the microscope, nor turned into aesthetic variations on pages, canvas or the stage. The blacks of course are locked into an unambiguous condition: on this occasion I do not need to address *us*. We know, and we embrace our mission. It is the *other* that this precedent seizes the opportunity to address, and not merely those who are trapped within the confines of that doomed camp, but those who live outside, on the fringes of conscience. Those specifically, who with shameless smugness invent arcane moral propositions that enable them to plead inaction in a language of unparalleled political flatulence: 'Personally, I find sanctions morally repugnant.' Or what shall we say of another leader for whom economic sanctions which work against an Eastern European country will not work in the Apartheid enclave of South Africa, that master of histrionics who takes to the world's airwaves to sing: 'Let Poland be', but turns off his hearing aid when the world shouts: 'Let Nicaragua be'. But enough of these world leaders of double-talk and multiple moralities.

It is baffling to any mind that pretends to the slightest claim to rationality, it is truly and formidably baffling. Can the same terrain of phenomenal assimilation—that is, one which produced evidence of a capacity to translate empirical observations into implications of rational human conduct—can this same terrain which, over half a century ago, fifty entire years, two, three generations ago produced the Buntings, the Roux, the Douglas Woltons, Solly Sachs, the Gideon Bothas—can that same terrain, fifty, sixty, even seventy years later, be peopled by a species of humanity so ahistorical that the declaration, so clearly spelt out in 1919 at the burning of the passes, remains only a troublesome event of no enduring significance?

Some atavistic bug is at work here which defies all scientific explanation, an arrest in time within the evolutionary mandate of nature, which puts all human experience of learning to serious question! We have to ask ourselves then, what event can speak to such a breed of people? How do we reactivate that petrified cell which houses historic apprehension and development? Is it possible, perhaps, that events, gatherings such as this might help? Dare we skirt the edge of hubris and say to them: Take a good look. Provide your response. In your anxiety to prove that this moment is not possible, you had killed, maimed, silenced, tortured, exiled, debased and dehumanised hundreds of thousands encased in this very skin, crowned with such hair, proudly content with their very being? How many potential partners in the science of heart transplant have you wasted? How do we know how many black South African scientists and writers would have stood here, by now, if you had had the vision to educate the rest of the world in the value of a great multi-racial society?

Jack Cope surely sums it up in his foreword to *The Adversary Within*, a study of dissidence in Afrikaner literature when he states:

> Looking back from the perspective of the present, I think it can justly be said that, at the core of the matter, the Afrikaaner leaders in 1924 took the wrong turning. Themselves the victims of imperialism in its most evil aspect, all their sufferings and enormous loss of life nevertheless failed to convey to them the obvious historical lesson. They became themselves the new imperialists. They took over from Britain the mantle of empire and colonialism. They could well have set their faces against annexation, aggression, colonial exploitation, and oppression, racial arrogance and barefaced hypocrisy, of which they had been themselves the victims. They could have opened the doors to humane ideas and civilizing processes and transformed the great territory with its incalculable resources into another New World.
>
> Instead they deliberately set the clock back wherever they could. Taking over ten million indigenous subjects from British

colonial rule, they stripped them of what limited rights they had gained over a century and tightened the screws on their subjection.

Well, perhaps the wars against Chaka and Dingaan and Diginswayo, even the Great Trek were then too fresh in your *laager* memory. But we are saying that over a century has passed since then, a century in which the world has leapt, in comparative tempo with the past, at least three centuries. And we have seen the potential of man and woman—of all races—contend with the most jealously guarded sovereignty of Nature and the Cosmos. In every field, both in the humanities and sciences, we have seen that human creativity has confronted and tempered the hostility of his environment, adapting, moderating, converting, harmonising and even subjugating. Triumphing over errors and resuming the surrendered fields, when man has had time to lick his wounds and listen again to the urgings of his spirit. History—distorted, opportunistic renderings of history have been cleansed and restored to truthful reality, because the traducers of the history of others have discovered that the further they advanced, the more their very progress was checked and vitiated by the lacunae they had purposefully inserted in the history of others. Self-interest dictated yet another round of revisionism—slight, niggardly concessions to begin with. But a breach had been made in the dam and an avalanche proved the logical progression. From the heart of jungles, even before the aid of high-precision cameras mounted on orbiting satellites, civilisations have resurrected, documenting their own existence with unassailable iconography and art. More amazing still, the records of the ancient voyagers, the merchant adventurers of the age when Europe did not yet require to dominate territories in order to feed its industrial mills—those objective recitals of mariners and adventurers from antiquity confirmed what the archeological remains affirmed so loudly. They spoke of living communities which regulated their own lives, which had evolved a working relationship with Nature, which ministered to their own wants and secured their future with their own genius. These narratives, uncluttered by the impure motives which needed to mystify the plain self-serving rush to dismantle independent societies for easy plundering—pointed accusing fingers unerringly in the direction of European savants, philosophers, scientists and theorists of human evolution. Gobineau is a notorious name, but how many students of European thought today, even among us Africans, recall that several of the most revered names in European philosophy—Hegel, Locke, Montesquieu, Hume, Voltaire—an endless list—were unabashed theorists of racial superiority and denigrators of the African history and being. As for the more prominent names among the theorists of revolution and class struggle—we will draw the curtain of extenuation on their own intellectual aberration, forgiving them a little for their vision of an end to human exploitation.

In any case, the purpose is not really to indict the past, but to summon it to the attention of a suicidal, anachronistic present. To say to that mutant present: you are a child of those centuries of lies, distortion and opportunism in high places, even among the holy of holies of intellectual objectivity. But the world is growing up, while you willfully remain a child, a stubborn, self-destructive child, with certain destructive powers, but a child nevertheless. And to say to the world, to call attention to its own historic passage of lies—as yet unabandoned by some—which sustains the evil precocity of this child. Wherein then lies the surprise that we, the victims of that intellectual dishonesty of others, demand from that world that is finally coming to itself, a measure of expiation? Demand that it rescues itself, by concrete acts, from the stigma of being the willful parent of a monstrosity, especially as that monstrous child still draws material nourishment, breath and human recognition from the strengths and devises of that world, with an umbilical cord which stretches across oceans, even across the cosmos via so-called programs of technological cooperation. We are saying very simply but urgently: Sever that cord. By any name, be it Total Sanction, Boycott, Disinvestment or whatever, sever this umbilical cord and leave this monster of a birth to atrophy and die or to rebuild itself on long-denied humane foundations. Let it collapse, shorn of its external sustenance, let it collapse of its own social disequilibrium, its economic lopsidedness, its war of attrition on its most productive labour. Let it wither like an aborted fetus of the human family if it persists in smothering the minds and sinews which constitute its authentic being.

This pariah society that is Apartheid South Africa plays many games on human intelligence. Listen to this, for example. When the whole world escalated its appeal for the release of Nelson Mandela, the South African government blandly declared that it continued to hold Nelson Mandela for the same reasons that the Allied powers continued to hold Rudolf Hess! Now a statement like that is an obvious appeal to the love of the ridiculous in everyone. Certainly it wrung a kind of satiric poem out of me—Rudolf Hess as Nelson Mandela in blackface! What else can a writer do to protect his humanity against such egregious assaults! But yet again to equate Nelson Mandela to the archcriminal Rudolf Hess is a macabre improvement on the attitude of regarding him as sub-human. It belongs on that same scale of Apartheid's self-improvement as the ratio between Sharpeville and Von Brandis Square, that near-kind, near-considerate, almost benevolent dispersal of the first Native Press rebellion.

That world which is so conveniently traduced by Apartheid thought is of course that which I so wholeheartedly embrace—and this is my choice—among several options—of the significance of my presence here. It is a world that nourishes my being, one which is so self-sufficient, so replete in all aspects of its productivity, so confident in itself and in its destiny that it experiences no fear in reaching out to others and in responding to the reach of others. It is the heart-stone of our creative existence. It constitutes the prism of our world perception and this means that our sight need not be and has never been permanently turned inwards. If it were, we could not so easily understand the enemy on our doorstep, nor understand how to obtain the means to disarm it. When this society which is Apartheid South Africa indulges from time to time in appeals to the outside world that it represents the last bastion of civilization against the hordes of barbarism from its north, we can even afford an indulgent smile. It is sufficient, imagines this state, to raise the spectre of a few renegade African leaders, psychopaths and robber barons who we ourselves are victims of—whom we denounce before the world and overthrow when we are able—this Apartheid society insists to the world that its picture of the future is the reality which only its policies can erase. This is a continent which only destroys, it proclaims, it is peopled by a race which has never contributed anything positive to the world's pool of knowledge. A vacuum, that will suck into its insatiable maw the entire fruits of centuries of European civilisation, then spew out the resulting mush with contempt. How strange that a society which claims to represent this endangered face of progress should itself be locked in centuries-old fantasies, blithely unaware of, or indifferent to the fact that it is the last, institutionally functioning product of archaic articles of faith in Euro-Judaic thought.

Take God and Law for example, especially the former. The black race has more than sufficient historic justification to be a little paranoid about the intrusion of alien deities into its destiny. For even today, Apartheid's mentality of the pre-ordained rests—according to its own unabashed claims, on what I can only describe as incidents in a testamentary Godism—I dare not call it Christianity. The sons of Ham on the one hand;

the descendants of Shem on the other. The once pronounced, utterly immutable curse. As for Law, these supremacists base their refusal to concede the right of equal political participation to blacks on a claim that Africans have neither respect for, nor the slightest proclivity for Law—that is, for any arbitrating concept between the individual and the collective.

Even the mildest, liberal, somewhat regretful but contented apologists for Apartheid, for at least some form of Apartheid which is not Apartheid but ensures the *status quo*—even this ambivalent breed bases its case on this lack of the idea of Law in the black mind. I need only refer to a recent contribution to this literature in the form of an autobiography by a famous heart transplant surgeon, one who in his own scientific right has probably been a candidate for a Nobel Prize in the sciences. Despite constant intellectual encounters on diverse levels, the sad phenomenon persists of Afrikaner minds which, in the words of Eddie Roux, is a product of that complete acceptance of the 'traditional attitudes of the time'.

They have, as already acknowledged, quite 'respectable' intellectual ancestors. Friedrich Wilhelm Hegel, to cite just my favourite example, found it convenient to pretend that the African had not yet developed to the level where he

> attained that realisation of any substantial objective existence—as for example, God, or Law—in which the interest of man's volition is involved and in which he realizes his own being.

He continues:

> This distinction between himself as an individual and the universality of his essential being, the African in the uniform, undeveloped oneness of his existence, has not yet attained: so that the knowledge of absolute Being, an Other and a Higher than his individual self, is entirely wanting.

Futile to waste a moment refuting the banal untruthfulness of this claim, I content myself with extracting from it only a lesson which escapes, even today, those who insist that the pinnacle of man's intellectual thirst is the capacity to project this universality in the direction of a Super-Other. There is, I believe, a very healthy school of thought which not only opposes this materially, but has produced effectively structured societies which operate independently of this seductive, even productively, inspiring but extravagant fable.

Once we thus overcome the temptation to contest the denial of this feat of imaginative projection to the African, we find ourselves left only with the dispassionate exercise of examining in what areas we encounter differences between the histories of societies which, according to Hegel and company, never conceived of this Omnipotent Extrusion into Infinite Space, and those who did—be these differences in the areas of economic or artistic life, social relations or scientific attainment—in short, in all those activities which are empirically verifiable, quite different from the racial consequences of imprecations arising from that post Adam-and-Eve nudist escapade in the Old Testament.

When we do this, we come upon a curious fact. The pre-colonial history of African societies—and I refer to both Euro-Christian and Arab-Islamic colonisation—indicates very clearly that African societies never at any time of their existence went to war with another over the issue of *their* religion. That is, at no time did the black race attempt to subjugate or forcibly convert others with any holier-than-thou evangelising zeal. Economic and political motives, yes. But not religion. Perhaps this unnatural fact was responsible for the conclusions of Hegel—we do not know. Certainly, the bloody histories of the world's major religions, localised skirmishes of which extend even to the present, lead to a sneaking suspicion that religion, as defined by these eminent philosophers, comes to self-knowledge only through the activity of war.

When, therefore, towards the close of the twentieth century, that is, centuries after the Crusades and Jihads that laid waste other and one another's civilisations, fragmented ancient cohesive social relations and trampled upon the spirituality of entire peoples, smashing their cultures in obedience to the strictures of unseen gods, when today, we encounter nations whose social reasoning is guided by canonical, theological claims, we believe, on our part, that the era of darkness has never truly left the world. A state whose justification for the continuing suppression of its indigenes, indigenes who constitute the majority on that land, rests on claims to divine selection is a menace to secure global relationship in a world that thrives on nationalism as common denominator. Such a society does not, in other words, belong in this modern world. We also have our myths, but we have never employed them as a base for the subjugation of others. We also inhabit a realistic world, however, and, for the recovery of the fullness of that world, the black race has no choice but to prepare itself and volunteer the supreme sacrifice.

In speaking of that world—both myth and reality—it is our duty, perhaps our very last peaceful duty to a doomed enemy—to remind it, and its supporters outside its boundaries, that the phenomenon of ambivalence induced by the African world has a very long history, but that most proponents of the slanderous aspects have long ago learnt to abandon the untenable. Indeed it is probably even more pertinent to remind this racist society that our African world, its cultural hoards and philosophical thought, have had concrete impacts on the racists' own forebears, have proved seminal to a number of movements and even created tributaries, both pure and polluted, among the white indigenes in their own homelands.

Such a variety of encounters and responses have been due, naturally, to profound searches for new directions in their cultural adventures, seeking solaces to counter the remorseless mechanisation of their existence, indeed seeking new meanings for the mystery of life and attempting to overcome the social malaise created by the very triumphs of their own civilisation. It has led to a profound respect for the African contribution to world knowledge, which did not, however, end the habitual denigration of the African world. It has created in places a near-deification of the African person—that phase in which every African had to be a prince—which yet again, was coupled with a primitive fear and loathing for the person of the African. To these paradoxical responses, the essentiality of our black being remains untouched. For the black race knows, and is content simply to know, itself. It is the European world that has sought, with the utmost zeal, to re-define itself through these encounters, even when it does appear that he is endeavouring to grant meaning to an experience of the African world.

We can make use of the example of that period of European Expressionism, a movement which saw African art, music and dramatic rituals share the same sphere of influence as the most disparate, astonishingly incompatible collection of ideas, ideologies and social tendencies—Freud, Karl Marx, Bakunin, Nietzsche, cocaine and free love. What wonder then, that the spiritual and plastic presence of the Bakota, Nimba, the Yoruba, Dogon, Dan etc., *should find themselves at once the inspiration* and the anathematised of a delirium that was most peculiarly European, mostly Teutonic and Gallic, spanning at least four decades across the last and the present centuries. Yet the vibrant goal remained the complete liberation of man, that freeing of his yet untapped potential that would carve marble blocks for the construction of a new world, debourgeoisify existing constrictions of European thought and light the flame to forge a new fraternity throughout this brave new world.

Yes, within this single movement that covered the vast spectrum of outright fascism, anarchism and revolutionary communism, the reality that was Africa was, as always, sniffed at, delicately tested, swallowed entire, regurgitated, appropriated, extolled and damned in the revelatory frenzy of a continent's recreative energies.

Oscar Kokoschka for instance: for this dramatist and painter African ritualism led mainly in the direction of sadism, sexual perversion, general self-gratification. It flowed naturally into a Nietzschean apocalyptic summons, full of self-induced, ecstatic rage against society, indeed, against the world. Vassily Kadinsky on his part, responded to the principles of African art by foreseeing: 'a science of art erected on a broad foundation which must be international in character', insisting that 'it is interesting, but certainly not sufficient, to create an exclusively European art theory'. The science of art would then lead, according to him, to 'a comprehensive synthesis which will extend far beyond the confines of art into the realm of the oneness of the human and the "divine"'.

This same movement, whose centenary will be due for celebrations in European artistic capitals in the next decade or two—among several paradoxes the phenomenon of European artists of later acknowledged giant stature—Modigliani, Matisse, Gauguin, Picasso, Brancusi etc. worshipping with varying degrees of fervour, at the shrine of African and Polynesian artistic revelations, even as Johannes Becher, in his Expressionist delirium, swore to build a new world on the eradication of all plagues, including: 'Negro tribes, fever, tuberculosis, venereal epidemics, intellectual psychic defects—I'll fight them, vanquish them.'

And was it by coincidence that contemporaneously with this stirring manifesto, yet another German enthusiast, Leo Frobenius—with no claims whatever to being part of, or indeed having the least interest in the Expressionist movement, was able to visit Ile-Ife, the heartland and cradle of the Yoruba race and be profoundly stirred by an object of beauty, the product of the Yoruba mind and hand, a classic expression of that serene portion of the world resolution of that race, in his own words:

> Before us stood a head of marvellous beauty, wonderfully cast in antique bronze, true to the life, incrusted with a patina of glorious dark green. This was, in very deed, the Olokun, Atlantic Africa's Poseidon.

Yet listen to what he had to write about the very people whose handiwork had lifted him into these realms of universal sublimity:

> Profoundly stirred, I stood for many minutes before the remnant of the erstwhile Lord and Ruler of the Empire of Atlantis. My companions were no less astounded. As though we have agreed to do so, we held our peace. Then I looked around and saw—the blacks—the circle of the sons of the 'venerable priest', his Holiness the Oni's friends, and his intelligent officials. I was moved to silent melancholy at the thought that this assembly of degenerate and feeble-minded posterity should be the legitimate guardians of so much loveliness.

A direct invitation to a free-for-all race for dispossession, justified on the grounds of the keeper's unworthiness, it recalls other schizophrenic conditions which are mother to, for instance, the far more lethal, dark mythopoeia of Van Lvyck Louw. For though this erstwhile Nazi sympathiser would later rain maledictions on the heads of the more extreme racists of his countrymen:

> Lord, teach us to think what 'own' is, Lord let us think! and then: over hate against blacks, browns, whites: over this and its cause, I dare to call down judgement.

Van Lvyck's powerful epic *Raka* was guaranteed to churn up the white cesspools of these primordial fears. A work of searing, visceral impact operating on racial memory, it would feed the Afrikaner Credo on the looming specter of a universal barbaric recession, bearing southwards on the cloven hooves of the Fifth Horseman of the Apocalypse, the black.

There is a deep lesson for the world in the black races' capacity to forgive, one which, I often think, has much to do with ethical precepts which spring from their world view and authentic religions, none of which is ever totally eradicated by the accretions of foreign faiths and their implicit ethnocentricism. For, not content with being a racial slanderer, one who did not hesitate to denigrate, in such uncompromisingly nihilistic terms, the ancestral fount of the black races—a belief which this ethnologist himself observed—Frobenius was also a notorious plunderer, one of a long line of European archeological raiders. The museums of Europe testify to this insatiable lust of Europe; the frustrations of the ministries of culture of the Third World and of organisations like UNESCO are a continuing testimony to the tenacity, even recidivist nature of your routine receiver of stolen goods. Yet, is it not amazing that Frobenius is today still honoured by black institutions, black leaders and scholars? That his anniversaries provide ready excuse for intellectual gatherings and symposia on the black continent, *that his racist condescensions*, assaults have not been permitted to obscure his contribution to their knowledge of Africa, or the role which he has played in the understanding of the phenomenon of human culture and society, even in spite of the frequent patchiness of his scholarship?

It is the same largeness of spirit which has informed the relationship today of erstwhile colonial nations, some of whom have undergone the most cruel forms of settler or plantation colonialism, where the human degradation that goes with greed and exploitation attained such levels of perversion that human ears, hands and noses served to atone for failures in production quota. Nations which underwent the agony of wars of liberation, whose earth freshly teems with the bodies of innocent victims and unsung martyrs, live side by side today with their recent enslavers, even sharing the control of their destiny with those who, barely four or five years ago, compelled them to witness the massacre of their kith and kin. Over and above Christian charity, they are content to rebuild, and share. This spirit of collaboration is easy to dismiss as the treacherous ploy of that special breed of leaders who settle for early compromises in order to safeguard, for their own use, the polished shoes of the departing oppressors. In many cases, the truth of this must be conceded. But we also have examples of regimes, allied to the aspirations of their masses on the black continent, which have adopted this same political philosophy. And, in any case, the final arbiters are the people themselves, from whose relationships any observations such as this obtain any validity. Let us simply content ourselves with remarking that it is a phenomenon worthy of note. There are, after all, European nations today whose memory of domination by other races remains so vivid more than two centuries after liberation, that a terrible vengeance culturally, socially and politically is still exacted, even at this very moment, from the descendants of those erstwhile conquerors. I have visited such nations whose cruel histories under foreign domination are enshrined as icons to daily consciousness in monuments, parks, in museums and churches, in documentation, woodcuts and photo gravures displayed under bullet-proof glass cases but, most telling of all, in the reduction of the remnants of the conquering hordes to the degraded status of aliens on sufferance, with reduced civic rights, privileges and social status, a barely tolerate marginality that expresses itself in the pathos of downcast faces, dropped shoulders and apologetic encounters in those rare times when intercourse with the latterly assertive race is unavoidable. Yes, all this I have seen, and much of it has been written about and debated in international gatherings. And even while acknowledging the poetic justice of it in the abstract, one cannot help but wonder if a physical pound of flesh, excised at birth, is not a kinder act than a lifelong visitation of the sins of the father on the sons even to the tenth and twelfth generations.

Confronted with such traditions of attenuating the racial and cultural pride of these marginalised or minority peoples, the mind travels back to our own societies where such causative histories are far fresher in the memory, where the ruins of formerly thriving communities still speak eloquent accusations and the fumes still rise from the scorched-earth strategies of colonial and racist myopia. Yet the streets bear the names of former oppressors, their statues and other symbols of subjugation are left to decorate their squares, the consciousness of a fully confident people having relegated them to mere decorations and roosting-places for bats and pigeons. And the libraries remain unpurged, so that new generations freely browse through the works of Frobenius, of Hume, Hegel or Montesquieu and others without first encountering, freshly stamped on the fly-leaf: WARNING! THIS WORK IS DANGEROUS FOR YOUR RACIAL SELF-ESTEEM.

Yet these proofs of accommodation, on the grand or minuscule scale, collective, institutional or individual, must not be taken as proof of an infinite, uncritical capacity of black patience. They constitute in their own nature, a body of tests, an accumulation of debt, an implicit offer that must be matched by concrete returns. They are the blocks in a suspended bridge begun from one end of a chasm which, whether the builders will it or not, must obey the law of matter and crash down beyond a certain point, settling definitively into the widening chasm of suspicion, frustration and redoubled hate. On that testing ground which, for us, is Southern Africa, that medieval camp of biblical terrors, primitive suspicions, a choice must be made by all lovers of peace: either to bring it into the modern world, into a rational state of being within that spirit of human partnership, a capacity for which has been so amply demonstrated by every liberated black nation on our continent, or—to bring it abjectly to its knees by ejecting it, in every aspect, from humane recognition, so that it caves in internally, through the strategies of its embattled majority. Whatever the choice, this inhuman affront cannot be allowed to pursue our twentieth century conscience into the twenty-first, that symbolic coming-of-age which peoples of all cultures appear to celebrate with rites of passage. That calendar, we know, is not universal, but time is, and so are the imperatives of time. And of those imperatives that challenge our being, our presence and humane definition at this time, none can be considered more pervasive than the end of racism, the eradication of human inequality and the dismantling of all their structures. The Prize is the consequent enthronement of its complement: universal suffrage, and peace.

Laureates
1901 to 2006

2006 Orhan Pamuk
2005 Harold Pinter
2004 Elfriede Jelinek
2003 J.M. Coetzee
2002 Imre Kertész
2001 V.S. Naipaul
2000 Gao Xingjian
1999 Günter Grass
1998 José Saramago
1997 Dario Fo
1996 Wislawa Szymborska
1995 Seamus Heaney
1994 Kenzaburo Oe
1993 Toni Morrison
1992 Derek Walcott
1991 Nadine Gordimer
1990 Octavio Paz
1989 Camilo José Cela
1988 Naguib Mahfouz
1987 Joseph Brodsky
1986 Wole Soyinka
1985 Claude Simon
1984 Jaroslav Seifert
1983 William Golding
1982 Gabriel García Márquez
1981 Elias Canetti
1980 Czeslaw Milosz
1979 Odysseus Elytis
1978 Isaac Bashevis Singer
1977 Vicente Aleixandre
1976 Saul Bellow
1975 Eugenio Montale
1974 Eyvind Johnson, Harry Martinson
1973 Patrick White
1972 Heinrich Böll
1971 Pablo Neruda
1970 Alexandr Solzhenitsyn
1969 Samuel Beckett
1968 Yasunari Kawabata
1967 Miguel Angel Asturias
1966 Samuel Agnon, Nelly Sachs
1965 Mikhail Sholokhov
1964 Jean-Paul Sartre
1963 Giorgos Seferis
1962 John Steinbeck
1961 Ivo Andric
1960 Saint-John Perse
1959 Salvatore Quasimodo
1958 Boris Pasternak
1957 Albert Camus
1956 Juan Ramón Jiménez
1955 Halldór Laxness
1954 Ernest Hemingway
1953 Winston Churchill
1952 François Mauriac
1951 Pär Lagerkvist
1950 Bertrand Russell
1949 William Faulkner
1948 T.S. Eliot

1947 André Gide
1946 Hermann Hesse
1945 Gabriela Mistral
1944 Johannes V. Jensen
1943 The prize money was 1/3 allocated to the Main Fund and 2/3 to the Special Fund of this prize section
1942 The prize money was 1/3 allocated to the Main Fund and 2/3 to the Special Fund of this prize section
1941 The prize money was 1/3 allocated to the Main Fund and 2/3 to the Special Fund of this prize section
1940 The prize money was 1/3 allocated to the Main Fund and 2/3 to the Special Fund of this prize section
1939 Frans Eemil Sillanpää
1938 Pearl Buck
1937 Roger Martin du Gard
1936 Eugene O'Neill
1935 The prize money was 1/3 allocated to the Main Fund and 2/3 to the Special Fund of this prize section
1934 Luigi Pirandello
1933 Ivan Bunin
1932 John Galsworthy
1931 Erik Axel Karlfeldt
1930 Sinclair Lewis
1929 Thomas Mann
1928 Sigrid Undset
1927 Henri Bergson
1926 Grazia Deledda
1925 George Bernard Shaw
1924 Wladyslaw Reymont
1923 William Butler Yeats
1922 Jacinto Benavente
1921 Anatole France
1920 Knut Hamsun
1919 Carl Spitteler
1918 The prize money was allocated to the Special Fund of this prize section
1917 Karl Gjellerup, Henrik Pontoppidan
1916 Verner von Heidenstam
1915 Romain Rolland
1914 The prize money was allocated to the Special Fund of this prize section
1913 Rabindranath Tagore
1912 Gerhart Hauptmann
1911 Maurice Maeterlinck
1910 Paul Heyse
1909 Selma Lagerlöf
1908 Rudolf Eucken
1907 Rudyard Kipling
1906 Giosuè Carducci
1905 Henryk Sienkiewicz
1904 Frédéric Mistral, José Echegaray
1903 Bjørnstjerne Bjørnson
1902 Theodor Mommsen
1901 Sully Prudhomme

Sources & Acknowledgements

The publishers wish to thank the Nobel Foundation for permission to reproduce the lectures in this book. The lecture by Seamus Heaney was reproduced from *Les Prix Nobel: The Nobel Prizes 1995*, edited by Tore Frängsmyr, Nobel Foundation, Stockholm, 1996. The lecture by Kenzaburo Oe was reproduced from *Les Prix Nobel: The Nobel Prizes 1994*, edited by Tore Frängsmyr, Nobel Foundation, Stockholm, 1995. Lectures by Toni Morrison, Derek Walcott and Nadine Gordimer were reproduced from *Nobel Lectures: Literature 1991–1995*, edited by Sture Allén, World Scientific Publishing Co., Singapore, 1997. Lectures by Octavio Paz, Camilo José Cela, Naguib Mahfouz, Joseph Brodsky and Wole Soyinka were reproduced from *Nobel Lectures: Literature 1981–1990*, edited by Grängsmyr & Allén, World Scientific Publishing Co., Singapore, 1993.

The extract from 'I'm Explaining a Few Things' translated by Nathaniel Tarn, from *Pablo Neruda: Selected Poems*, published by Jonathan Cape, is reprinted by permission of The Random House Group Ltd. Extracts from 'Exposure', from *North* by Seamus Heaney and from 'The Novelist' by W.H. Auden, are reproduced with permission from Faber and Faber Ltd. The extracts from 'The Municipal Gallery Revisited', 'Meditations in Time of Civil War' and 'Vacillation' by W.B. Yeats are reproduced by permission of A.P. Watt Ltd on behalf of Gráinne Yeats. Every effort has been made to contact copyright holders for other extracts contained in this book.

The Truth That Sticks

Martin Bell

A timely, heartfelt and tough analysis of Britain's New Labour years from a hugely respected journalist and former politician.

Ten years after Labour surged to power on the spoils of Tory sleaze, their lies, corruption, warmongering and maltreatment of high office have proved a bitter disappointment for millions for whom New Labour represented new hope. What happened?

Martin Bell dissects scandals from Bernie Ecclestone to David Blunkett; explores Labour's contempt for democracy; attacks the illegal and utterly disastrous decision to go to war in Iraq, and questions the deployment in Afghanistan – he visited both countries in the course of writing the book.

Wide-ranging and pulling no punches, *The Truth That Sticks* is a crushing analysis of Labour's decade of deception, dishonesty and abuse of power, delivered with precision and great passion.

ISBN: 978-1840468-22-9   Hardback £16.99

Best of Enemies

Richard Milton

Richard Milton exposes the secrets of a relationship steeped in mutual admiration, blood and propaganda.

For a century, Britain and Germany had been closer than any other two countries. Germany was Britain's biggest export market, and vice versa. Germans adopted English dress, customs and manners. Even as late as the Nazi era, Hess, Himmler, Goering and Hitler himself remained passionate Anglophiles.

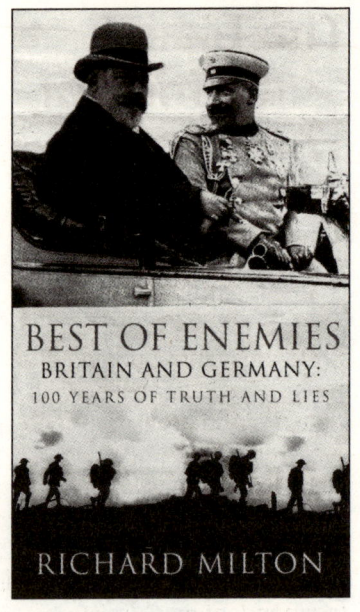

During the First World War, however, Germany and Britain spent billions on clandestine propaganda to blacken each other's reputations. This gargantuan effort gave birth to the PR industry itself – later seized upon by Nazi propagandist Goebbels to devastating effect.

Richard Milton's expertly written popular history gives a fresh perspective on this tumultuous, painful love-hate relationship, and is also a brilliant study of propaganda itself – now more than ever a vital weapon of war.

ISBN: 978-1840468-28-1   Hardback £14.99

The Lives and Times of The Great Composers

Michael Steen

'A glorious plum-pudding of a book … to be consulted with pleasure and profit, over and over again.'
Sir Jeremy Isaacs

'Michael Steen's beautifully illustrated book packs [in] an astonishing amount of detail.' *Independent on Sunday*

'Hugely informative and deliciously gossipy' *The Spectator*

'An absolute delight … a superbly eclectic work of modern reference.' *Times Literary Supplement*

Michael Steen's highly acclaimed history of the giants of classical music is a new, unique and lovingly constructed modern reference work. Grand and panoramic in its scope, it is also a beguiling and absorbing read from beginning to end.

Beautifully presented, with over 50 colour plates and many more black and white pictures, maps and family trees, *The Great Composers* is an enticing biography of the giants of European music and the tumultuous times in which they lived.

ISBN: 978-1840466-79-9   Paperback £16.99

China: Friend or Foe?

Hugo de Burgh

China is growing phenomenally, with half the world's cranes currently on its soil. Its 1.3 billion people have around 300 million mobile phones and a purchasing power second only to the US, although, especially in rural areas, there is widespread poverty. Government censorship is a fact of life – with 30,000 workers manning a firewall restricting citizens' access to the internet.

Yet few in the West know much about China. Popular press coverage is limited to stereotypes, the serious media to economics and business, and that's about it. What *does* China mean to the rest of the world?

Hugo de Burgh explores the key questions: How is China managed? What do we need to know about Chinese nationalism? Will the Chinese economy provide huge new opportunities for trade, or will it kill off our own livelihoods? What about China's human rights record? Is China a friend to be welcomed or a foe to be guarded against?

Accessible, straightforward and often astonishing, *China: Friend or Foe?* is the first popular exploration of one of the biggest issues of the next hundred years.

ISBN: 978-1840467-33-8   Paperback £7.99

50 Facts that Should Change the World

Emma Hartley

'Provides proof of why we cannot be complacent about the world as it is today. Should become the bible of political activists everywhere.'
New Statesman

Cars kill two people every minute
More than 150 countries use torture
Ten languages die out every year
There are 44 million child labourers in India

50
facts that should change the world
Jessica Williams

'A research handbook for the *No Logo* generation'
Guardian

'Fearless and compelling. You need to know what's in this book.'
Monica Ali

'Fearless and compelling. You need to know what's in this book.' Monica Ali

- Landmines kill or main at least one person every hour
- Brazil has more Avon ladies than members of its armed services
- A third of the world's obese people live in the developing world

In this brand new edition of her bestseller, Jessica Williams tests the temperature of our world – and diagnoses a malaise with some shocking symptoms.

Get the facts but also the human side of the story on the world's hunger, poverty, material and emotional deprivation; its human rights abuses and unimaginable wealth; the unstoppable rise of consumerism, mental illness, the drugs trade, corruption, gun culture, the abuse of our environment and more.

The prognosis might look bleak, yet there is hope, Williams argues – and it's down to us to act now to change things.

ISBN: 978-1840468-46-5   Paperback £8.99

Why Do People Hate America?

Ziauddin Sardar and Merryl Wyn Davies

The economic power of US corporations and the virus-like power of American popular culture affect the lives and infect the indigenous cultures of millions around the world. The foreign policy of the US government, backed by its military strength, has unprecedented global influence now that the USA is the world's only superpower – its first 'hyperpower'.

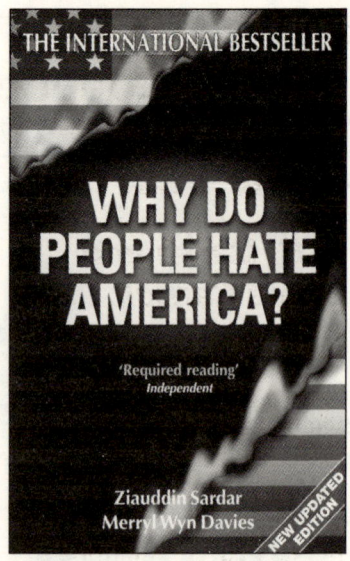

America also exports its value systems, defining what it means to be civilised, rational, developed and democratic – indeed, what it is to be human. Meanwhile, the US itself is impervious to outside influence, and if most Americans think of the rest of the world at all, it is in terms of deeply ingrained cultural stereotypes.

Many people *do* hate America, in the Middle East and the developing countries as well as in Europe. Ziauddin Sardar and Merryl Wyn Davies explore the global impact of America's foreign policy and its corporate and cultural power, placing this unprecedented dominance in the context of America's own perception of itself. Their analysis provides an important contribution to a debate which needs to be addressed by people of all nations, cultures, religions and political persuasions.

ISBN 978-1840465-25-9   Paperback £7.99

366: A Leap Year of Stories for Every Day of the Year

W.B. Marsh and Bruce Carrick

The unputdownable sequel to *365* – highly addictive, bite-size chunks of history.

16 Jan 1920: Prohibition is born
14 Feb 270: St Valentine's martyrdom gives birth to a romantic tradition
5 Jul 1946: The bikini swimsuit makes its debut at a Paris fashion show
22 Dec 1849: Dostoyevsky is led out for a pretend execution

It's strange sometimes to think that even the biggest events of world history happened on a particular day – a rainy 25 February, a sweltering 2 July, your father's birthday …

W. B. Marsh and Bruce Carrick present a leap year of historical stories by turns amazing, horrifying, touching and tearful.

Read about the first-ever tanks going into combat on the Somme, Pushkin's death in a duel, Nietzsche's dramatic breakdown in Turin, Jesse Owens humiliating the Nazis at the Olympic Games and much, much more. The ideal book for any history junkie.

ISBN: 978-1840468-27-4   Hardback £16.99

Torture Taxi

Trevor Paglen and A.C. Thompson

Praise for *Torture Taxi*:

'Exhilarating ... Paglen and Thompson provide a comprehensive look at the ways the CIA hides its operations, and at the brave citizens who have cracked its codes. It paints a mysterious and frightening picture.' *Time Out Chicago*

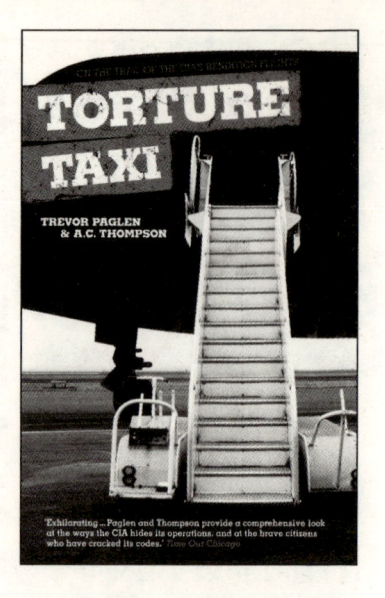

The incredible story of how the CIA's darkest secret of the 'war on terror' – the 'extraordinary rendition' programme – was exposed.

It's no longer a secret: since 9/11, the CIA has quietly kidnapped more than a hundred people and detained them at prisons throughout the world. Often, the detainees are tortured or disappear entirely.

In this shocking book, an award-winning investigative journalist and a 'military geographer' explore the programme in journeys around the world: to suburban Massachusetts to profile a CIA front company supplying the agency with planes; to the San Francisco suburbs to study with a planespotter who monitors the CIA's movements; and to Afghanistan, where they interview released Afghan detainees.

A chilling look at the logistics of torture which shows how far Bush is prepared to go in the 'war on terror'.

ISBN: 978-1840468-30-4   Paperback £9.99